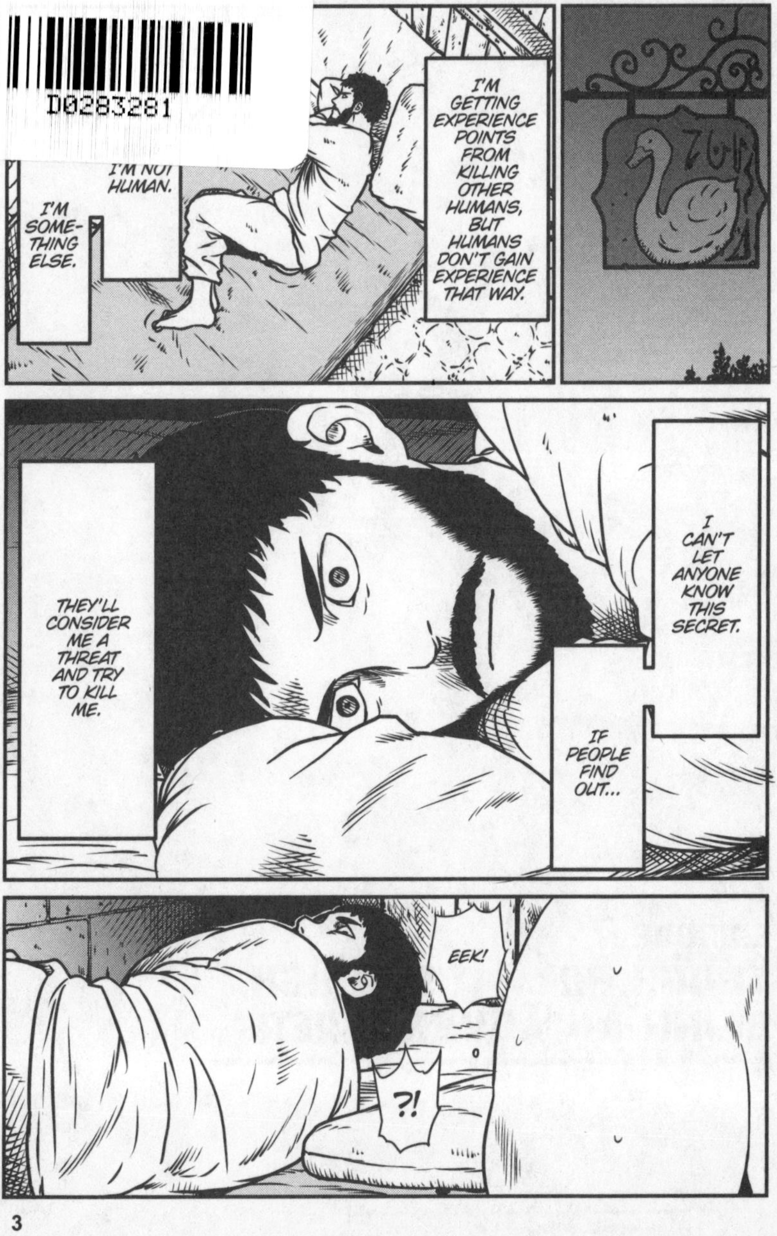
I'M GETTING EXPERIENCE POINTS FROM KILLING OTHER HUMANS, BUT HUMANS DON'T GAIN EXPERIENCE THAT WAY.
I'M NOT HUMAN.
I'M SOME-THING ELSE.
I CAN'T LET ANYONE KNOW THIS SECRET.
IF PEOPLE FIND OUT...
THEY'LL CONSIDER ME A THREAT AND TRY TO KILL ME.
EEK!
?!

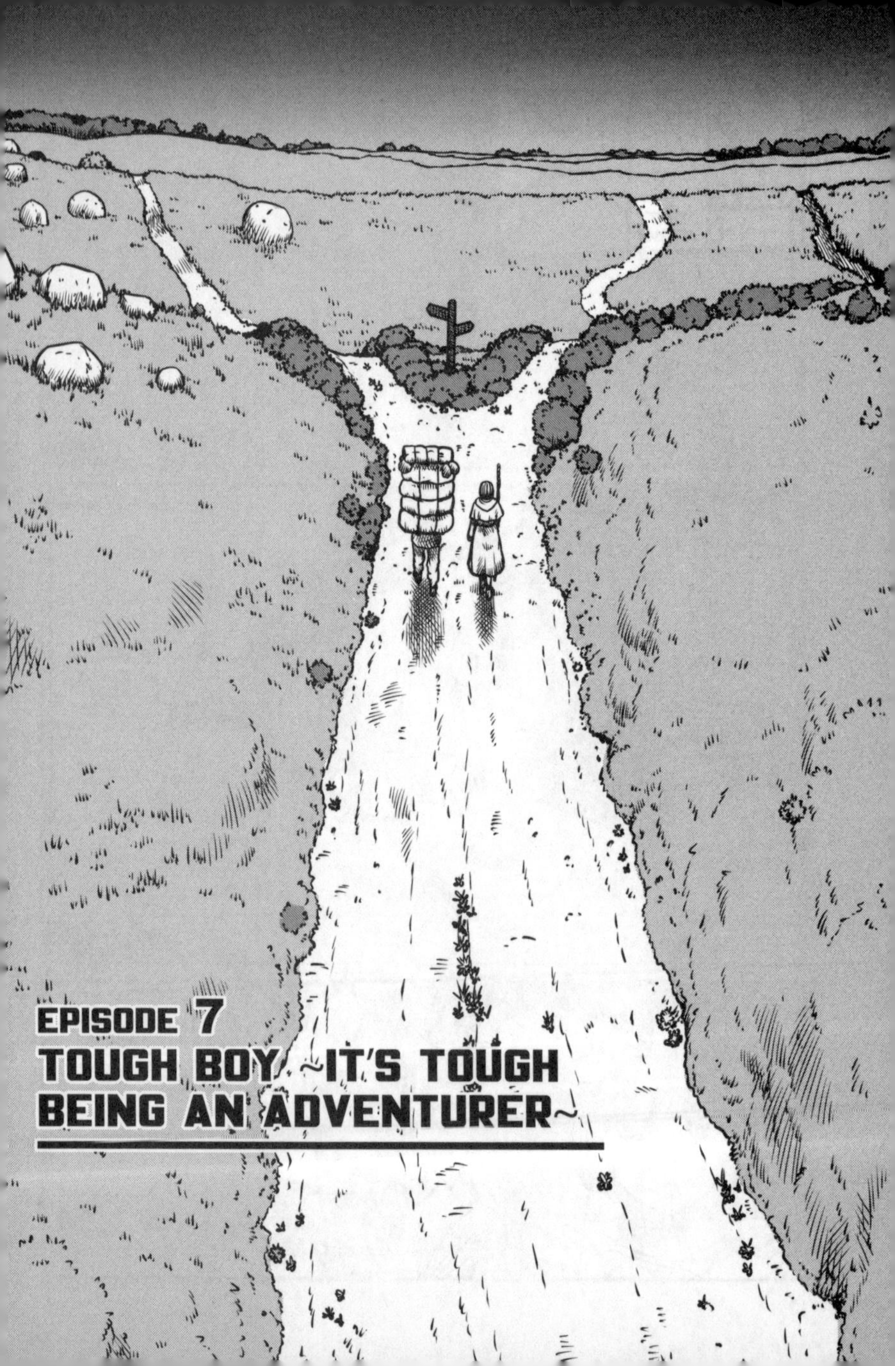
EPISODE 7
TOUGH BOY ~IT'S TOUGH BEING AN ADVENTURER~

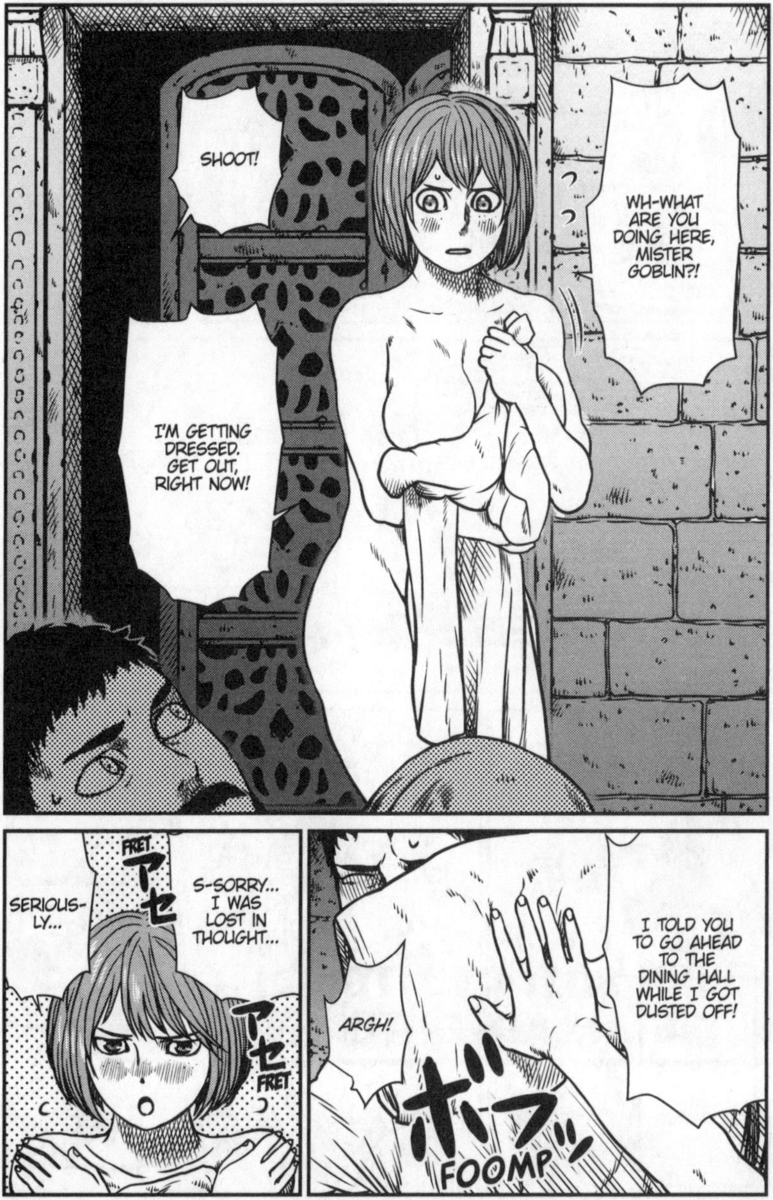
WH-WHAT ARE YOU DOING HERE, MISTER GOBLIN?!
SHOOT!
I'M GETTING DRESSED. GET OUT, RIGHT NOW!
I TOLD YOU TO GO AHEAD TO THE DINING HALL WHILE I GOT DUSTED OFF!
ARGH!
FOOMP
S-SORRY... I WAS LOST IN THOUGHT...
FRET
SERIOUS-LY...
FRET

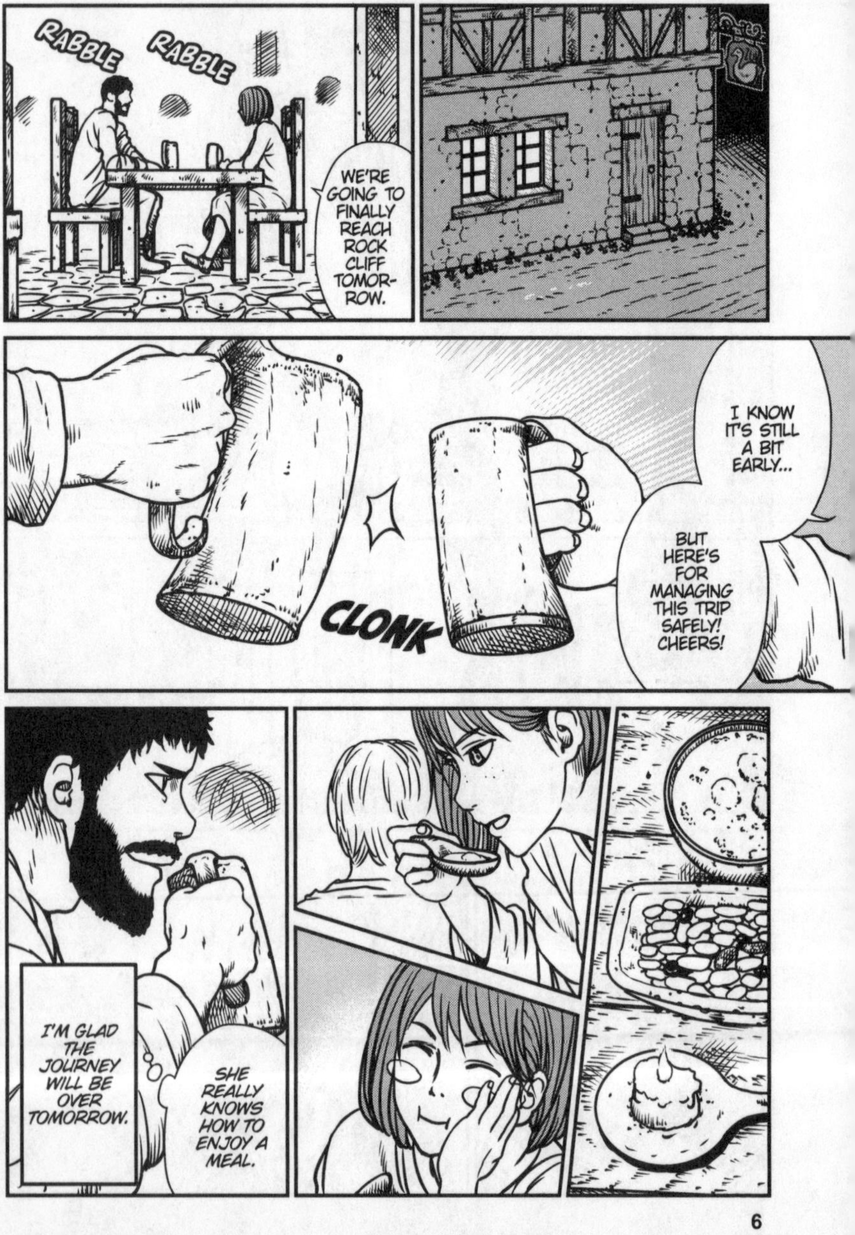
RABBLE RABBLE
WE'RE GOING TO FINALLY REACH ROCK CLIFF TOMORROW.
I KNOW IT'S STILL A BIT EARLY...
BUT HERE'S FOR MANAGING THIS TRIP SAFELY! CHEERS!
CLONK
I'M GLAD THE JOURNEY WILL BE OVER TOMORROW.
SHE REALLY KNOWS HOW TO ENJOY A MEAL.

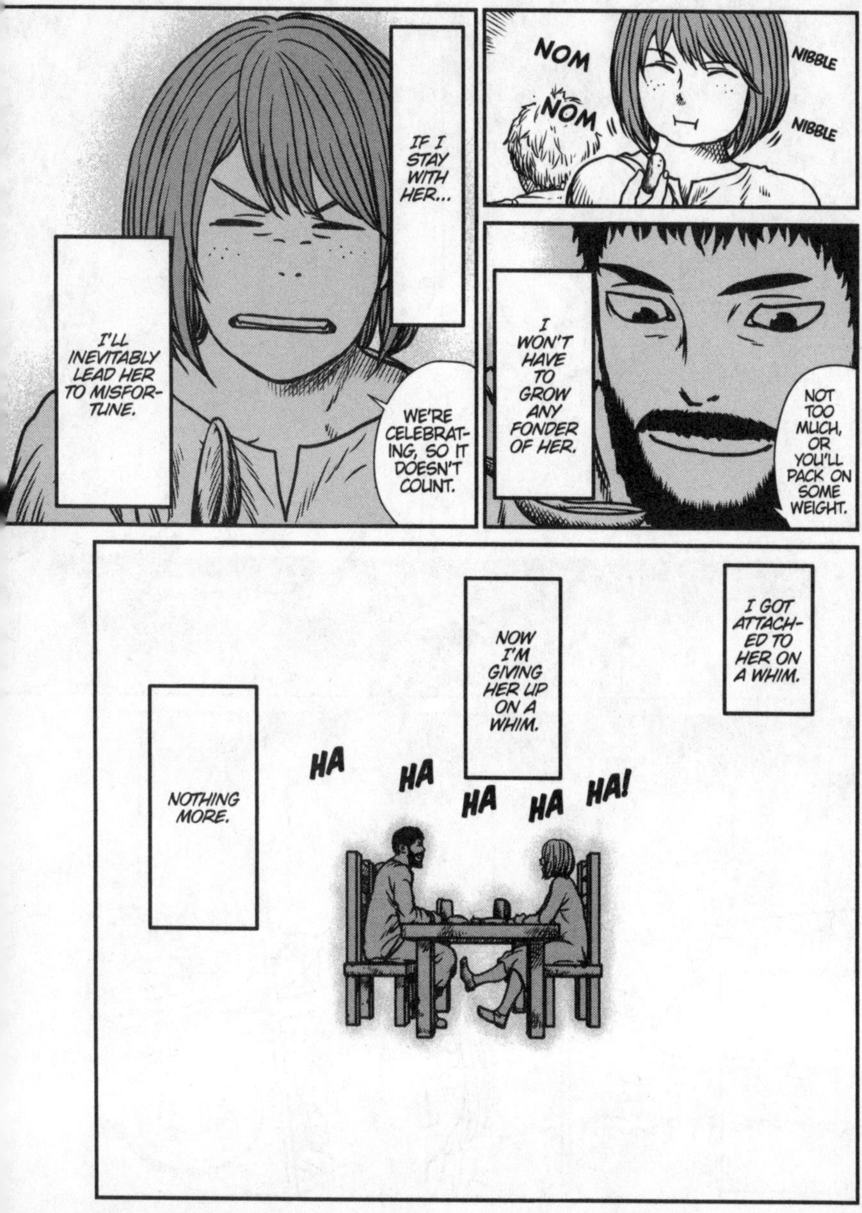
NIBBLE NIBBLE
NOM NOM
NOT TOO MUCH, OR YOU'LL PACK ON SOME WEIGHT.
I WON'T HAVE TO GROW ANY FONDER OF HER.
IF I STAY WITH HER...
WE'RE CELEBRATING, SO IT DOESN'T COUNT.
I'LL INEVITABLY LEAD HER TO MISFORTUNE.
I GOT ATTACHED TO HER ON A WHIM.
NOW I'M GIVING HER UP ON A WHIM.
HA HA HA HA HA!
NOTHING MORE.

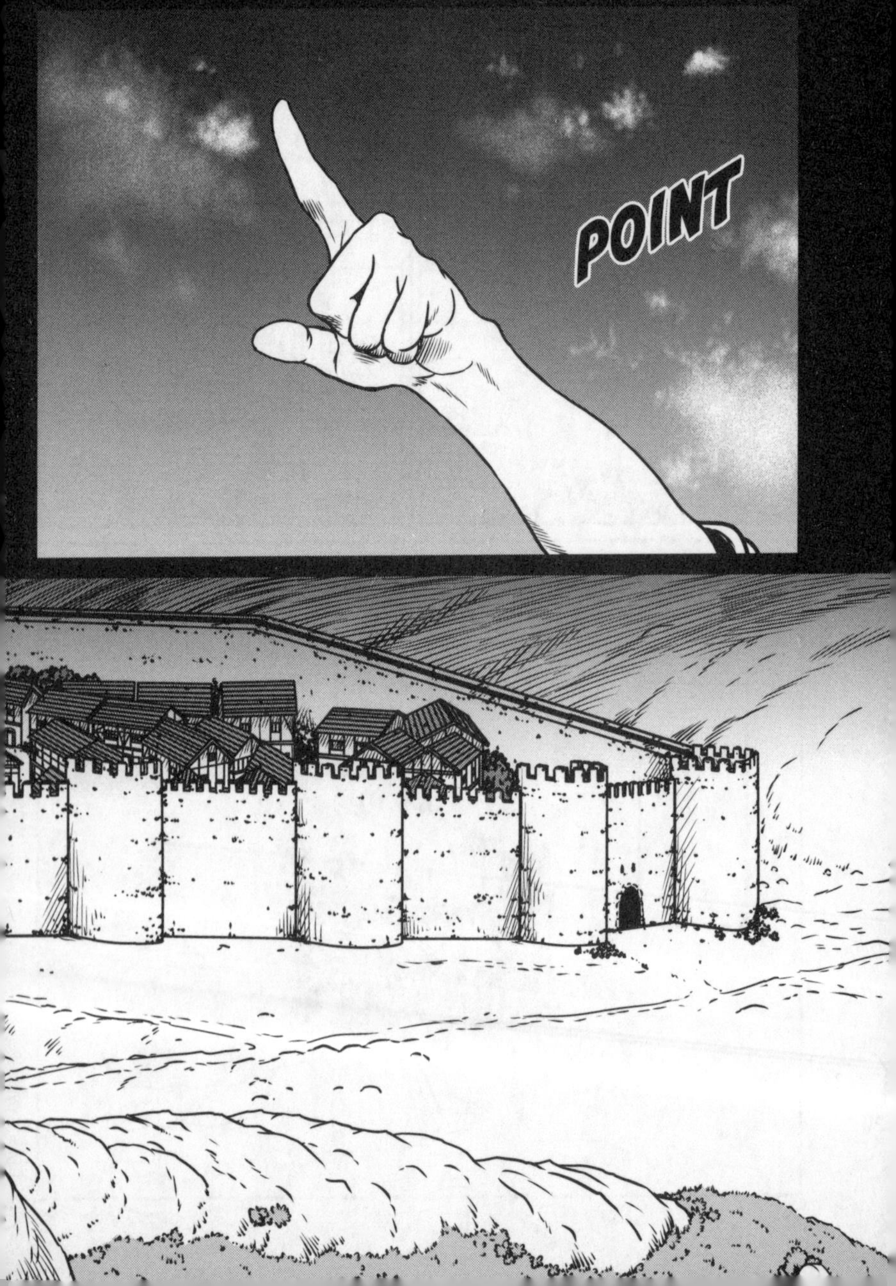
POINT

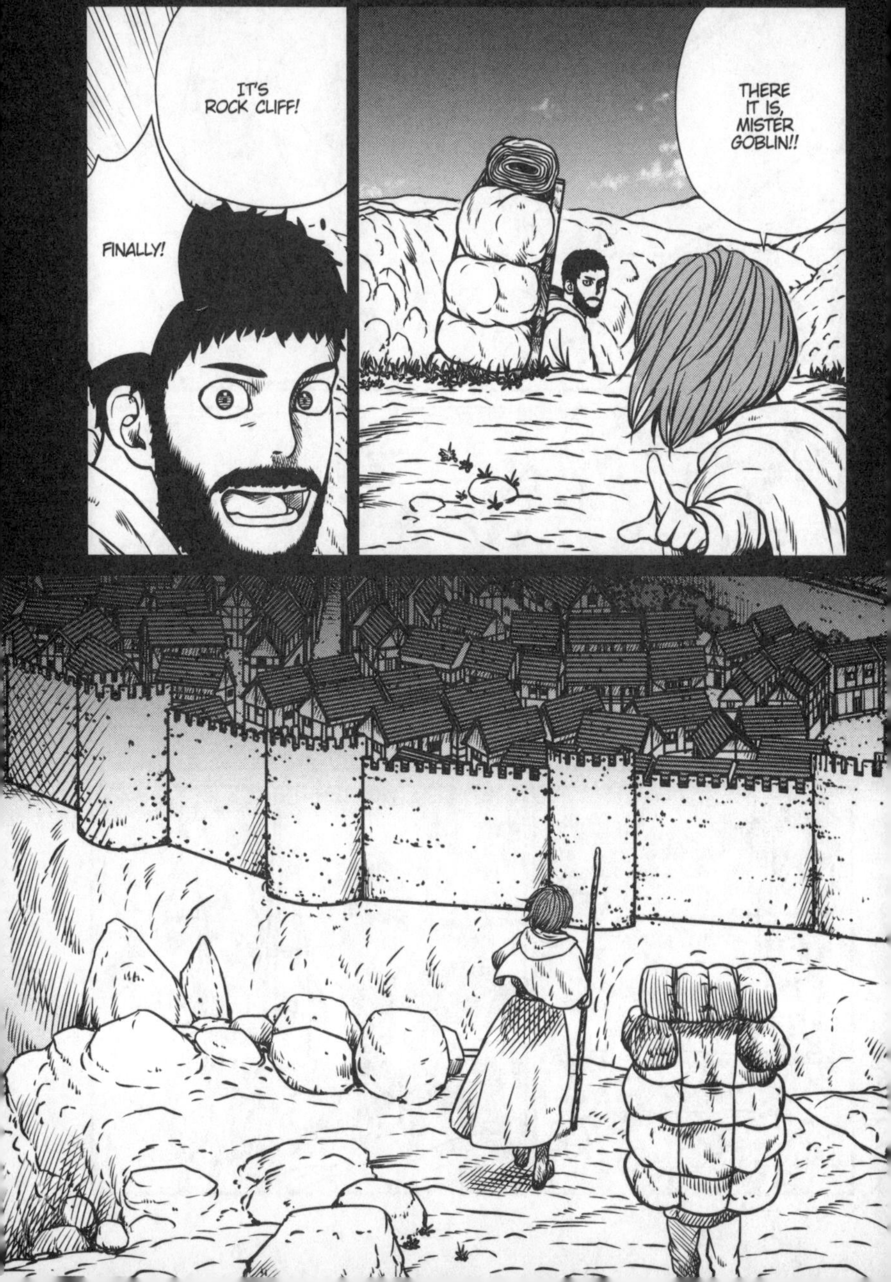
THERE IT IS, MISTER GOBLIN!!
IT'S ROCK CLIFF!
FINALLY!

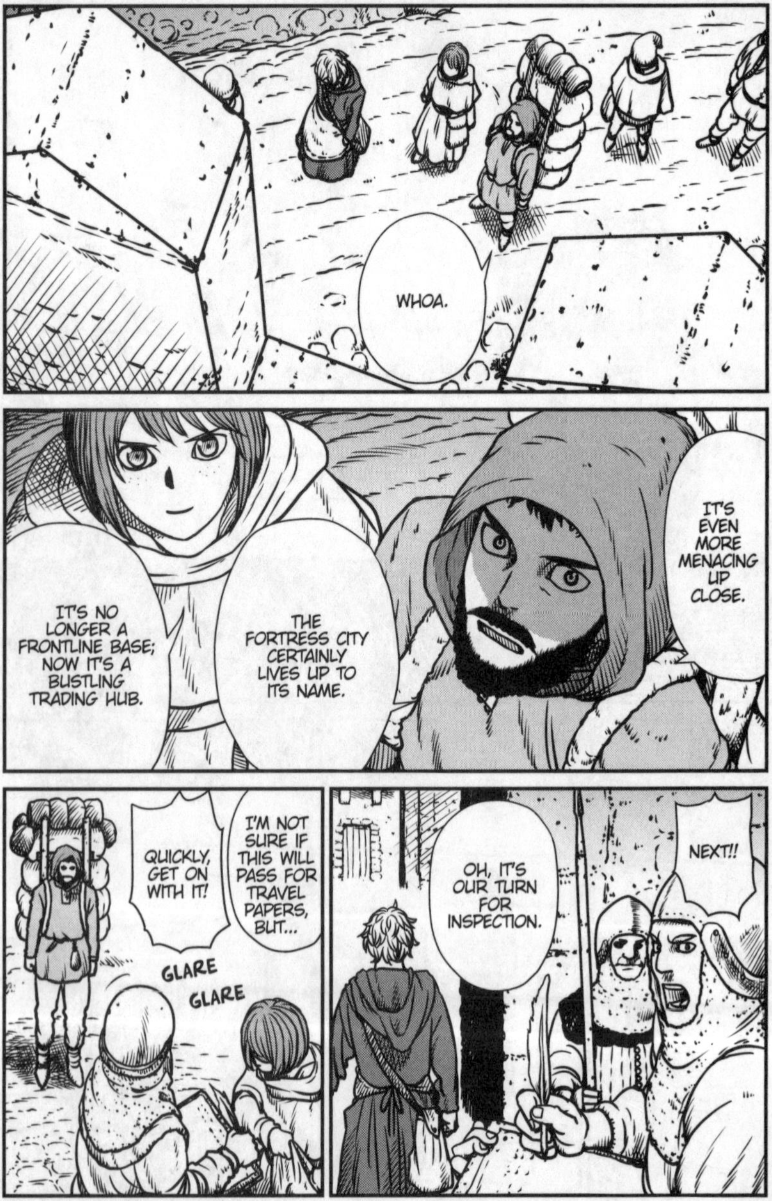
WHOA.
IT'S EVEN MORE MENACING UP CLOSE.
THE FORTRESS CITY CERTAINLY LIVES UP TO ITS NAME.
IT'S NO LONGER A FRONTLINE BASE; NOW IT'S A BUSTLING TRADING HUB.
NEXT!!
OH, IT'S OUR TURN FOR INSPECTION.
I'M NOT SURE IF THIS WILL PASS FOR TRAVEL PAPERS, BUT...
QUICKLY, GET ON WITH IT!
GLARE
GLARE

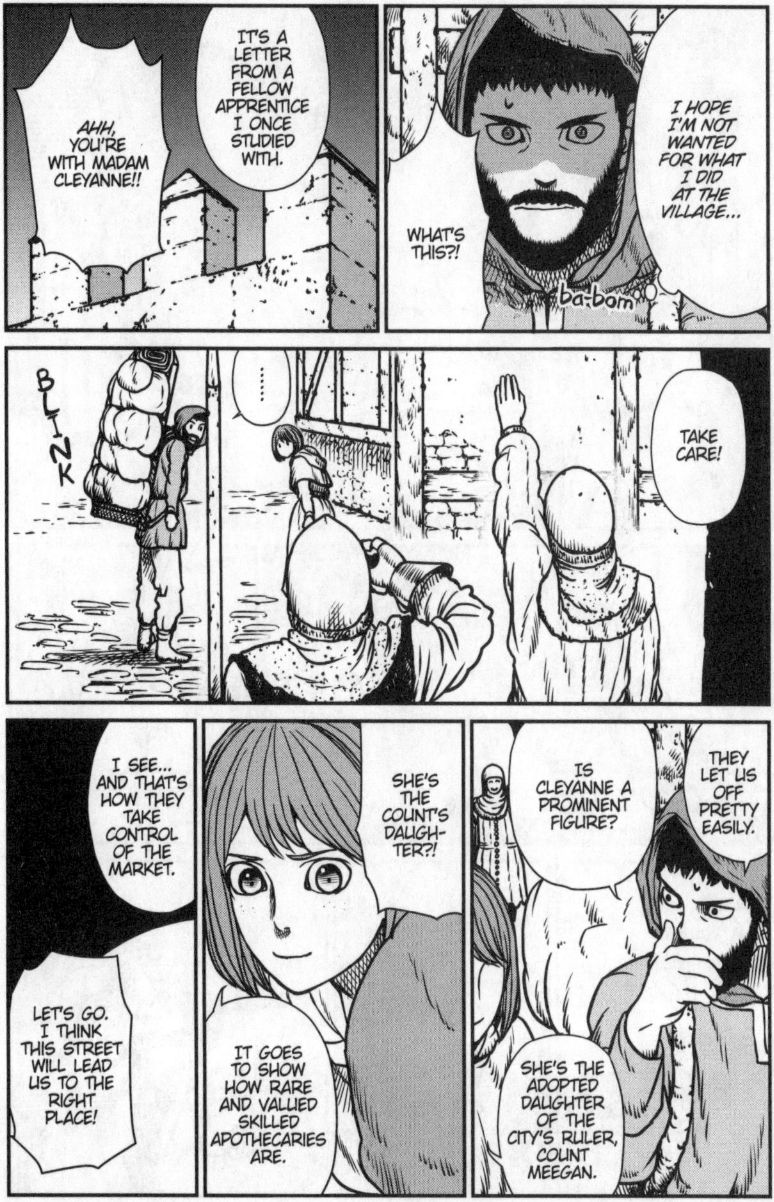
I HOPE I'M NOT WANTED FOR WHAT I DID AT THE VILLAGE...
WHAT'S THIS?!
ba-bom
IT'S A LETTER FROM A FELLOW APPRENTICE I ONCE STUDIED WITH.
AHH, YOU'RE WITH MADAM CLEYANNE!!
TAKE CARE!
......
BLINK
THEY LET US OFF PRETTY EASILY.
IS CLEYANNE A PROMINENT FIGURE?
SHE'S THE ADOPTED DAUGHTER OF THE CITY'S RULER, COUNT MEEGAN.
SHE'S THE COUNT'S DAUGH-TER?!
IT GOES TO SHOW HOW RARE AND VALUED SKILLED APOTHECARIES ARE.
I SEE... AND THAT'S HOW THEY TAKE CONTROL OF THE MARKET.
LET'S GO. I THINK THIS STREET WILL LEAD US TO THE RIGHT PLACE!

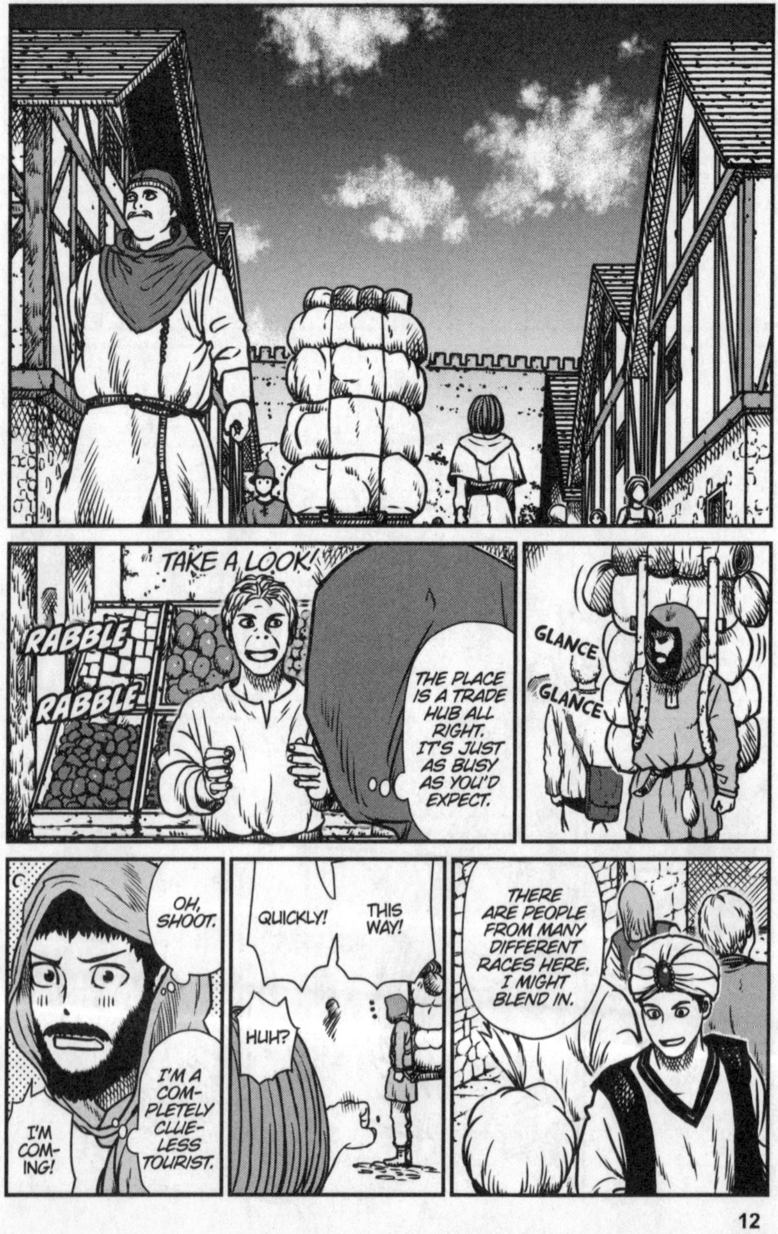
GLANCE
GLANCE
TAKE A LOOK!
THE PLACE IS A TRADE HUB ALL RIGHT. IT'S JUST AS BUSY AS YOU'D EXPECT.
RABBLE
RABBLE
THERE ARE PEOPLE FROM MANY DIFFERENT RACES HERE. I MIGHT BLEND IN.
THIS WAY!
QUICKLY!
HUH?
OH, SHOOT.
I'M A COMPLETELY CLUELESS TOURIST.
I'M COMING!

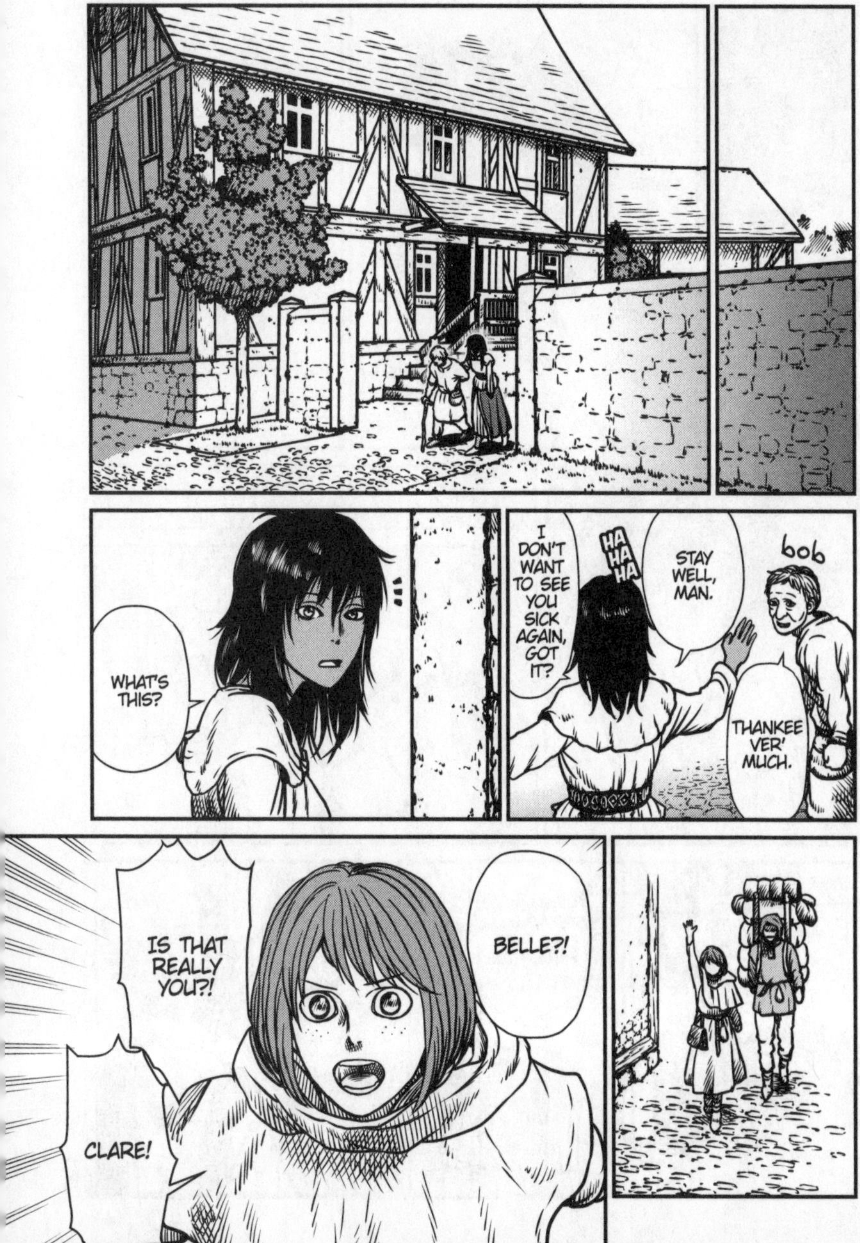
bob
STAY WELL, MAN.
HA HA HA
I DON'T WANT TO SEE YOU SICK AGAIN, GOT IT?
THANKEE VER' MUCH.
WHAT'S THIS?
BELLE?!
IS THAT REALLY YOU?!
CLARE!

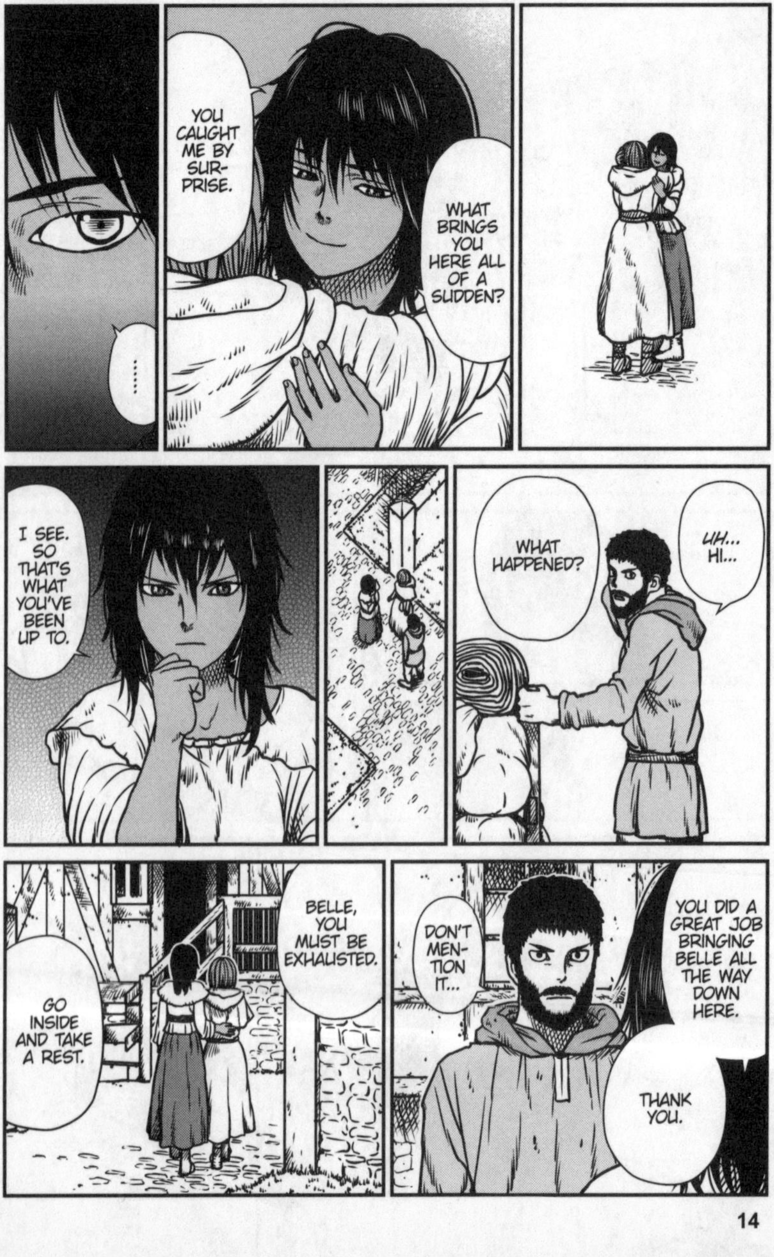
YOU CAUGHT ME BY SURPRISE.
WHAT BRINGS YOU HERE ALL OF A SUDDEN?
……
UH... HI...
WHAT HAPPENED?
I SEE. SO THAT'S WHAT YOU'VE BEEN UP TO.
YOU DID A GREAT JOB BRINGING BELLE ALL THE WAY DOWN HERE.
THANK YOU.
DON'T MENTION IT...
BELLE, YOU MUST BE EXHAUSTED.
GO INSIDE AND TAKE A REST.

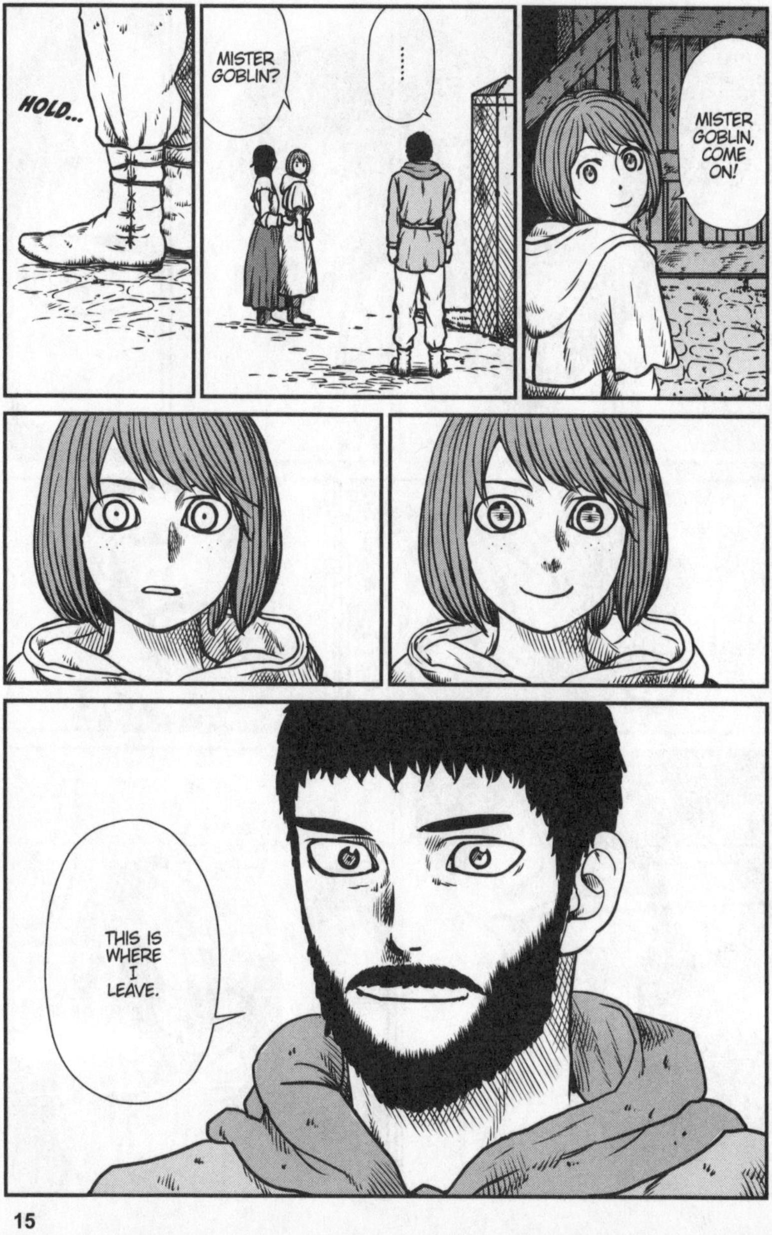
MISTER GOBLIN, COME ON!
......
MISTER GOBLIN?
HOLD...
THIS IS WHERE I LEAVE.

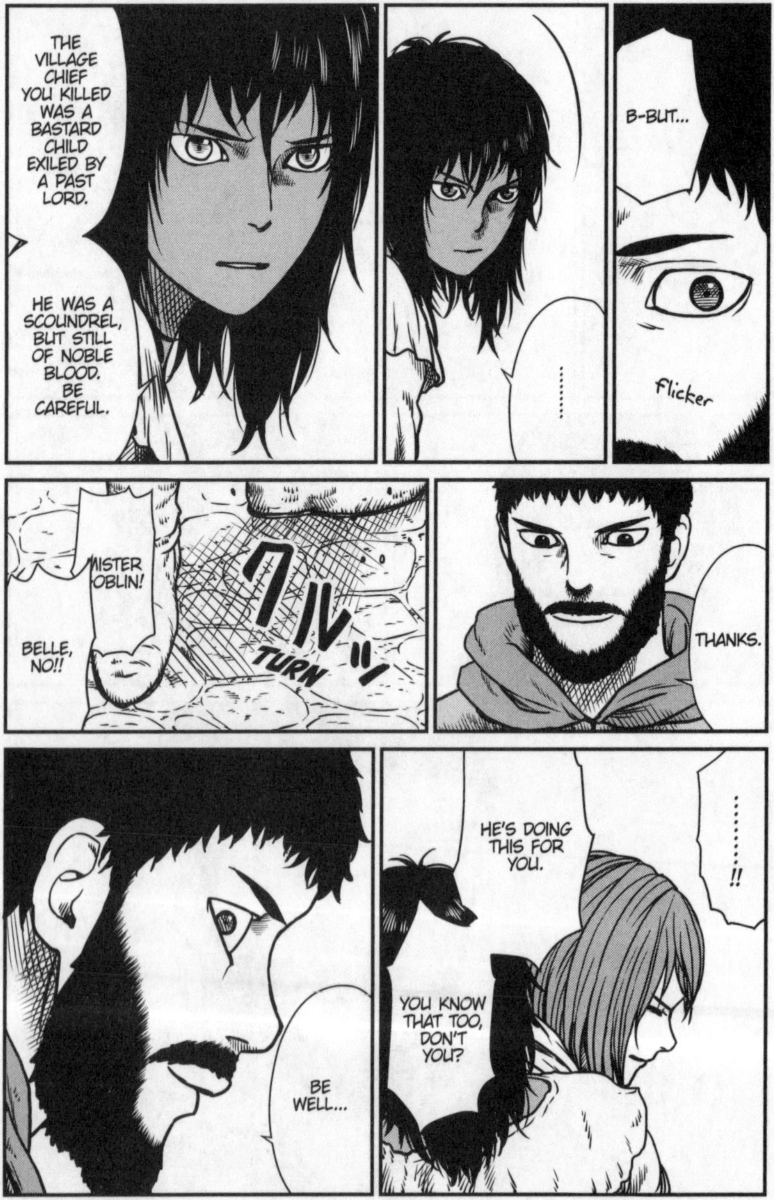
B-BUT...
Flicker
......
THE VILLAGE CHIEF YOU KILLED WAS A BASTARD CHILD EXILED BY A PAST LORD.
HE WAS A SCOUNDREL, BUT STILL OF NOBLE BLOOD. BE CAREFUL.
THANKS.
TURN
MISTER OBLIN!
BELLE, NO!!
......!!
HE'S DOING THIS FOR YOU.
YOU KNOW THAT TOO, DON'T YOU?
BE WELL...

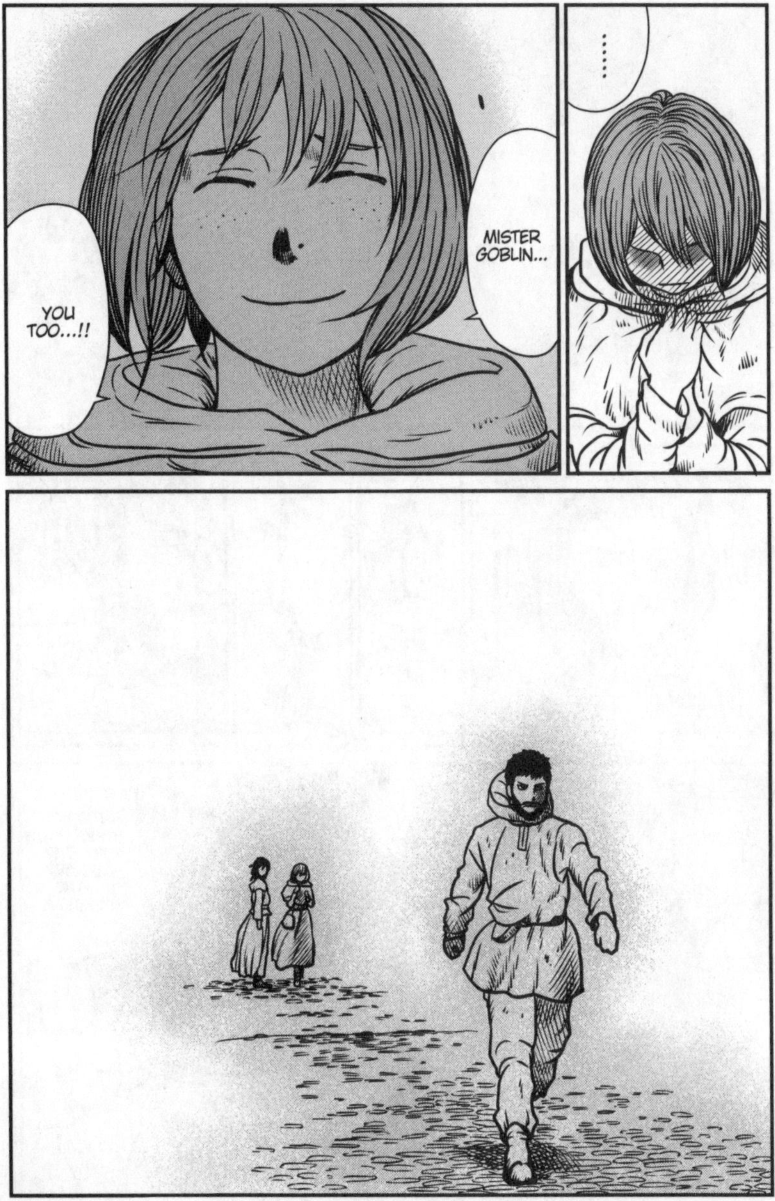
......
MISTER GOBLIN...
YOU TOO...!!

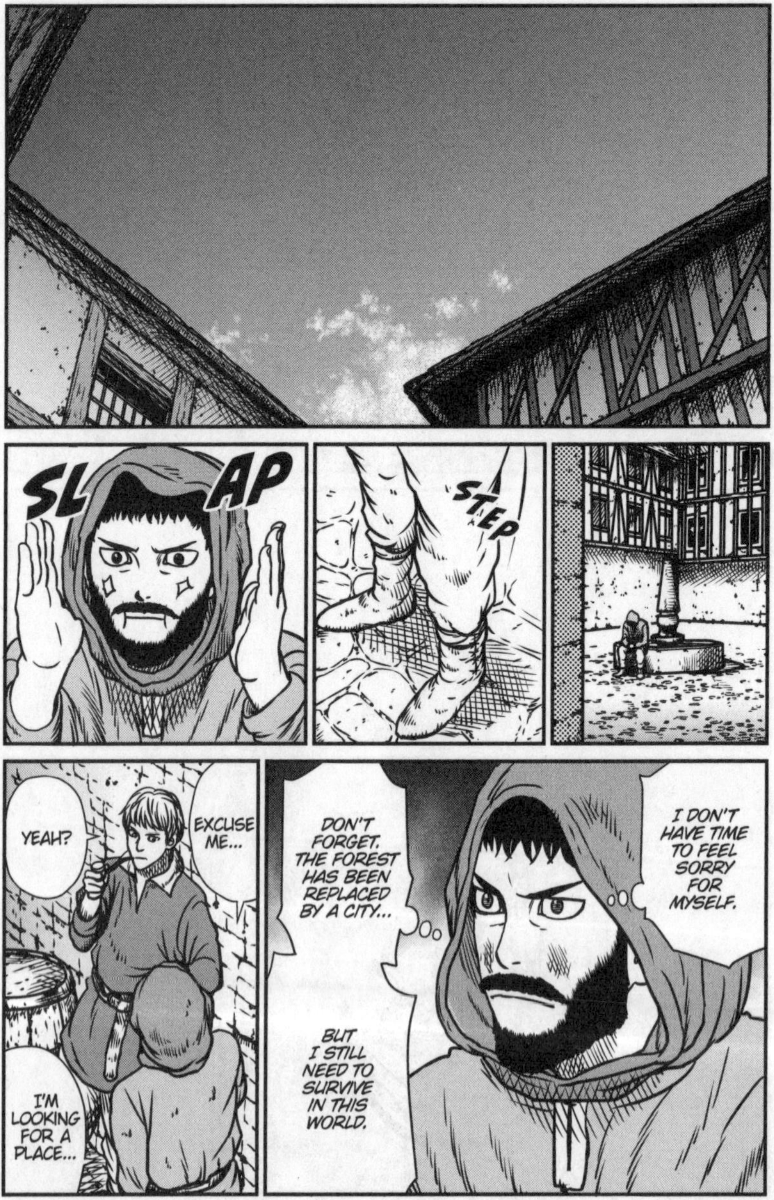
STEP
SLAP
I DON'T HAVE TIME TO FEEL SORRY FOR MYSELF.
DON'T FORGET. THE FOREST HAS BEEN REPLACED BY A CITY...
BUT I STILL NEED TO SURVIVE IN THIS WORLD.
EXCUSE ME...
YEAH?
I'M LOOKING FOR A PLACE...

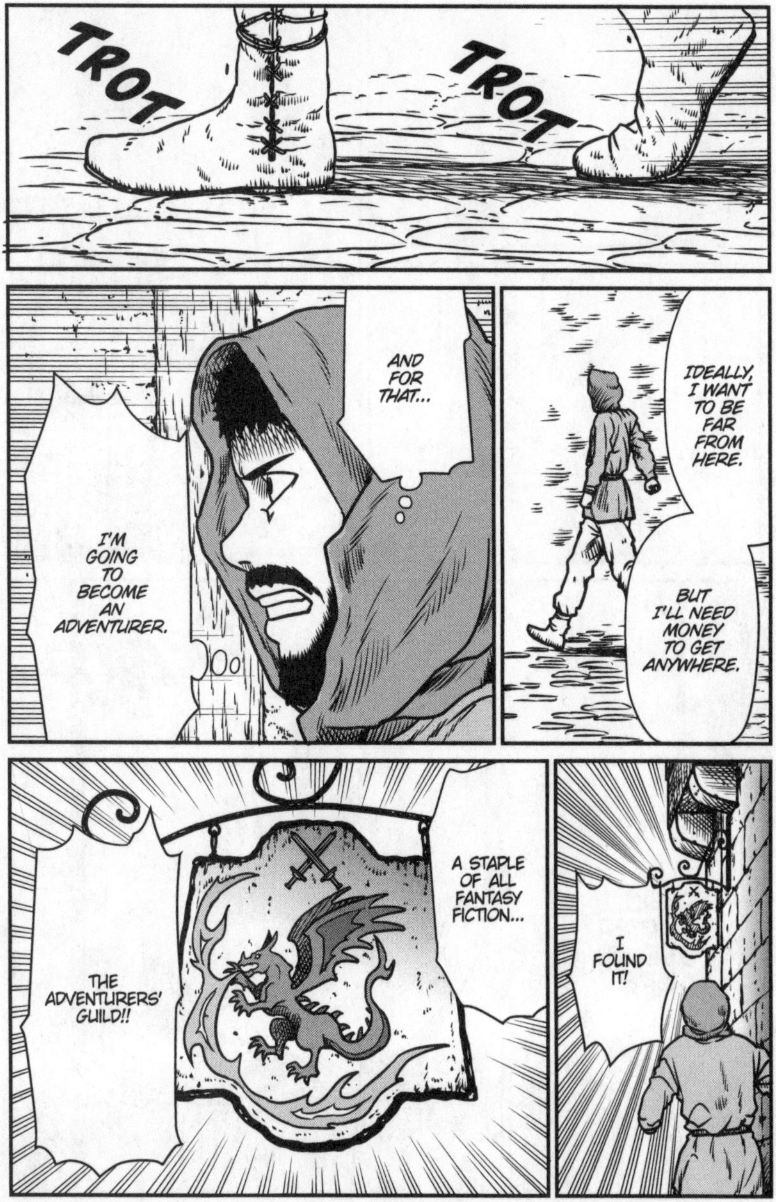
TROT
TROT
IDEALLY, I WANT TO BE FAR FROM HERE.
BUT I'LL NEED MONEY TO GET ANYWHERE.
AND FOR THAT...
I'M GOING TO BECOME AN ADVENTURER.
I FOUND IT!
A STAPLE OF ALL FANTASY FICTION...
THE ADVENTURERS' GUILD!!

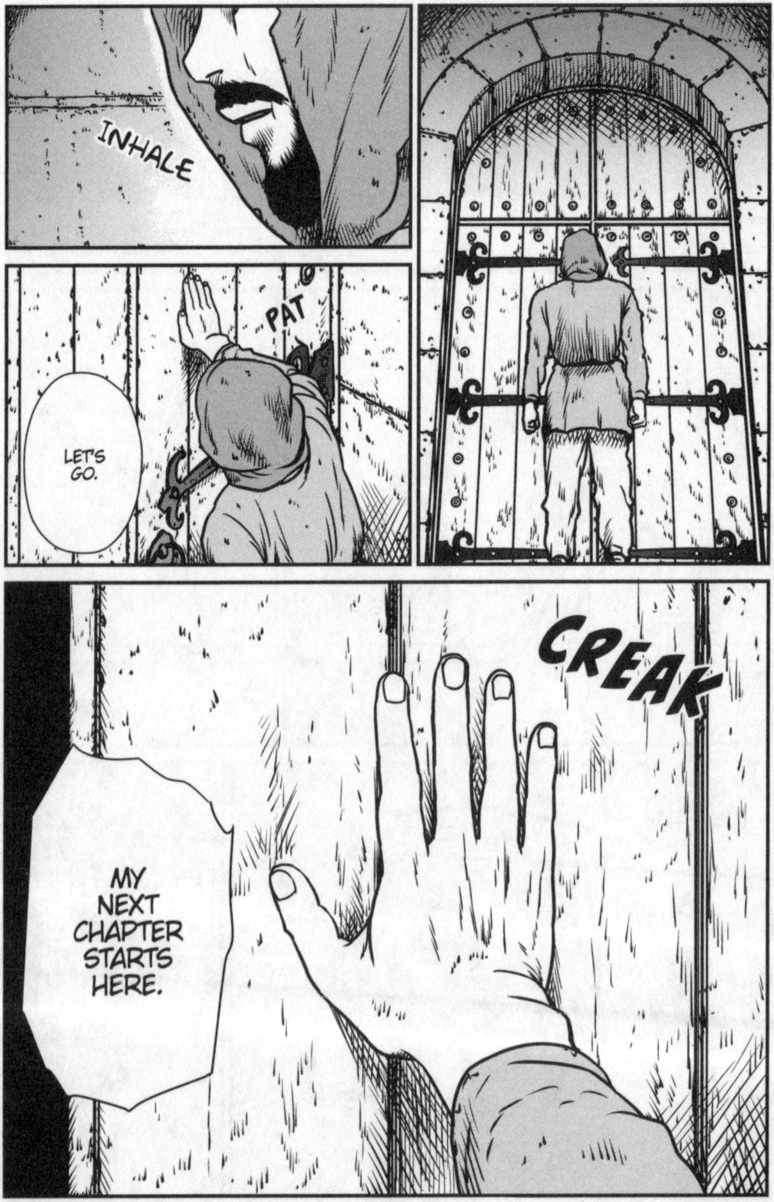
INHALE
PAT
LET'S GO.
CREAK
MY NEXT CHAPTER STARTS HERE.

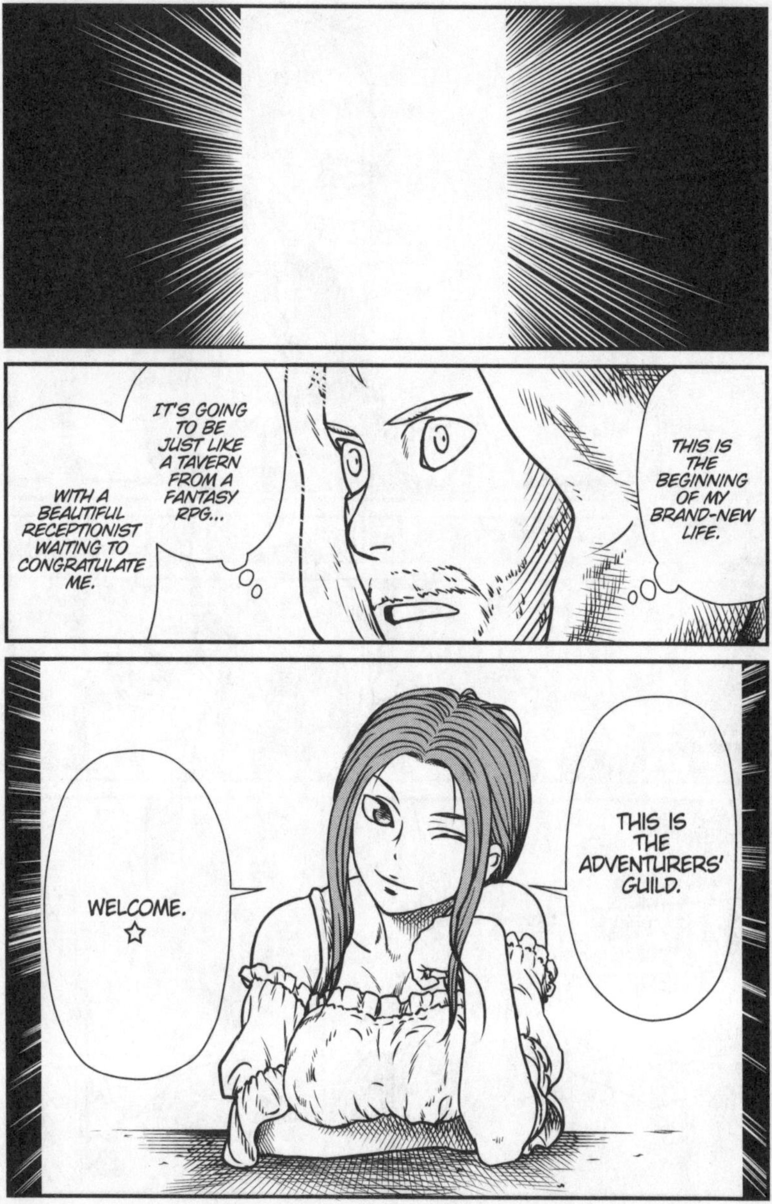
THIS IS THE BEGINNING OF MY BRAND-NEW LIFE.
IT'S GOING TO BE JUST LIKE A TAVERN FROM A FANTASY RPG...
WITH A BEAUTIFUL RECEPTIONIST WAITING TO CONGRATULATE ME.
THIS IS THE ADVENTURERS' GUILD.
WELCOME. ☆

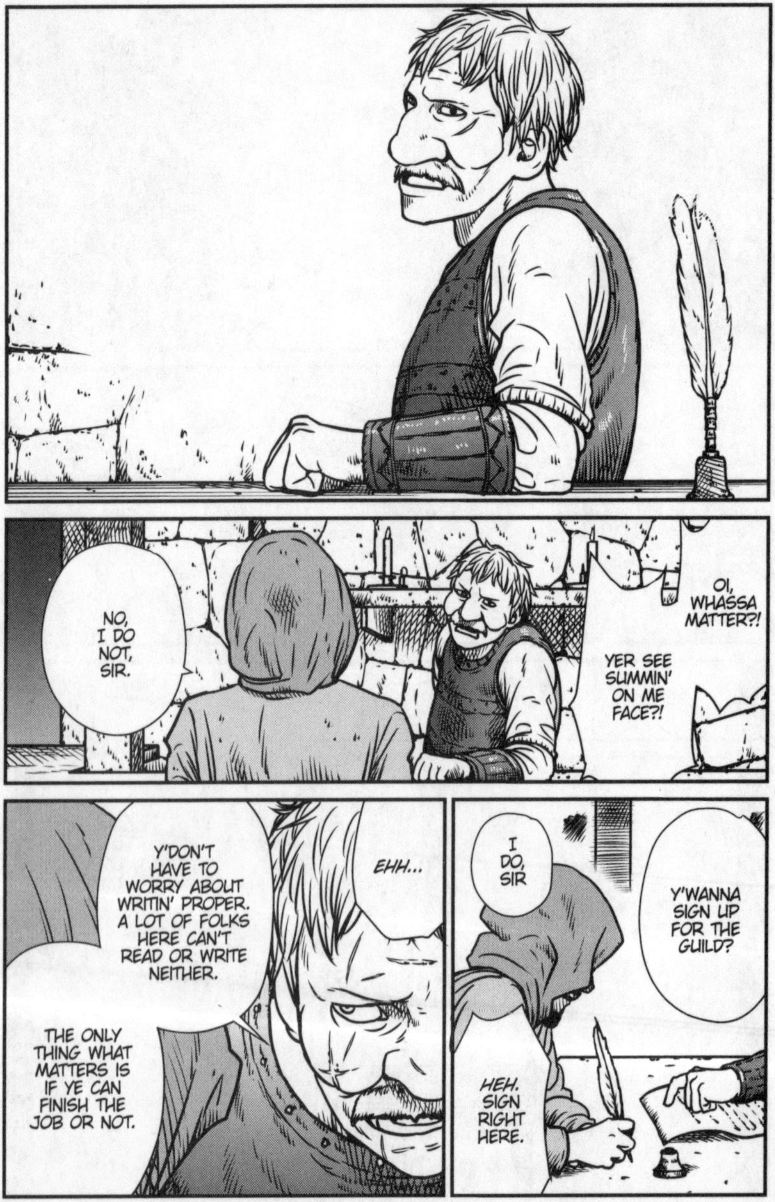
OI, WHASSA MATTER?!
YER SEE SUMMIN' ON ME FACE?!
NO, I DO NOT, SIR.
Y'WANNA SIGN UP FOR THE GUILD?
I DO, SIR
HEH. SIGN RIGHT HERE.
EHH...
Y'DON'T HAVE TO WORRY ABOUT WRITIN' PROPER. A LOT OF FOLKS HERE CAN'T READ OR WRITE NEITHER.
THE ONLY THING WHAT MATTERS IS IF YE CAN FINISH THE JOB OR NOT.

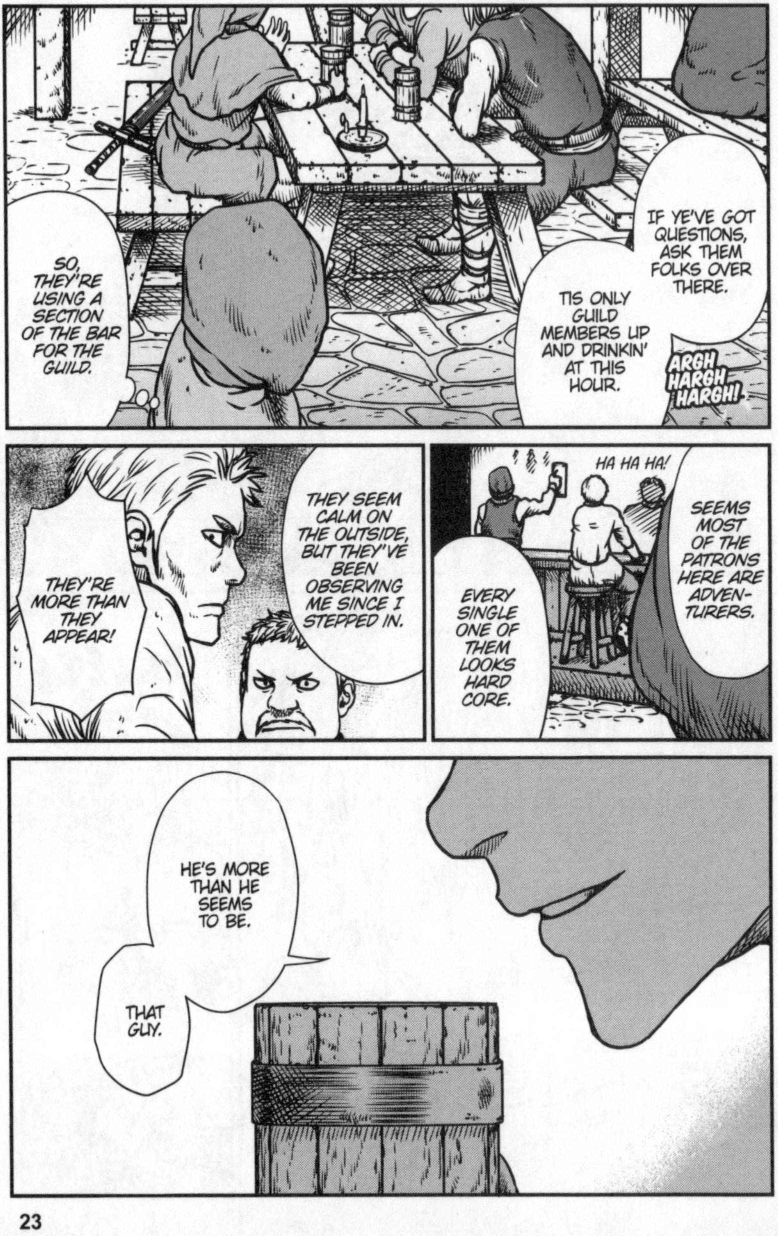
IF YE'VE GOT QUESTIONS, ASK THEM FOLKS OVER THERE.
TIS ONLY GUILD MEMBERS UP AND DRINKIN' AT THIS HOUR.
ARGH HARGH HARGH!
SO, THEY'RE USING A SECTION OF THE BAR FOR THE GUILD.
SEEMS MOST OF THE PATRONS HERE ARE ADVEN-TURERS.
HA HA HA!
EVERY SINGLE ONE OF THEM LOOKS HARD CORE.
THEY SEEM CALM ON THE OUTSIDE, BUT THEY'VE BEEN OBSERVING ME SINCE I STEPPED IN.
THEY'RE MORE THAN THEY APPEAR!
HE'S MORE THAN HE SEEMS TO BE.
THAT GUY.

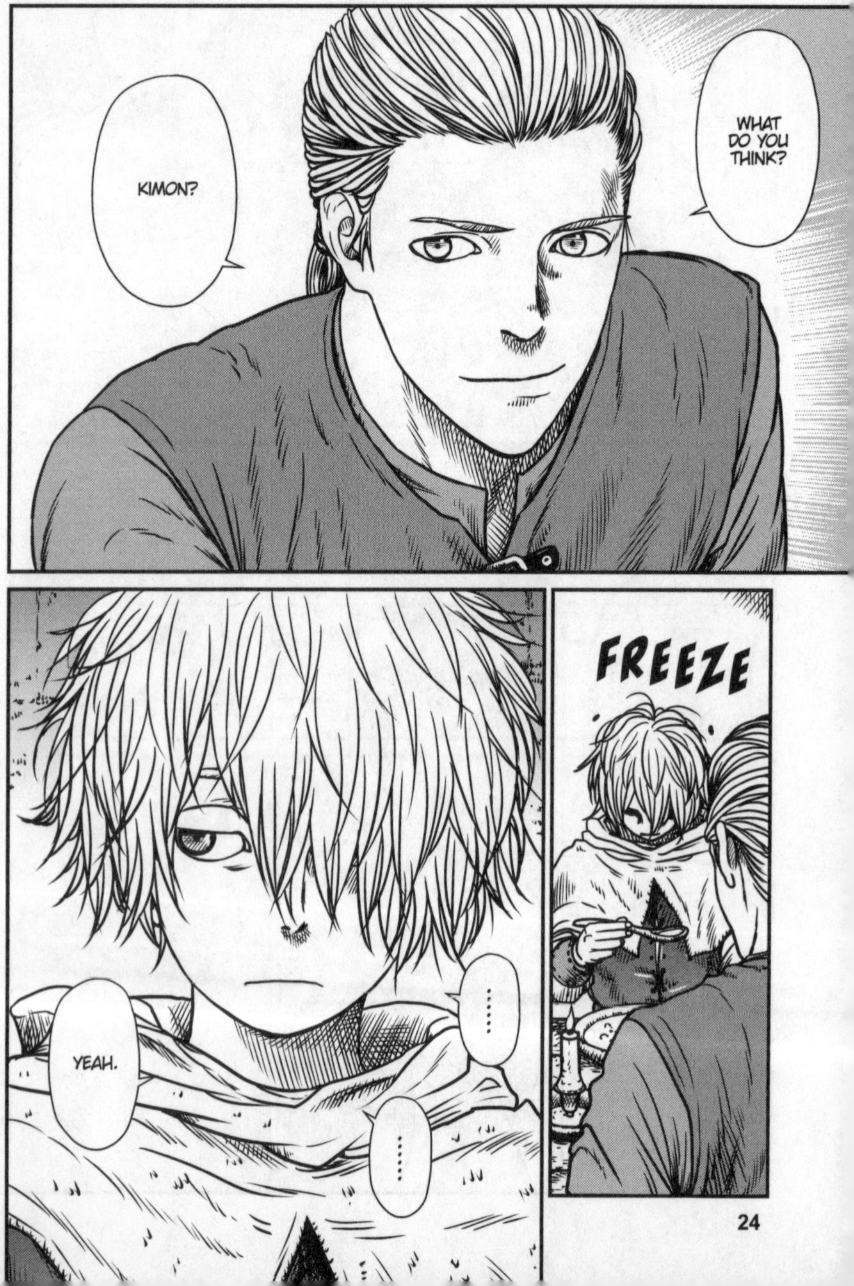
WHAT DO YOU THINK?
KIMON?
FREEZE
......
YEAH.
......

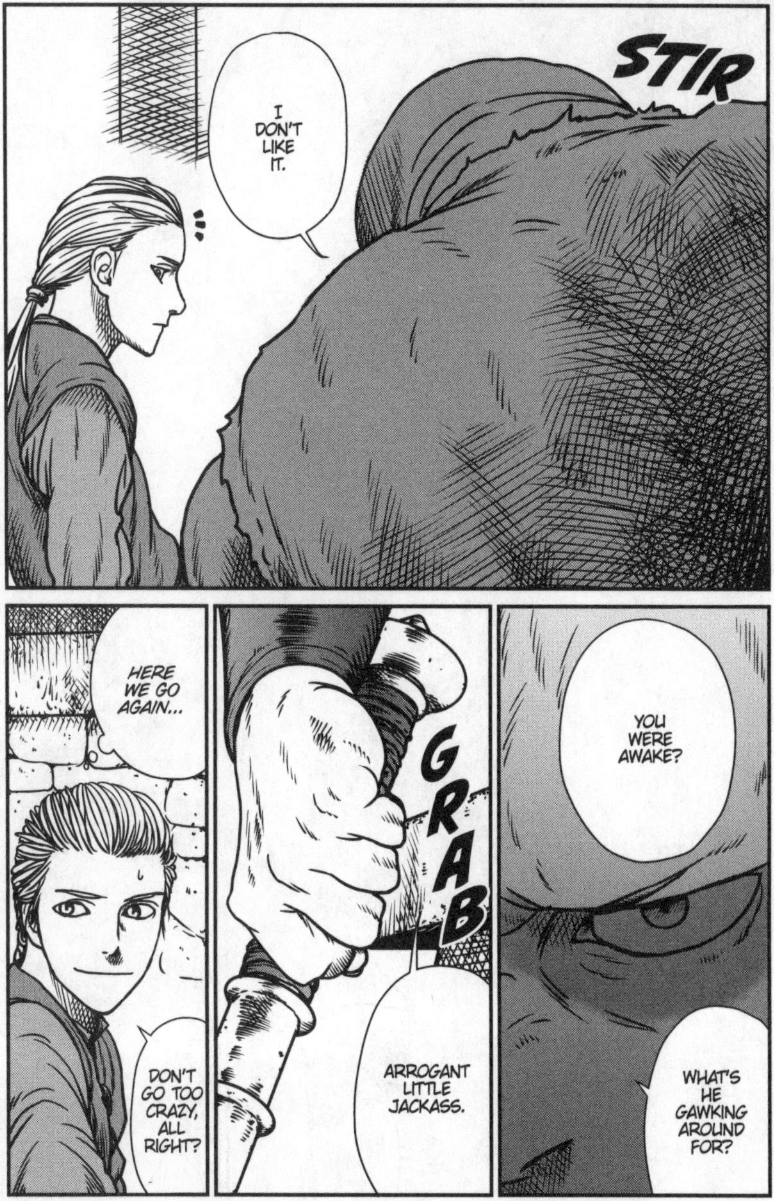
STIR
I DON'T LIKE IT.
YOU WERE AWAKE?
WHAT'S HE GAWKING AROUND FOR?
GRAB
ARROGANT LITTLE JACKASS.
HERE WE GO AGAIN...
DON'T GO TOO CRAZY, ALL RIGHT?

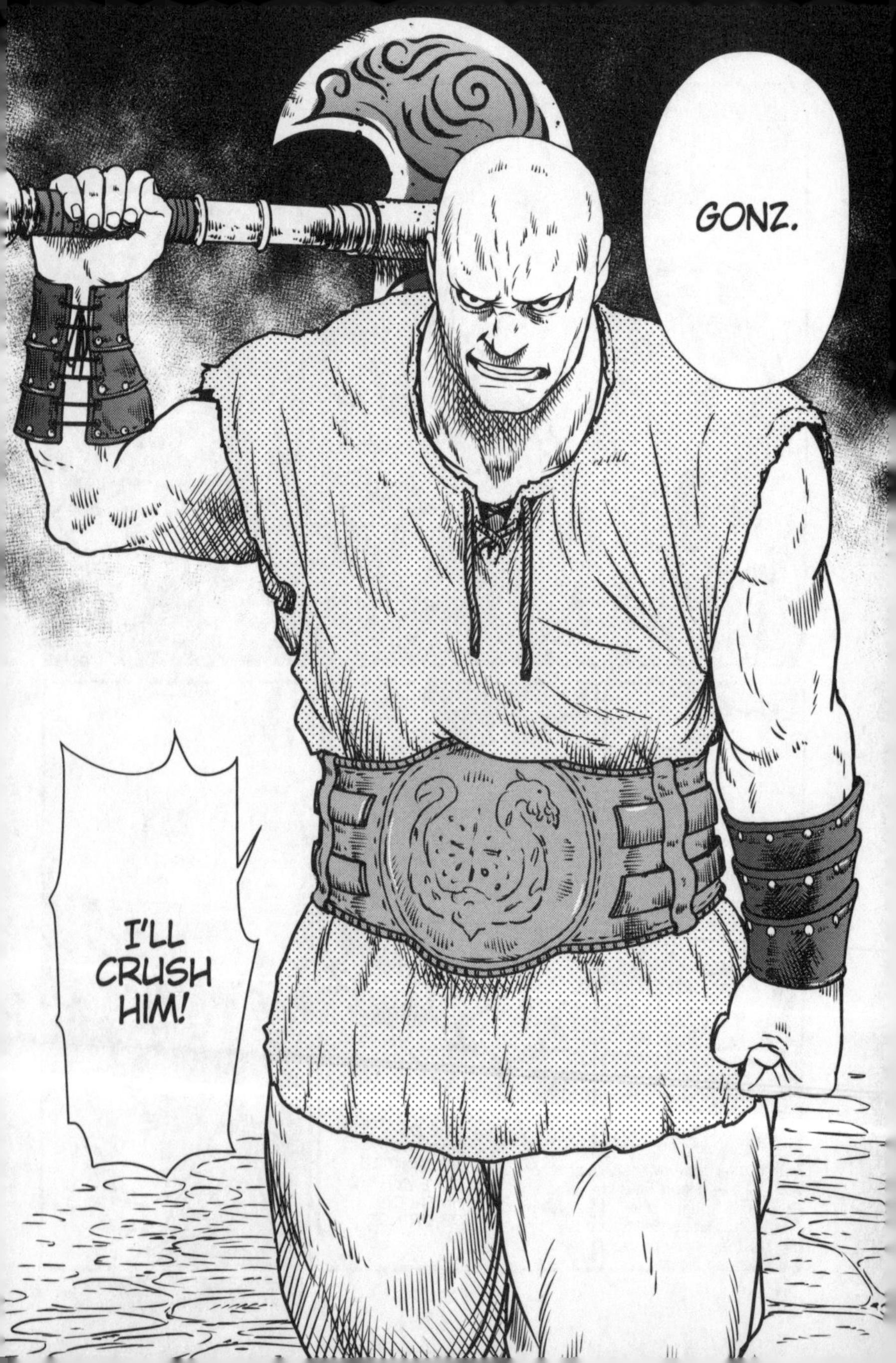
GONZ.
I'LL CRUSH HIM!

SPECIAL COLUMN BY AUTHOR, YAZIN

KARATE SURVIVOR IN ANOTHER WORLD

INTERMISSION

SAVAGE RULES 7

THE ADVENTURER'S ROLE

The history of human civilization is the history of war, and with war comes mercenaries. As citizens of a nation currently not at war, it is easy to forget that peace does not come cheap. Armies are a massive financial drain, and this is not a fact exclusive to medieval times or fantasy worlds. According to the Stockholm International Peace Research Institute, the nations of the world spent a total of almost $2 trillion on military expenses in 2019. This is the cost of securing the safety and fruits of a nation's population.

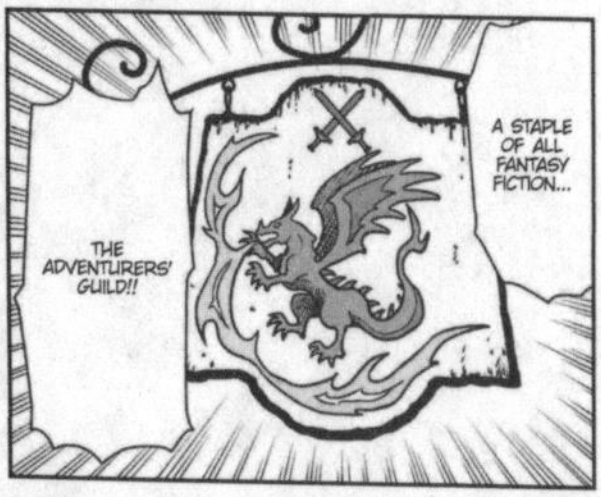
A STAPLE OF ALL FANTASY FICTION...
THE ADVENTURERS' GUILD!!

In the world Nozaki is sent to, both monsters and other nations are dangerous threats. To prevent the invasion of competing states, troops are stationed at the borders. Monsters within national borders must also be periodically culled to keep them from launching incursions into human settlements. Despite the discontent of the populace, defense costs cannot be cut. A possible invasion or incursion could be the downfall of the nation. The military is a mere drain on resources during times of peace, but completely necessary in an emergency.

While every other country was struggling with military expenditure, a ruler of a certain state proposed a solution. This ruler wondered, if a military under regular employ is so costly, is it possible for them to be employed only when necessary?

Ordinarily, it would be unwise to entrust the safety of the nation to "hired hands." They cannot be relied upon and there is always the possibility that they would abandon their duties at a time of crisis. This opens the country up to an enemy invasion.

However, the extermination of monsters is a different matter. This ruler proposed using independent fighters to deal with these monsters. Peasants without farmland to inherit leave the countryside to live in the cities, but not all of them are able to find employment. These people live in slums and increase crime on the streets. Monster-hunting would provide jobs for these people, and as act as a social safety net. Furthermore, taxes could be collected from these people, too. This scheme had the chance to hit three birds with one stone. Battling and defeating monsters would also increase the strength of these fighters. If a warrior could prove themselves powerful and worthy, they could be recruited into the regular army to strengthen the nation.

This ruler chartered a guild, to be managed by a high-level warrior, and to be responsible for collecting taxes from its members. Despite a rocky start, the trial proved to be a success and the system was adopted in other states. The guild was called the adventurers' guild to differentiate itself from existing hunters' guilds and mercenary groups. The guild has evolved over the years but continues operating to this day.

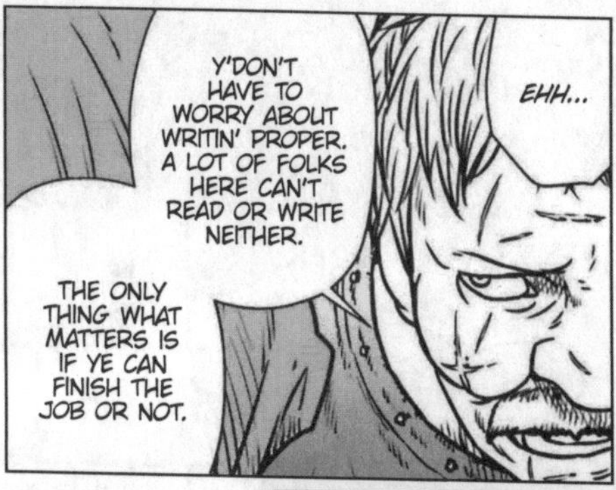
EHH...
Y'DON'T HAVE TO WORRY ABOUT WRITIN' PROPER. A LOT OF FOLKS HERE CAN'T READ OR WRITE NEITHER.
THE ONLY THING WHAT MATTERS IS IF YE CAN FINISH THE JOB OR NOT.

Even in our modern times, contractors such as freelancers and day-laborers are highly sought after to save on unnecessary costs. Our world is not so different than the one being explored by the nomad Nozaki.

KARATE SURVIVOR IN ANOTHER WORLD

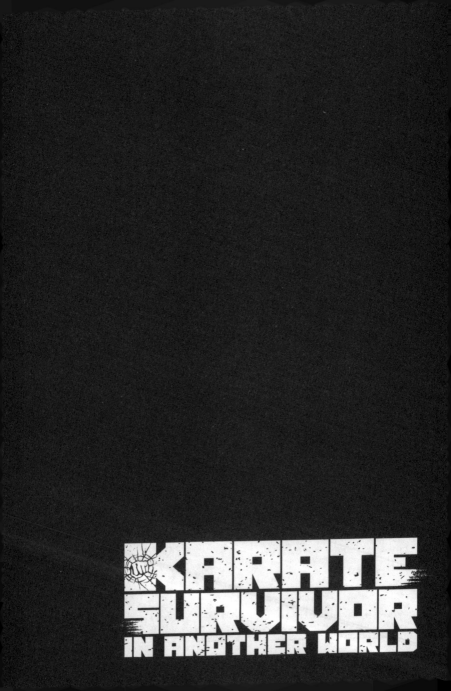

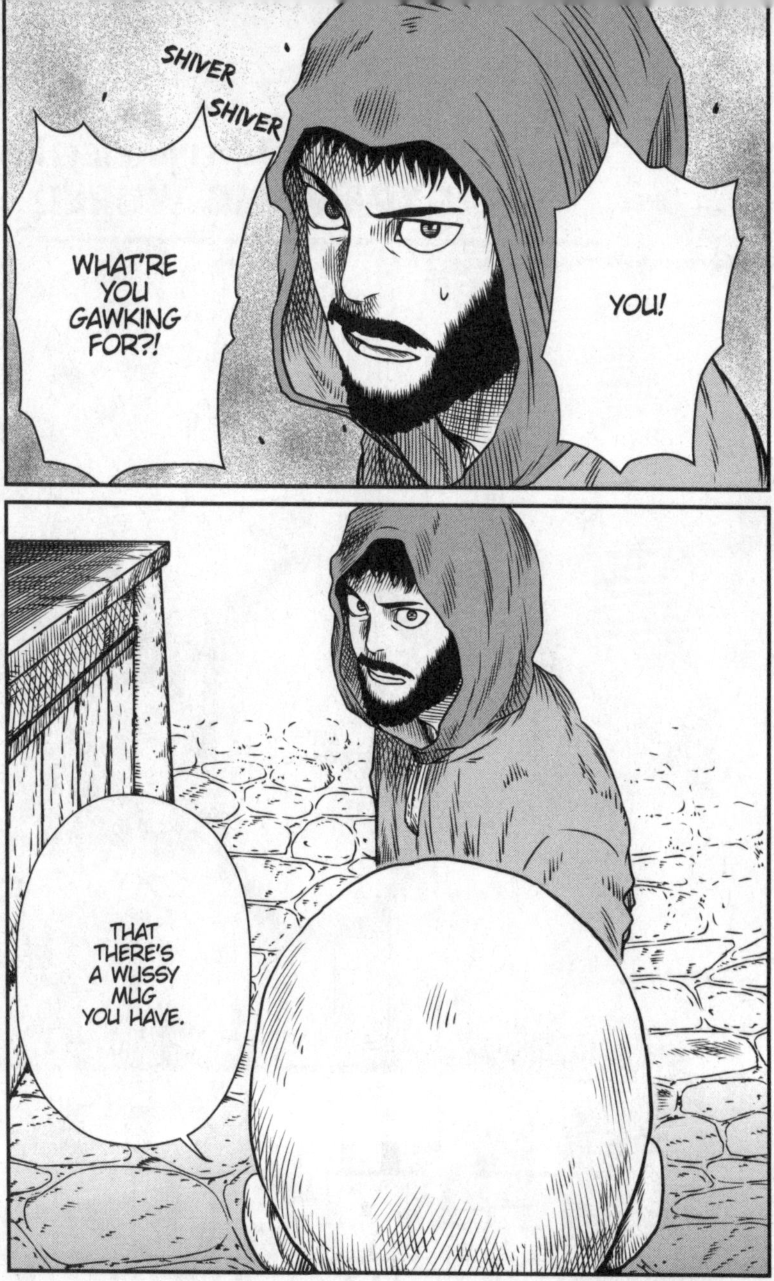
SHIVER
SHIVER
YOU!
WHAT'RE YOU GAWKING FOR?!
THAT THERE'S A WUSSY MUG YOU HAVE.

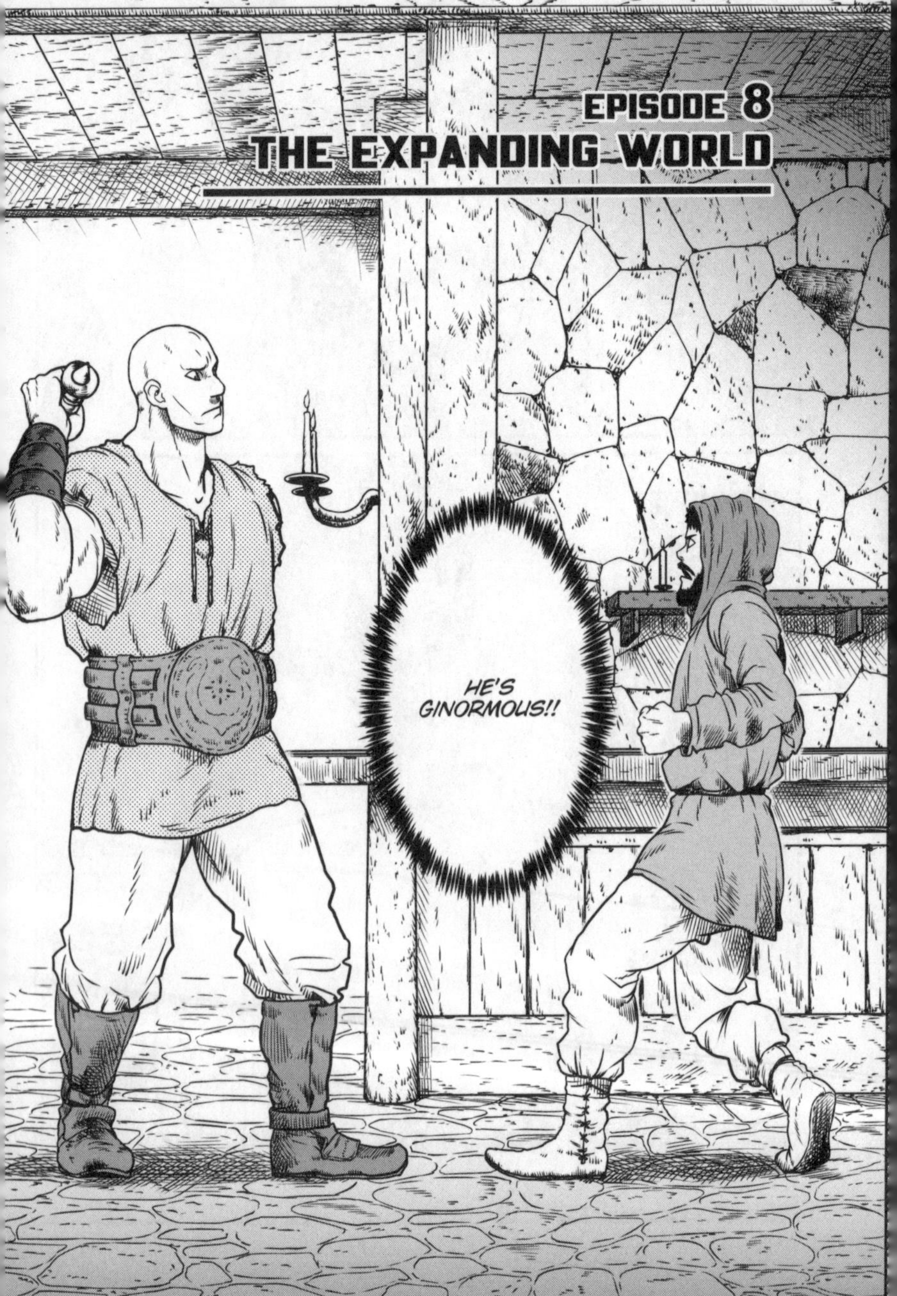
EPISODE 8
THE EXPANDING WORLD
HE'S GINORMOUS!!

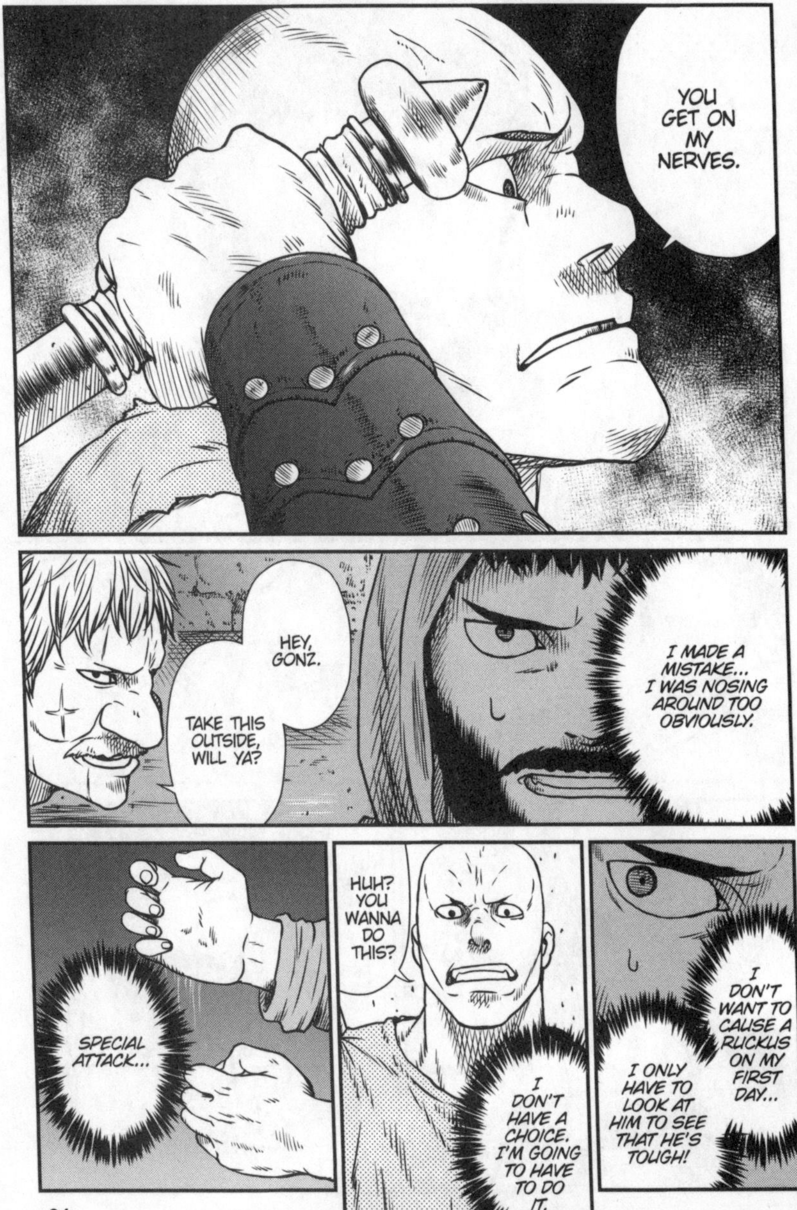
YOU GET ON MY NERVES.
I MADE A MISTAKE... I WAS NOSING AROUND TOO OBVIOUSLY.
HEY, GONZ.
TAKE THIS OUTSIDE, WILL YA?
I DON'T WANT TO CAUSE A RUCKUS ON MY FIRST DAY...
I ONLY HAVE TO LOOK AT HIM TO SEE THAT HE'S TOUGH!
HUH? YOU WANNA DO THIS?
I DON'T HAVE A CHOICE. I'M GOING TO HAVE TO DO IT.
SPECIAL ATTACK...

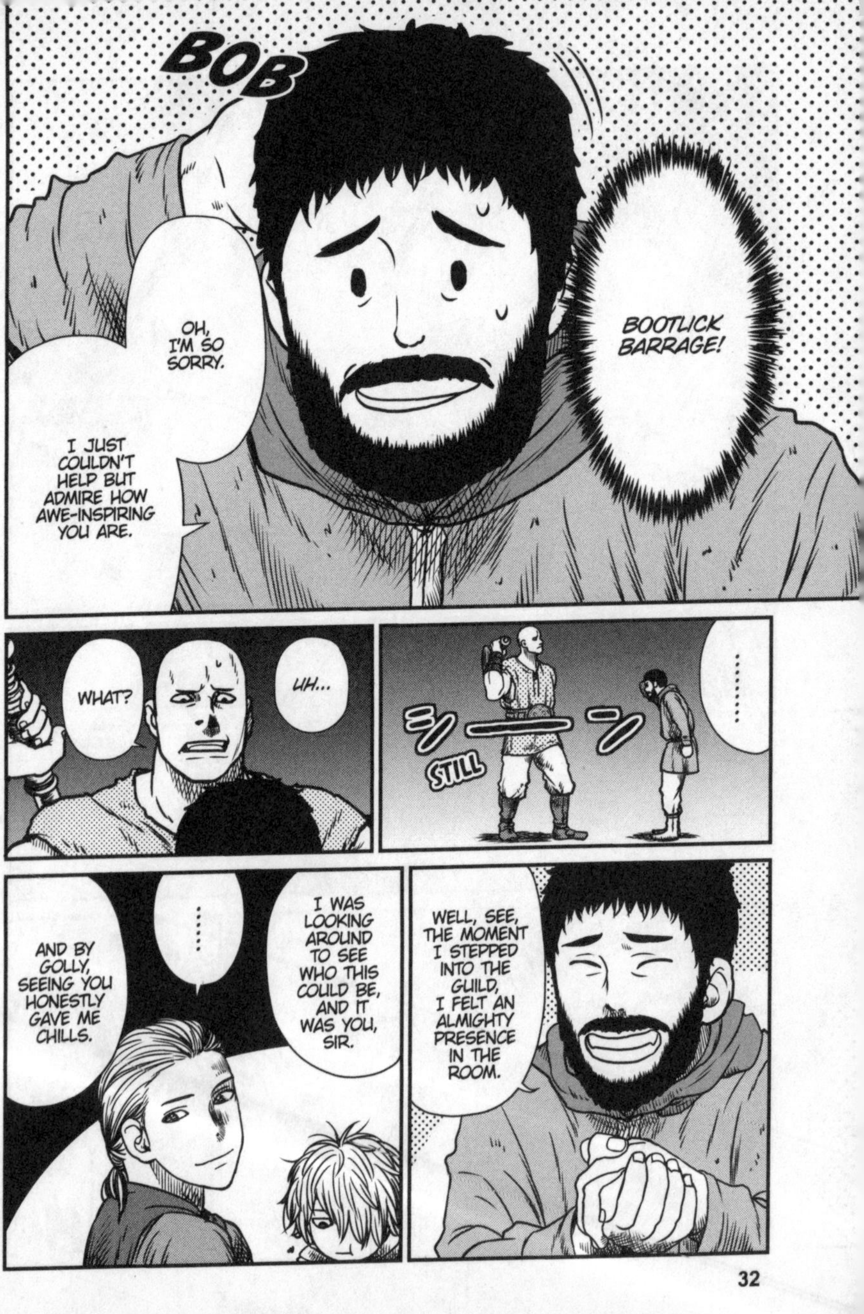
BOB
BOOTLICK BARRAGE!
OH, I'M SO SORRY.
I JUST COULDN'T HELP BUT ADMIRE HOW AWE-INSPIRING YOU ARE.
......
STILL
UH...
WHAT?
WELL, SEE, THE MOMENT I STEPPED INTO THE GUILD, I FELT AN ALMIGHTY PRESENCE IN THE ROOM.
I WAS LOOKING AROUND TO SEE WHO THIS COULD BE, AND IT WAS YOU, SIR.
......
AND BY GOLLY, SEEING YOU HONESTLY GAVE ME CHILLS.

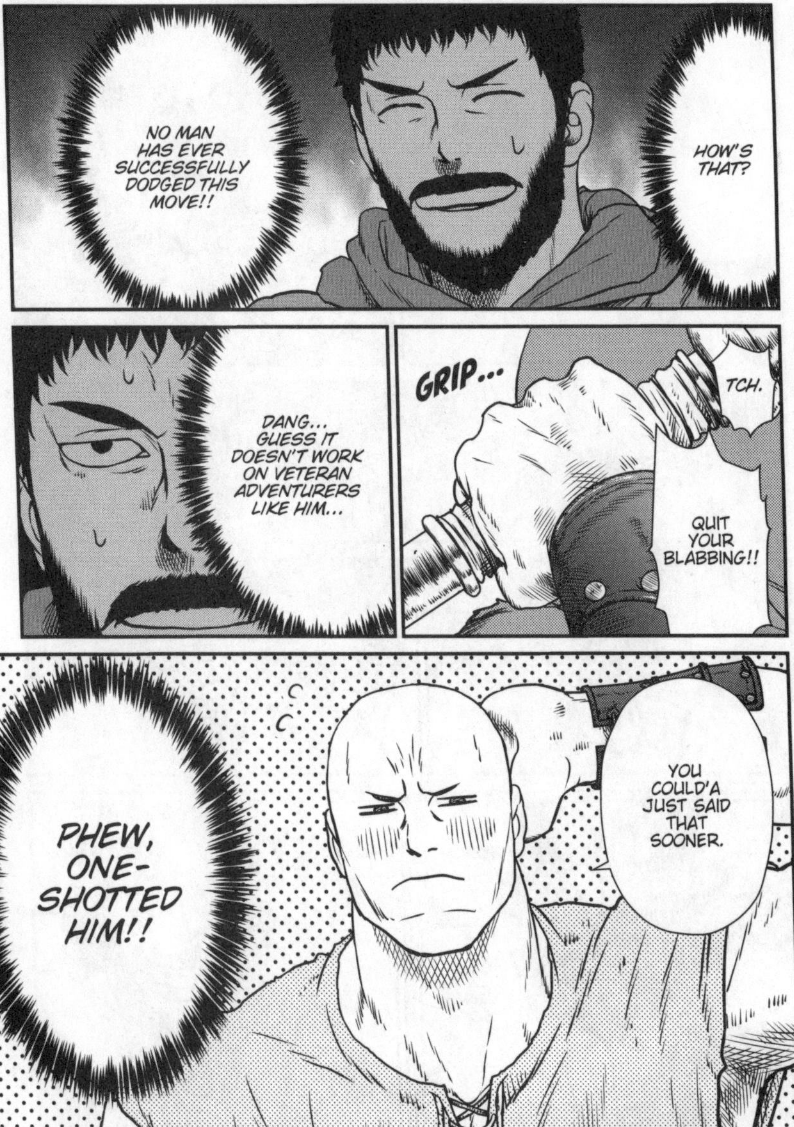
HOW'S THAT?
NO MAN HAS EVER SUCCESSFULLY DODGED THIS MOVE!!
GRIP...
TCH.
QUIT YOUR BLABBING!!
DANG... GUESS IT DOESN'T WORK ON VETERAN ADVENTURERS LIKE HIM...
YOU COULD'A JUST SAID THAT SOONER.
PHEW, ONE-SHOTTED HIM!!

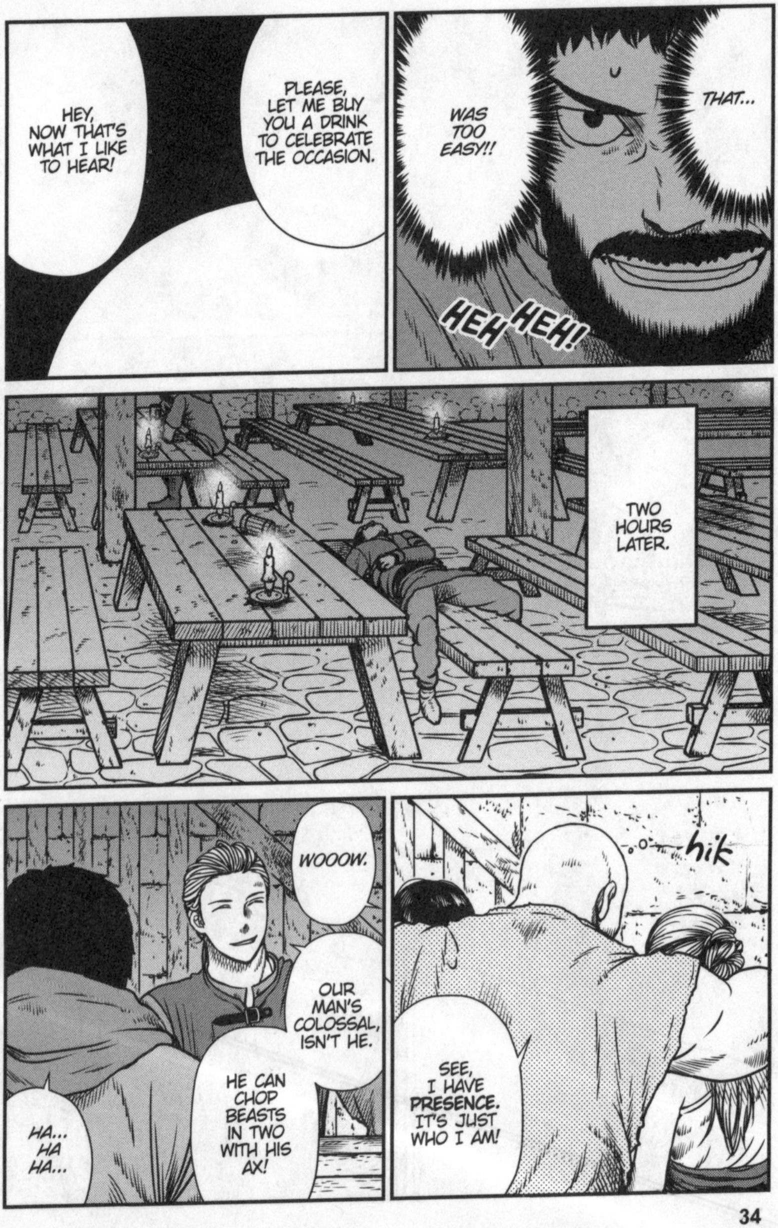

THAT...
WAS TOO EASY!!
HEH HEH!
PLEASE, LET ME BUY YOU A DRINK TO CELEBRATE THE OCCASION.
HEY, NOW THAT'S WHAT I LIKE TO HEAR!
TWO HOURS LATER.
hik
SEE, I HAVE PRESENCE. IT'S JUST WHO I AM!
WOOOW.
OUR MAN'S COLOSSAL, ISN'T HE.
HE CAN CHOP BEASTS IN TWO WITH HIS AX!
HA... HA HA...

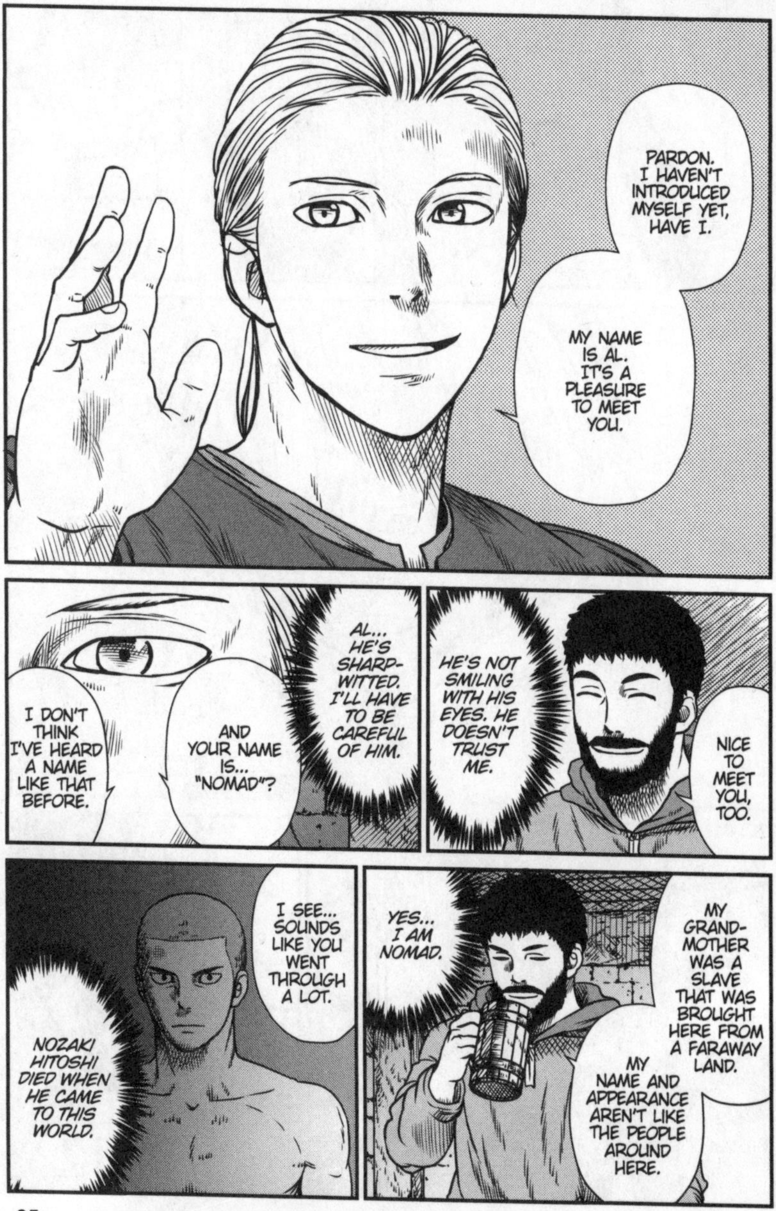
PARDON. I HAVEN'T INTRODUCED MYSELF YET, HAVE I.
MY NAME IS AL. IT'S A PLEASURE TO MEET YOU.
NICE TO MEET YOU, TOO.
HE'S NOT SMILING WITH HIS EYES. HE DOESN'T TRUST ME.
AL... HE'S SHARP-WITTED. I'LL HAVE TO BE CAREFUL OF HIM.
AND YOUR NAME IS... "NOMAD"?
I DON'T THINK I'VE HEARD A NAME LIKE THAT BEFORE.
YES... I AM NOMAD.
MY GRANDMOTHER WAS A SLAVE THAT WAS BROUGHT HERE FROM A FARAWAY LAND.
MY NAME AND APPEARANCE AREN'T LIKE THE PEOPLE AROUND HERE.
I SEE... SOUNDS LIKE YOU WENT THROUGH A LOT.
NOZAKI HITOSHI DIED WHEN HE CAME TO THIS WORLD.

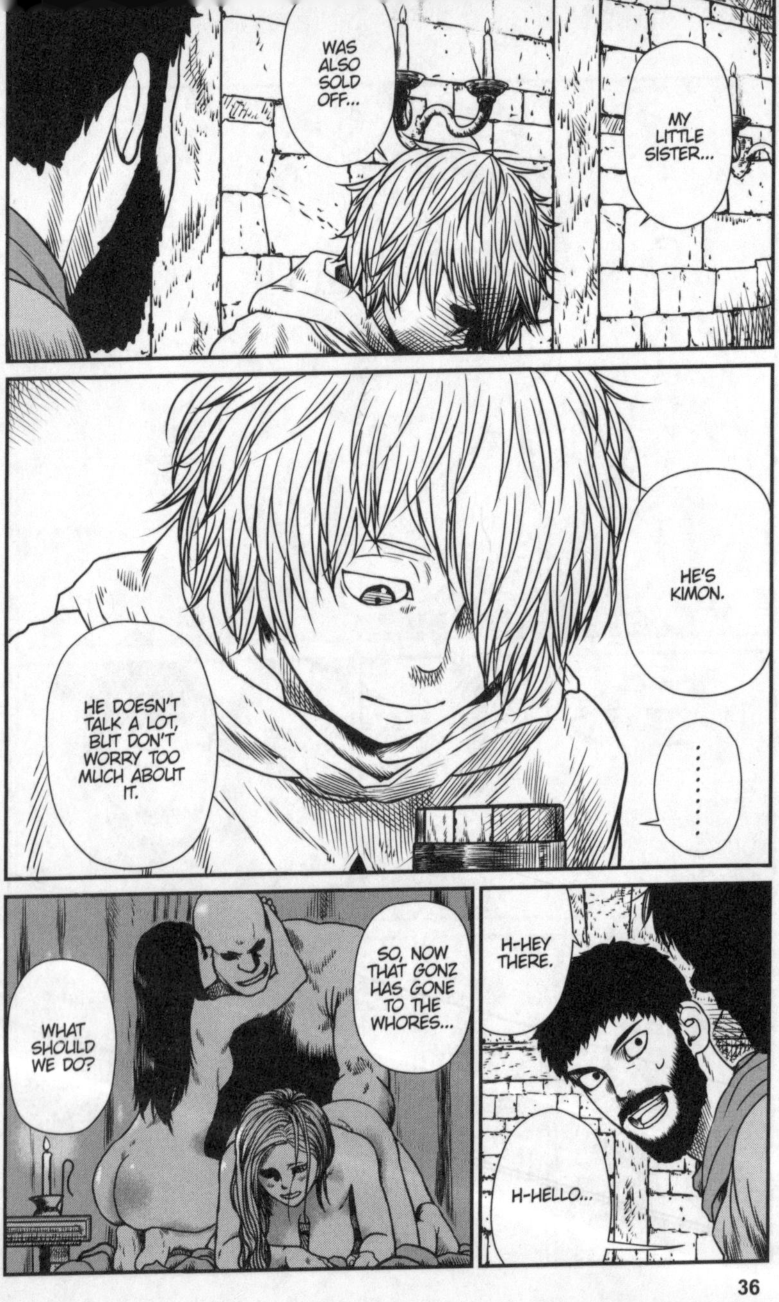
MY LITTLE SISTER...
WAS ALSO SOLD OFF...
HE'S KIMON.
......
HE DOESN'T TALK A LOT, BUT DON'T WORRY TOO MUCH ABOUT IT.
H-HEY THERE.
H-HELLO...
SO, NOW THAT GONZ HAS GONE TO THE WHORES...
WHAT SHOULD WE DO?

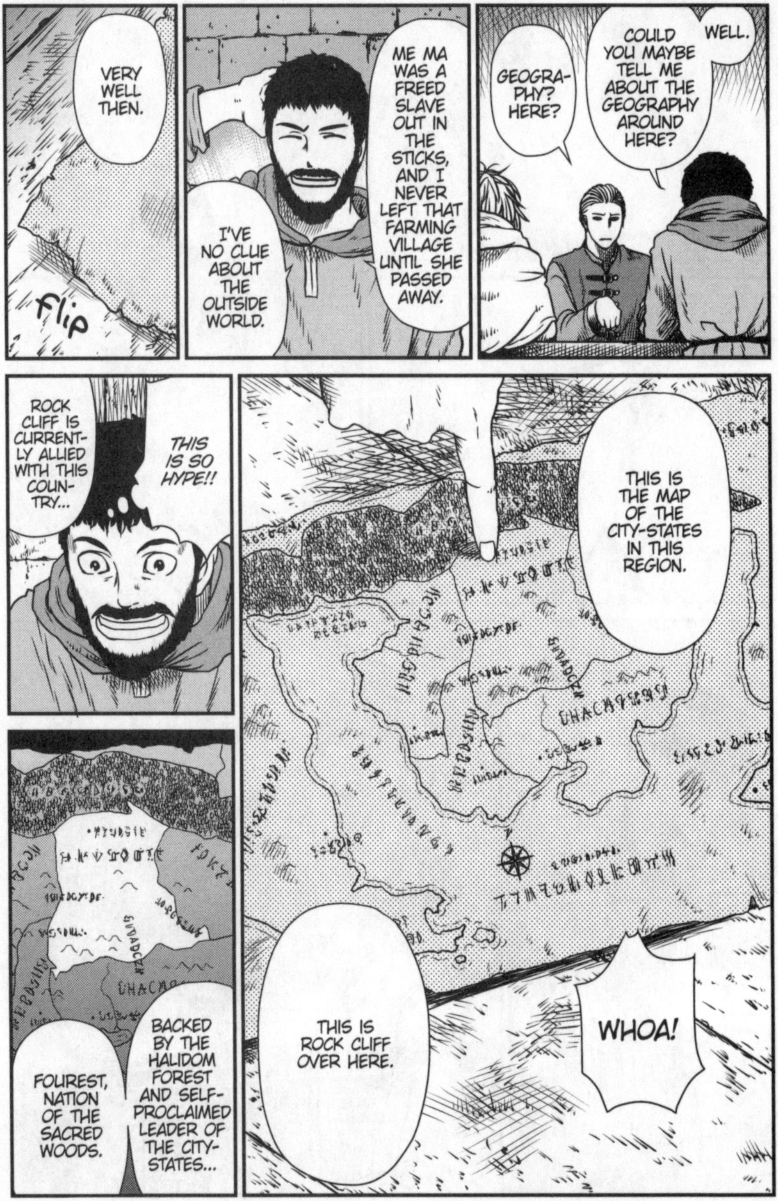
WELL.
COULD YOU MAYBE TELL ME ABOUT THE GEOGRAPHY AROUND HERE?
GEOGRA-PHY? HERE?
ME MA WAS A FREED SLAVE OUT IN THE STICKS, AND I NEVER LEFT THAT FARMING VILLAGE UNTIL SHE PASSED AWAY.
I'VE NO CLUE ABOUT THE OUTSIDE WORLD.
VERY WELL THEN.
Flip
THIS IS THE MAP OF THE CITY-STATES IN THIS REGION.
WHOA!
THIS IS ROCK CLIFF OVER HERE.
THIS IS SO HYPE!!
ROCK CLIFF IS CURRENT-LY ALLIED WITH THIS COUN-TRY...
BACKED BY THE HALIDOM FOREST AND SELF-PROCLAIMED LEADER OF THE CITY-STATES...
FOUREST, NATION OF THE SACRED WOODS.

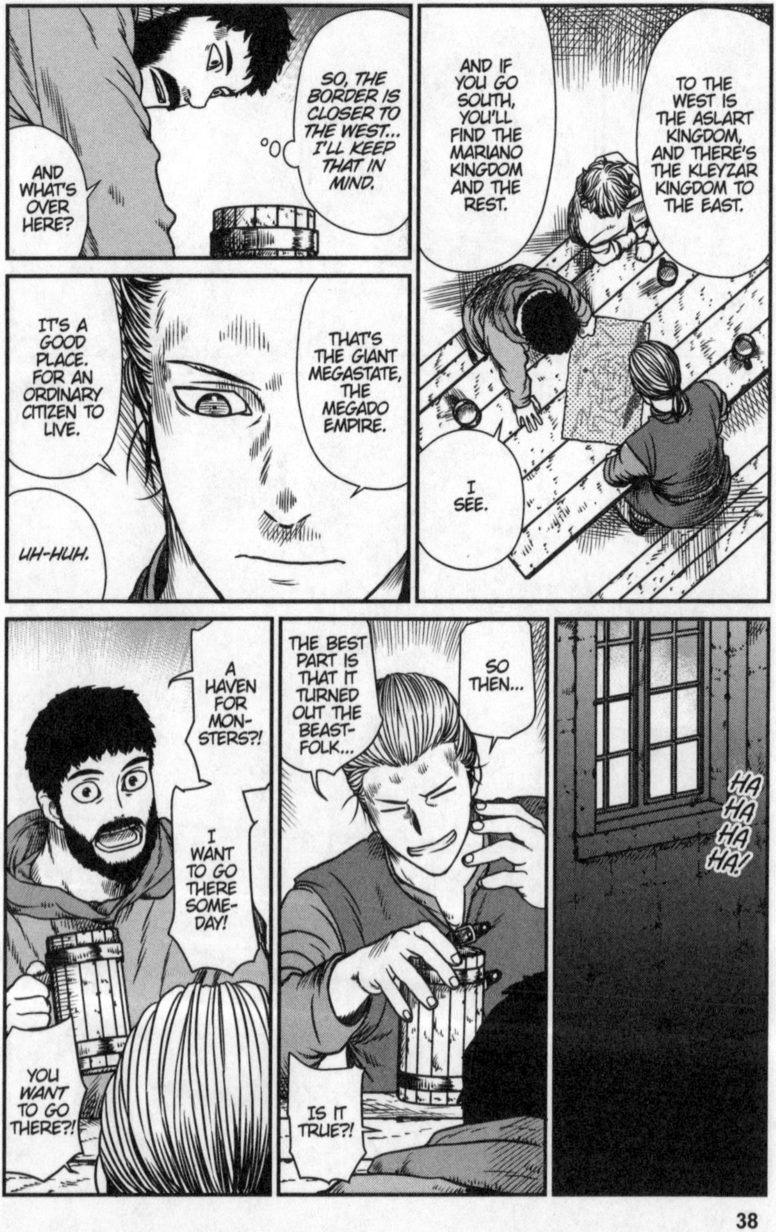
TO THE WEST IS THE ASLART KINGDOM, AND THERE'S THE KLEYZAR KINGDOM TO THE EAST.
AND IF YOU GO SOUTH, YOU'LL FIND THE MARIANO KINGDOM AND THE REST.
I SEE.
SO, THE BORDER IS CLOSER TO THE WEST... I'LL KEEP THAT IN MIND.
AND WHAT'S OVER HERE?
THAT'S THE GIANT MEGASTATE, THE MEGADO EMPIRE.
IT'S A GOOD PLACE. FOR AN ORDINARY CITIZEN TO LIVE.
UH-HUH.
HA HA HA HA!
SO THEN...
THE BEST PART IS THAT IT TURNED OUT THE BEAST-FOLK...
IS IT TRUE?!
A HAVEN FOR MON-STERS?!
I WANT TO GO THERE SOME-DAY!
YOU WANT TO GO THERE?!

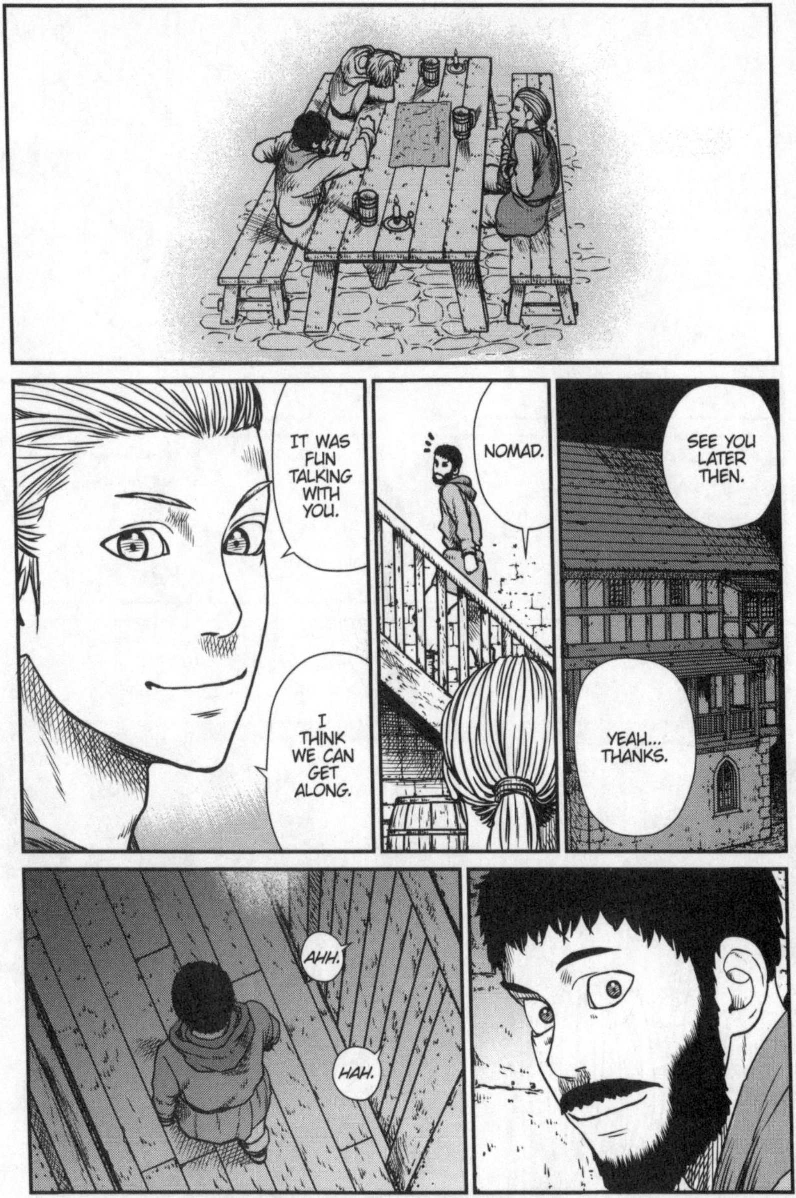
SEE YOU LATER THEN.
YEAH... THANKS.
NOMAD.
IT WAS FUN TALKING WITH YOU.
I THINK WE CAN GET ALONG.
AHH.
HAH.

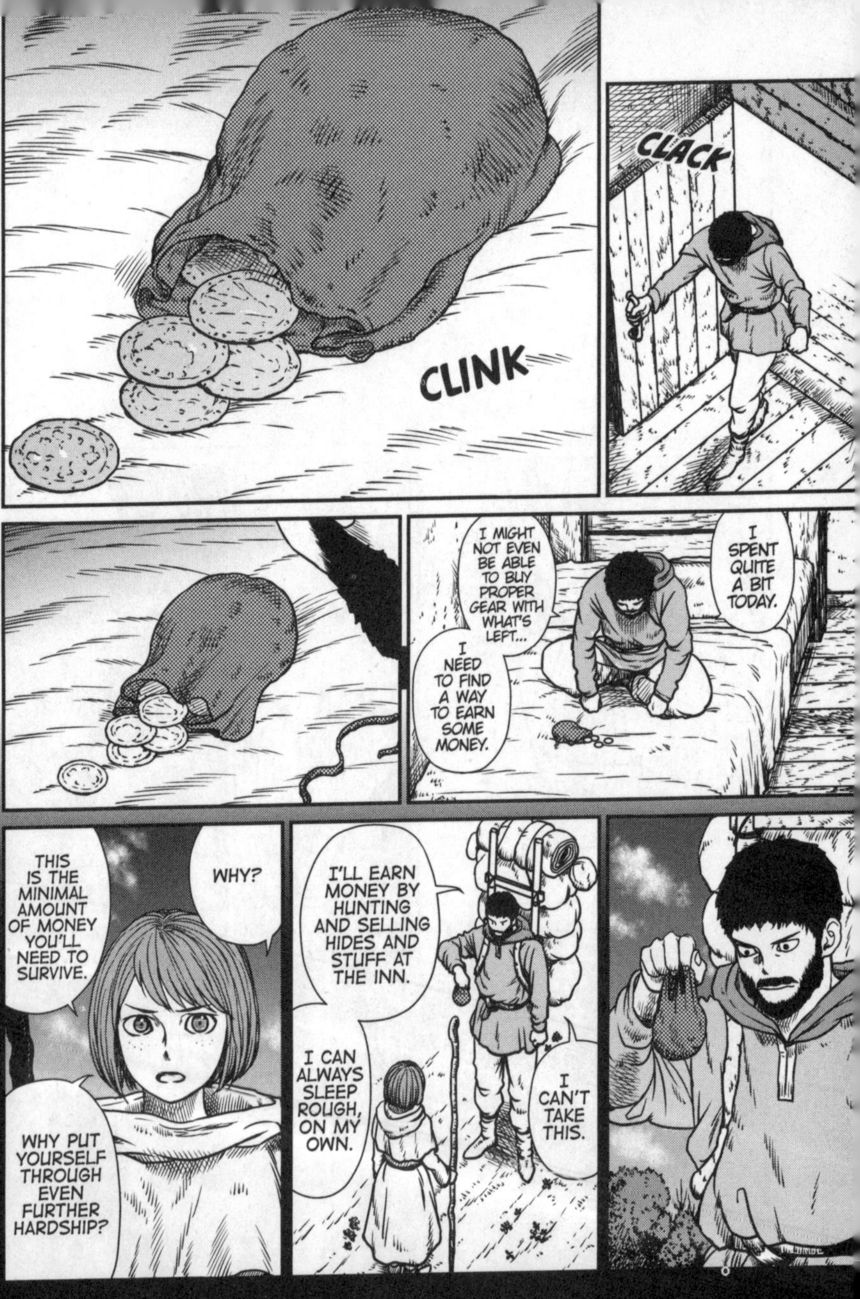
CLACK
CLINK
I SPENT QUITE A BIT TODAY.
I MIGHT NOT EVEN BE ABLE TO BUY PROPER GEAR WITH WHAT'S LEFT...
I NEED TO FIND A WAY TO EARN SOME MONEY.
I CAN'T TAKE THIS.
I'LL EARN MONEY BY HUNTING AND SELLING HIDES AND STUFF AT THE INN.
I CAN ALWAYS SLEEP ROUGH, ON MY OWN.
WHY?
THIS IS THE MINIMAL AMOUNT OF MONEY YOU'LL NEED TO SURVIVE.
WHY PUT YOURSELF THROUGH EVEN FURTHER HARDSHIP?

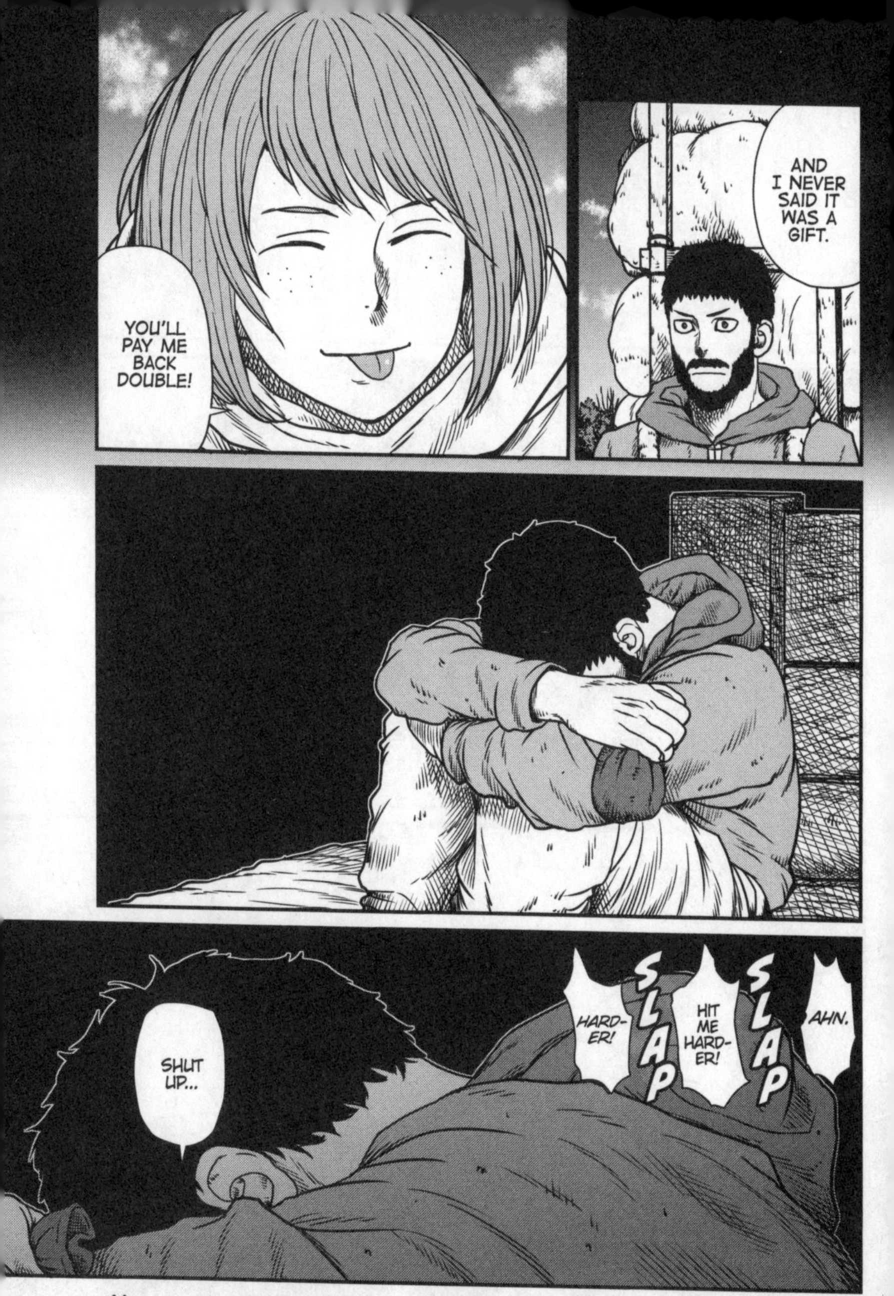
AND I NEVER SAID IT WAS A GIFT.
YOU'LL PAY ME BACK DOUBLE!
AHN.
SLAP
HIT ME HARDER!
SLAP
HARDER!
SHUT UP...

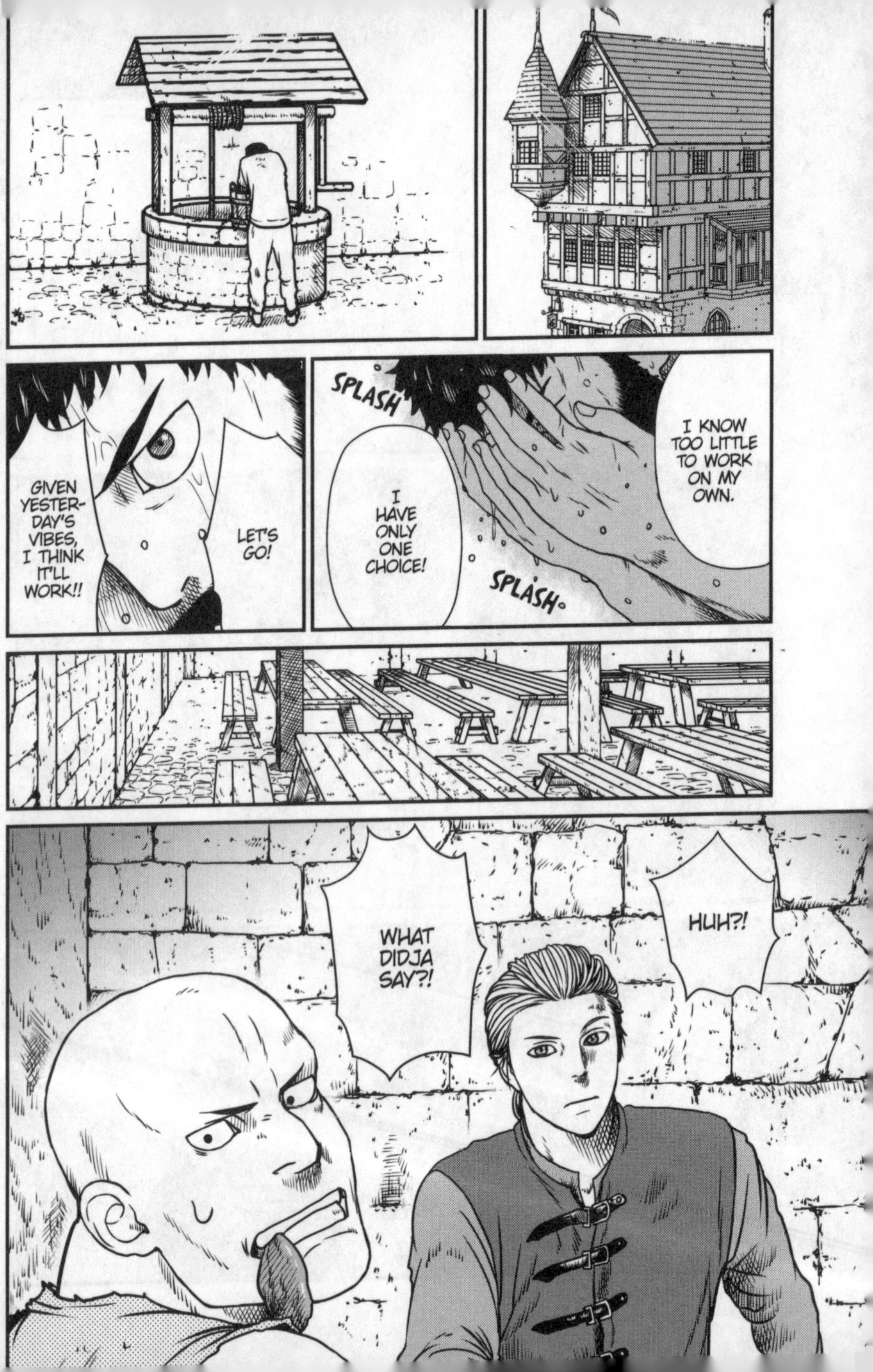
I KNOW TOO LITTLE TO WORK ON MY OWN.
SPLASH
I HAVE ONLY ONE CHOICE!
SPLASH
LET'S GO!
GIVEN YESTER-DAY'S VIBES, I THINK IT'LL WORK!!
HUH?!
WHAT DIDJA SAY?!

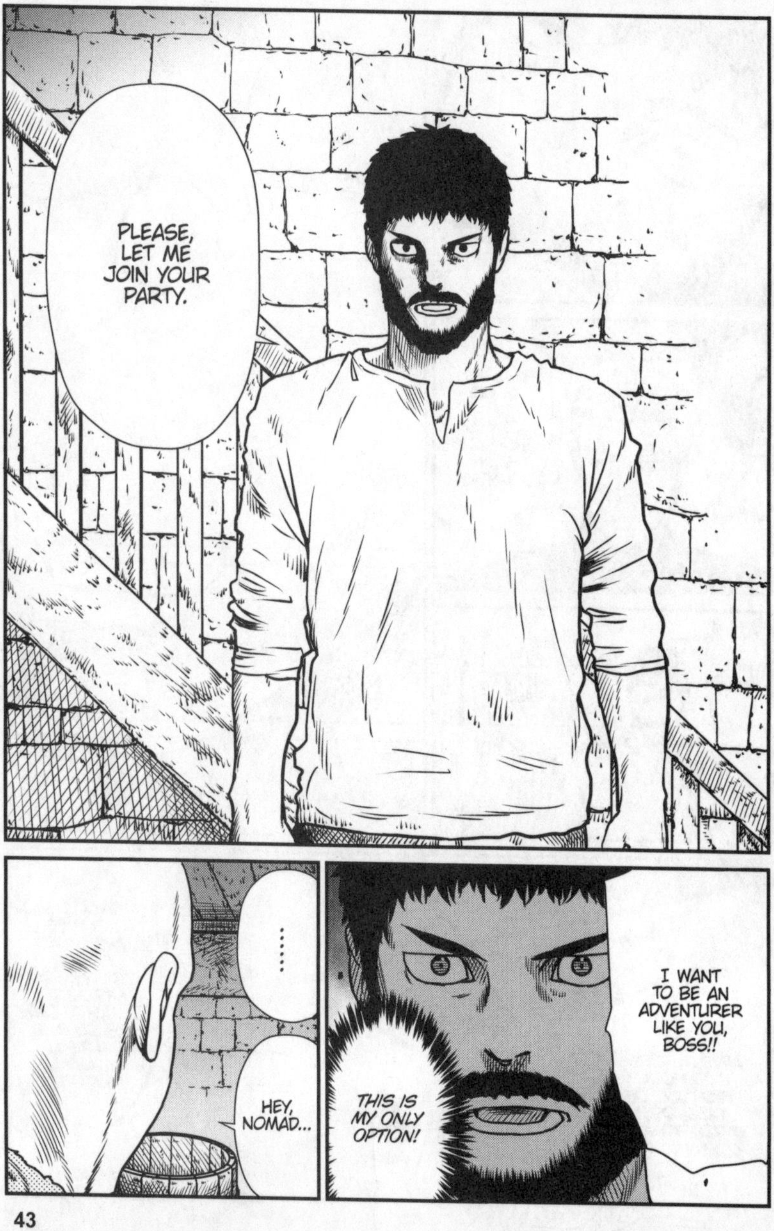
PLEASE, LET ME JOIN YOUR PARTY.
I WANT TO BE AN ADVENTURER LIKE YOU, BOSS!!
THIS IS MY ONLY OPTION!
......
HEY, NOMAD...

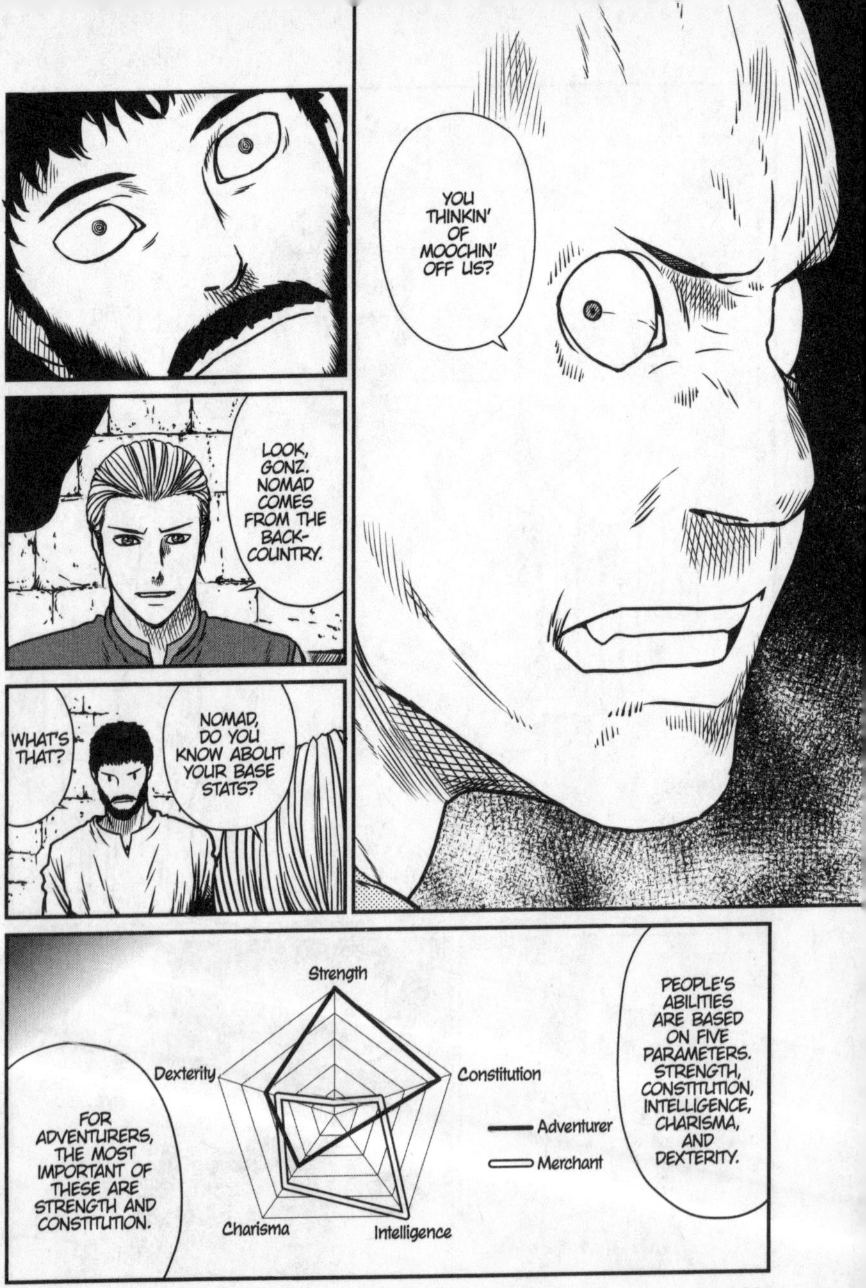
YOU THINKIN' OF MOOCHIN' OFF US?
LOOK, GONZ. NOMAD COMES FROM THE BACK-COUNTRY.
NOMAD, DO YOU KNOW ABOUT YOUR BASE STATS?
WHAT'S THAT?
PEOPLE'S ABILITIES ARE BASED ON FIVE PARAMETERS. STRENGTH, CONSTITUTION, INTELLIGENCE, CHARISMA, AND DEXTERITY.
Strength
Constitution
Intelligence
Charisma
Dexterity
Adventurer
Merchant
FOR ADVENTURERS, THE MOST IMPORTANT OF THESE ARE STRENGTH AND CONSTITUTION.

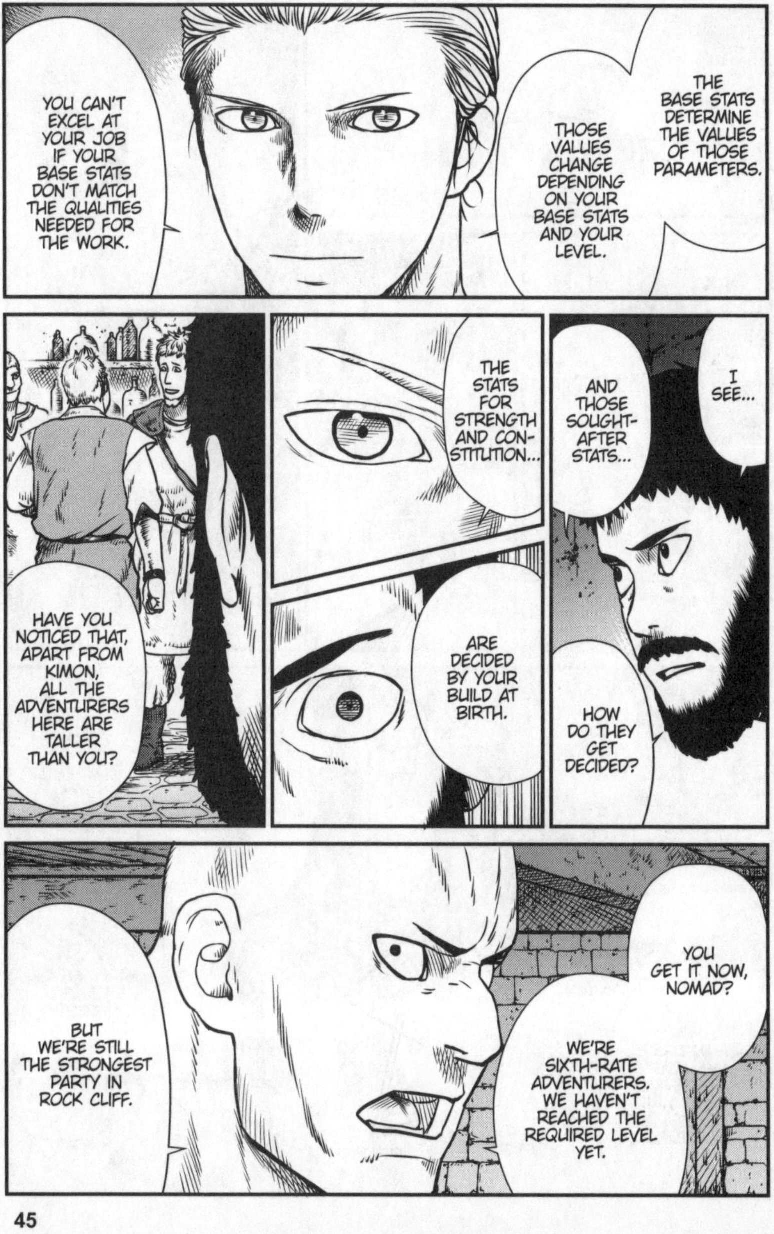
THE BASE STATS DETERMINE THE VALUES OF THOSE PARAMETERS.
THOSE VALUES CHANGE DEPENDING ON YOUR BASE STATS AND YOUR LEVEL.
YOU CAN'T EXCEL AT YOUR JOB IF YOUR BASE STATS DON'T MATCH THE QUALITIES NEEDED FOR THE WORK.
I SEE...
AND THOSE SOUGHT-AFTER STATS...
HOW DO THEY GET DECIDED?
THE STATS FOR STRENGTH AND CON-STITUTION...
ARE DECIDED BY YOUR BUILD AT BIRTH.
HAVE YOU NOTICED THAT, APART FROM KIMON, ALL THE ADVENTURERS HERE ARE TALLER THAN YOU?
YOU GET IT NOW, NOMAD?
WE'RE SIXTH-RATE ADVENTURERS. WE HAVEN'T REACHED THE REQUIRED LEVEL YET.
BUT WE'RE STILL THE STRONGEST PARTY IN ROCK CLIFF.

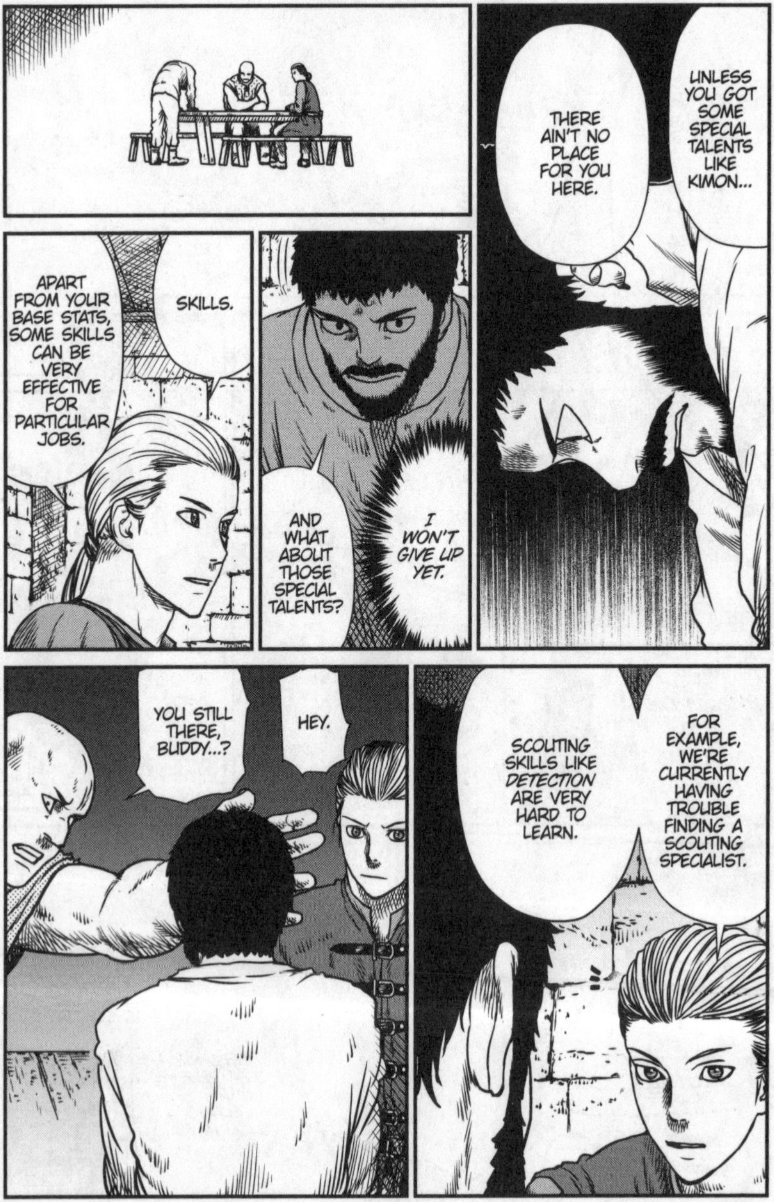
UNLESS YOU GOT SOME SPECIAL TALENTS LIKE KIMON...
THERE AIN'T NO PLACE FOR YOU HERE.
I WON'T GIVE UP YET.
AND WHAT ABOUT THOSE SPECIAL TALENTS?
SKILLS.
APART FROM YOUR BASE STATS, SOME SKILLS CAN BE VERY EFFECTIVE FOR PARTICULAR JOBS.
FOR EXAMPLE, WE'RE CURRENTLY HAVING TROUBLE FINDING A SCOUTING SPECIALIST.
SCOUTING SKILLS LIKE *DETECTION* ARE VERY HARD TO LEARN.
HEY.
YOU STILL THERE, BUDDY...?

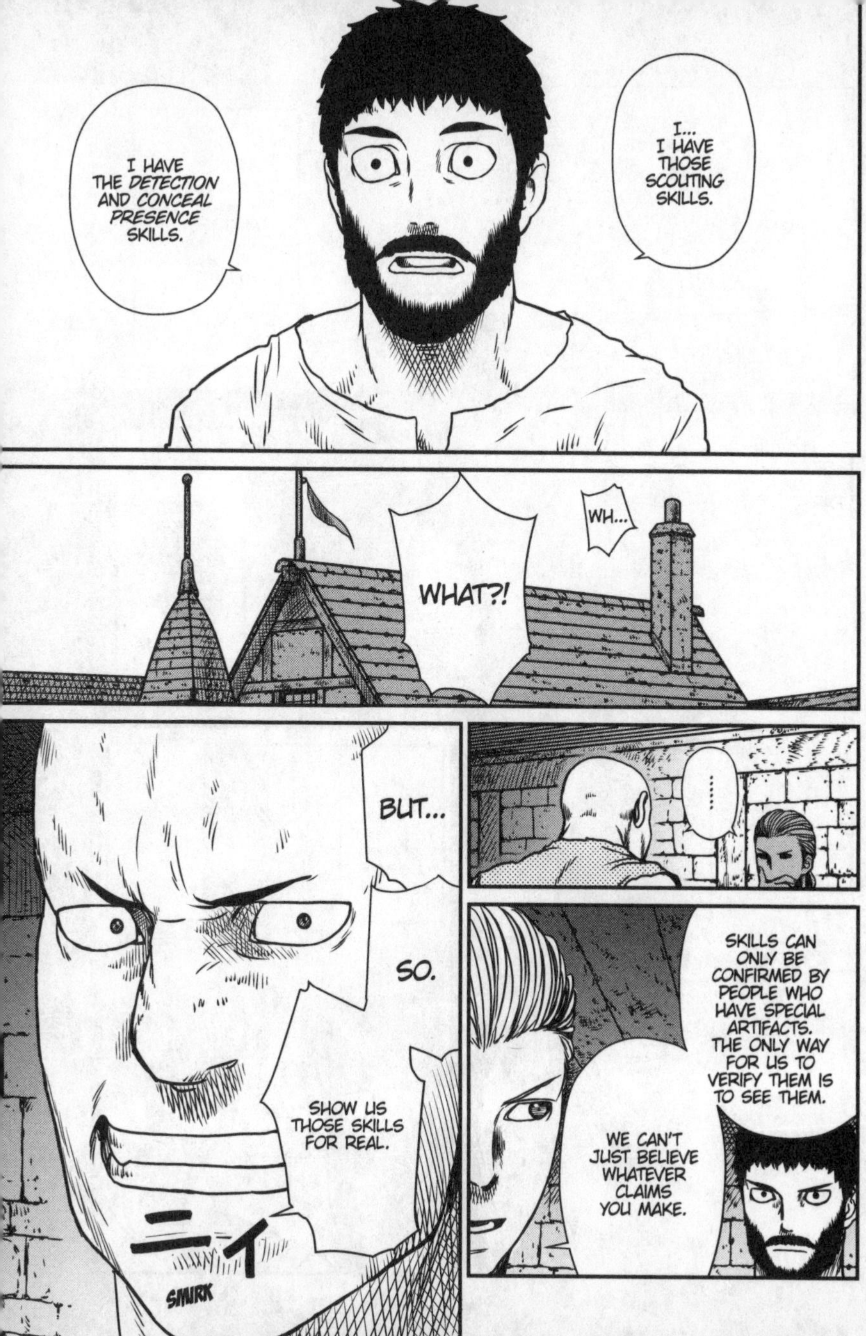
I... I HAVE THOSE SCOUTING SKILLS.
I HAVE THE *DETECTION* AND *CONCEAL PRESENCE* SKILLS.
WH...
WHAT?!
......
SKILLS CAN ONLY BE CONFIRMED BY PEOPLE WHO HAVE SPECIAL ARTIFACTS. THE ONLY WAY FOR US TO VERIFY THEM IS TO SEE THEM.
WE CAN'T JUST BELIEVE WHATEVER CLAIMS YOU MAKE.
BUT...
SO.
SHOW US THOSE SKILLS FOR REAL.
SMIRK

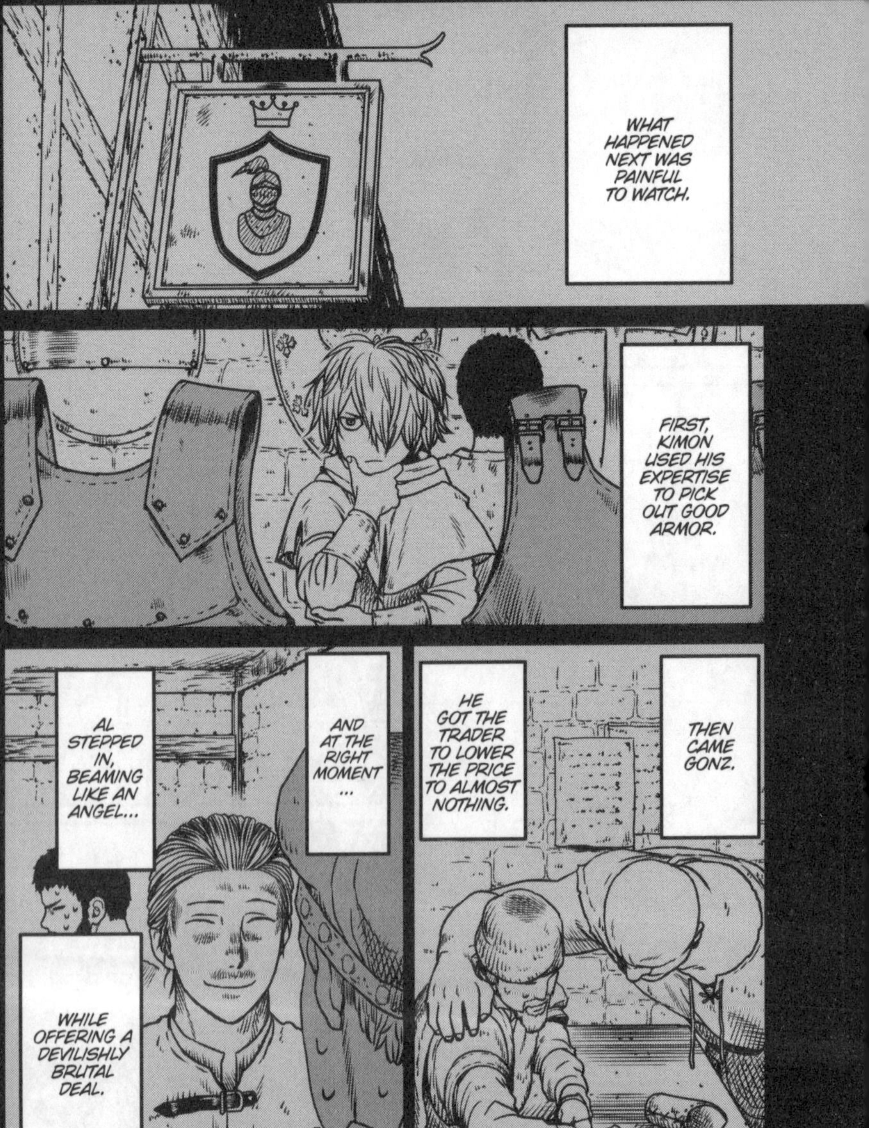
WHAT HAPPENED NEXT WAS PAINFUL TO WATCH.
FIRST, KIMON USED HIS EXPERTISE TO PICK OUT GOOD ARMOR.
THEN CAME GONZ.
HE GOT THE TRADER TO LOWER THE PRICE TO ALMOST NOTHING.
AND AT THE RIGHT MOMENT ...
AL STEPPED IN, BEAMING LIKE AN ANGEL...
WHILE OFFERING A DEVILISHLY BRUTAL DEAL.

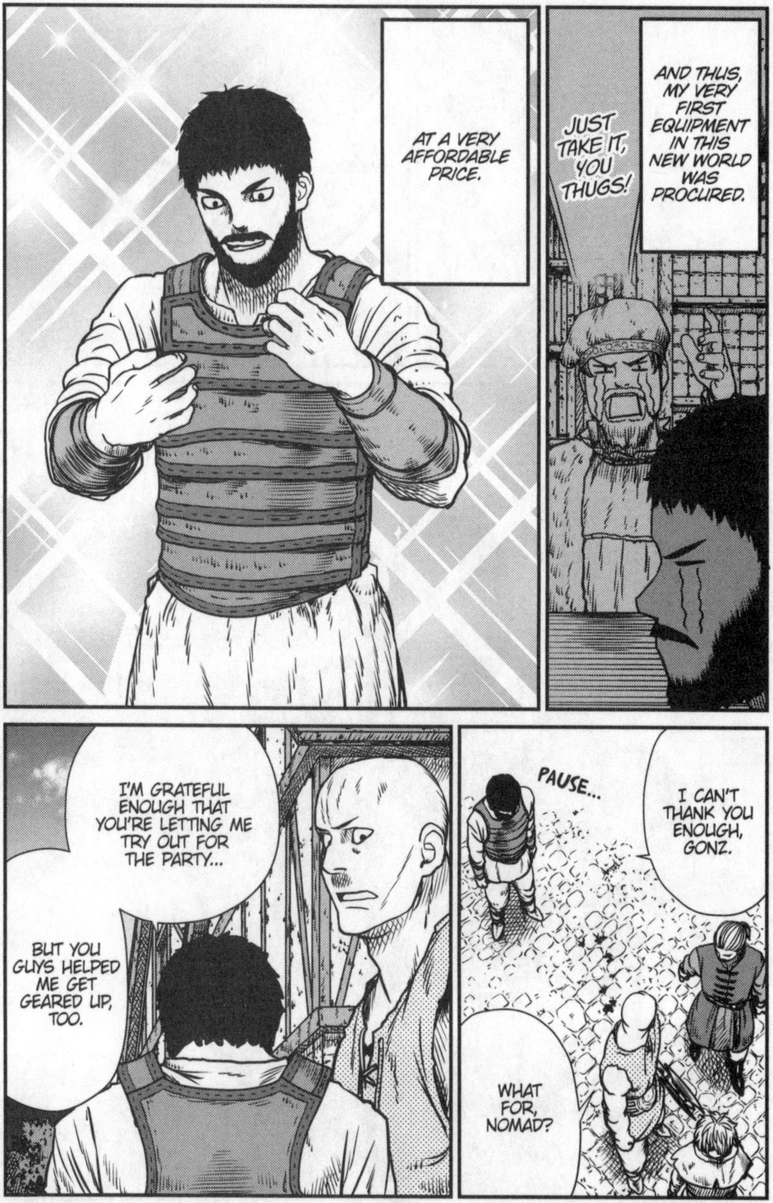
AND THUS, MY VERY FIRST EQUIPMENT IN THIS NEW WORLD WAS PROCURED.
JUST TAKE IT, YOU THUGS!
AT A VERY AFFORDABLE PRICE.
I CAN'T THANK YOU ENOUGH, GONZ.
PAUSE...
WHAT FOR, NOMAD?
I'M GRATEFUL ENOUGH THAT YOU'RE LETTING ME TRY OUT FOR THE PARTY...
BUT YOU GUYS HELPED ME GET GEARED UP, TOO.

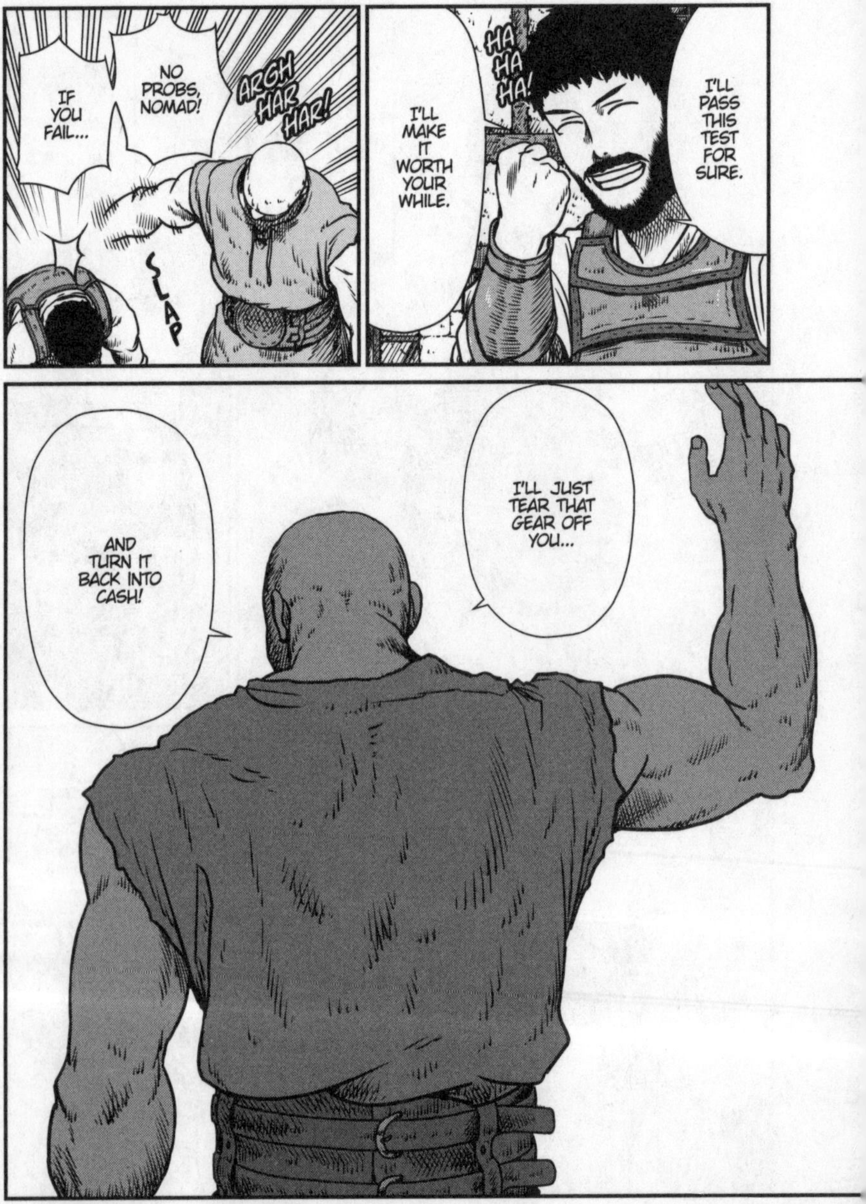
I'LL PASS THIS TEST FOR SURE.
HA HA HA!
I'LL MAKE IT WORTH YOUR WHILE.
ARGH HAR HAR!
NO PROBS, NOMAD!
IF YOU FAIL...
SLAP
I'LL JUST TEAR THAT GEAR OFF YOU...
AND TURN IT BACK INTO CASH!

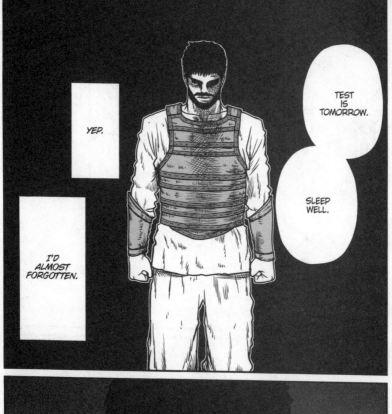

TEST IS TOMORROW.

SLEEP WELL.

YEP.

I'D ALMOST FORGOTTEN.

THIS IS THE WORLD I LIVE IN NOW.

JUST GREAT.

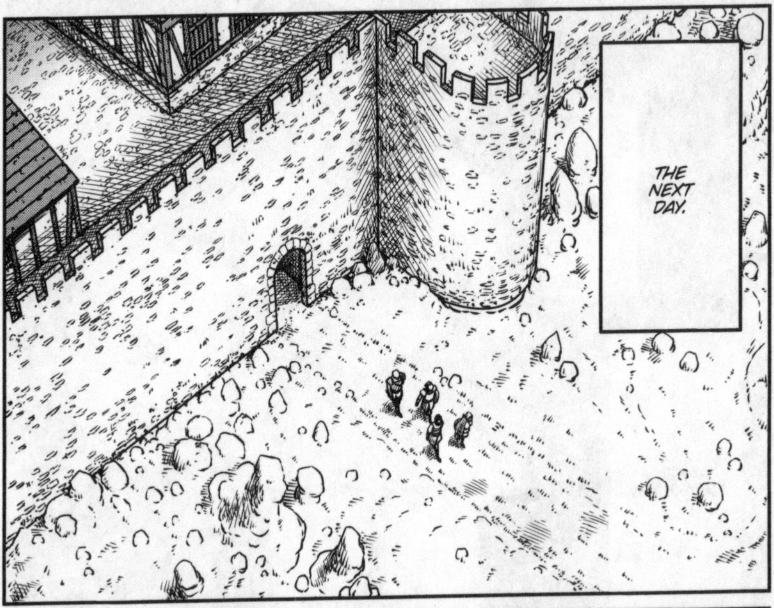
THE NEXT DAY.
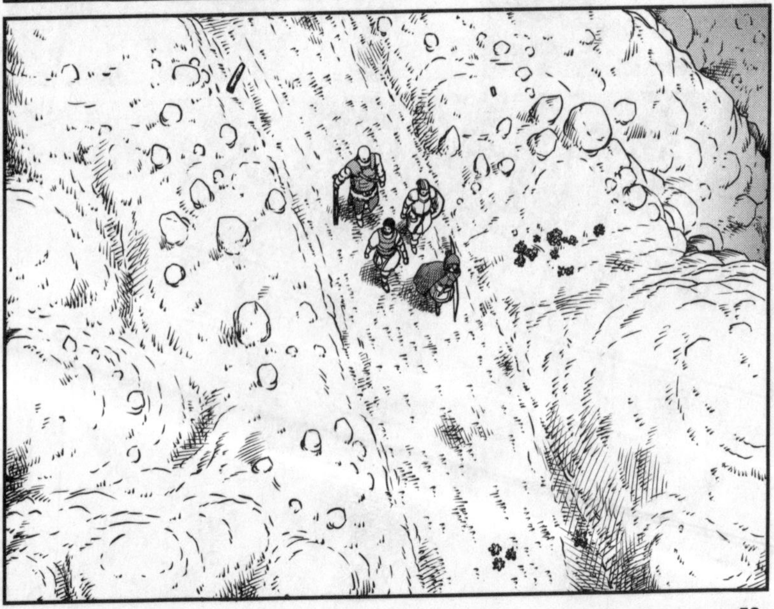

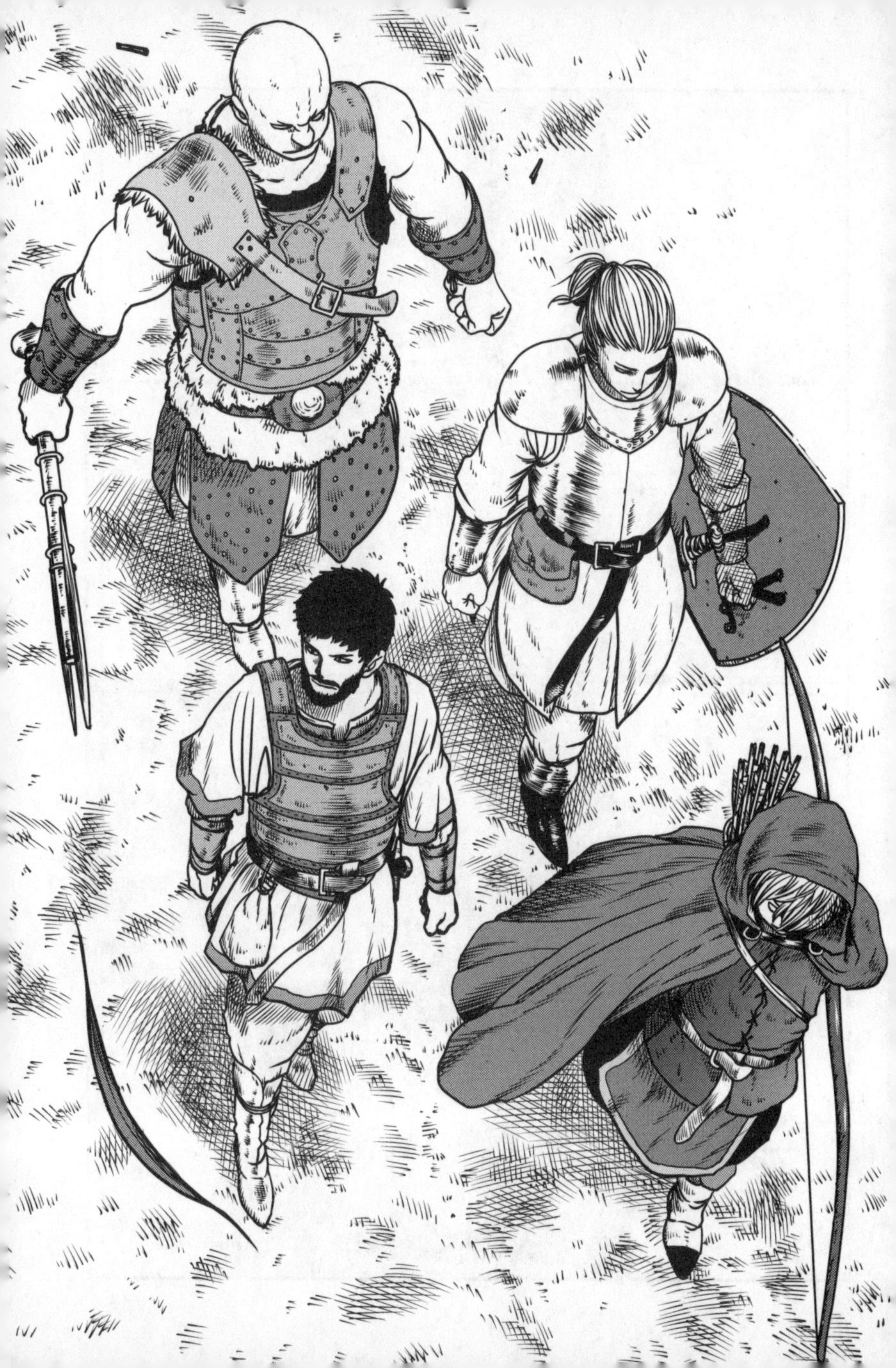

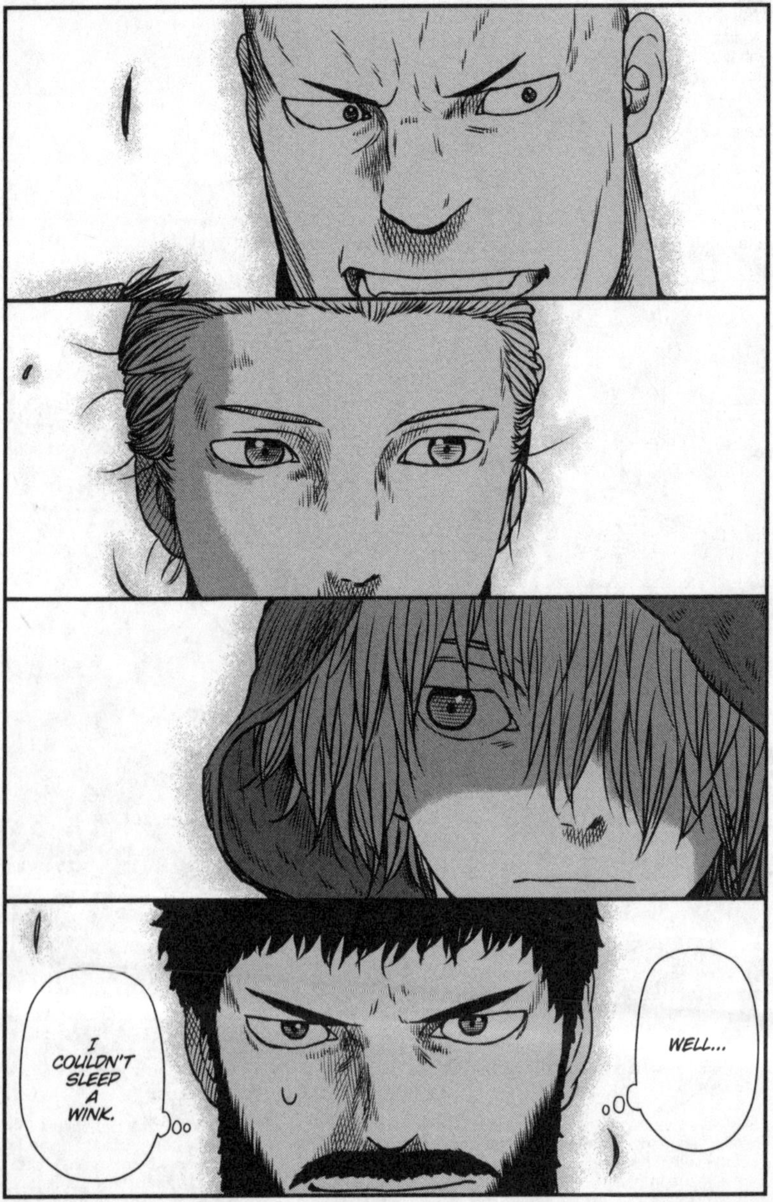
WELL...
I COULDN'T SLEEP A WINK.

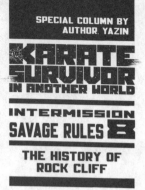

SPECIAL COLUMN BY
AUTHOR, YAZIN

KARATE SURVIVOR IN ANOTHER WORLD

INTERMISSION
SAVAGE RULES 8
THE HISTORY OF ROCK CLIFF

The fortress city of Rock Cliff was built during the conflict against the barbarian forces. The region was previously inhabited by the beastfolk, dubbed "barbarians" by the local human population. While the Megado Empire and the Reagam Kingdom were expanding their territories, they exiled their convicts to the peninsula that would later be the domain of several city-states.

With the Halidom Forest to the north and ocean on the three other sides, it was an isolated area in all but name. The region was uncharted, dominated by the inhuman barbarians. The area was a place of banishment for nobles and other criminals that could not be outright executed for various political reasons.

THIS IS THE MAP OF THE CITY-STATES IN THIS REGION.
WHOA!
THIS IS ROCK CLIFF OVER HERE.

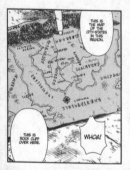

However, the exiles more resilient than expected. They first befriended the beastfolk and gradually increased their own numbers. Eventually, the humans massacred most of the barbarians and took the rest as slaves.

Rock Cliff was built at the height of the human assault. As the humans increased their strength through trade with the Megado Empire and the Reagam Kingdom, they expanded their territories southward, neglecting the north . The northern region did not face the ocean and offered few opportunities for trade. It was also home to the few straggling beastfolk that remained. There was little incentive for humans to expand north.

However, human population growth continued. It's not easy to develop land overrun with monsters, and not many areas left were safe for people. Living space was limited, and eventually the humans had to migrate northward. The beastfolk were pushed northward as well and were driven nearer to the Halidom Forest. The fortress, Rock Cliff, was built to finally annihilate the remaining beast-folk.

Beastfolk are more physically capable than humans of the same level. However, they were courageous and simple, weak against coordinated attacks, and were not skilled in siege warfare. The humans exploited the beastfolk's weaknesses and achieved a final victory.

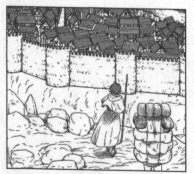

Humans used tactics such as kidnapping beastfolk children as bait and displaying the desecrated bodies of beastfolk to lure them to Rock Cliff. The brave but simple beastfolk repeatedly engaged in disadvantageous battles to rescue their children and exact revenge for the disrespectful displays.

The beastfolk, having lost all their fighters, had to escape further north and were swallowed by the depths of the Halidom Forest. Any remaining individuals near Rock Cliff were taken as slaves by the humans.

Nomad arrived at Rock Cliff two hundred years after the humans established the city-states. The brutal treatment of the beastfolk at Rock Cliff brought them to the brink of extinction. However, countries that frequently trade with the Megado Empire and Reagam Kingdom have ironically seen an increase in beastfolk numbers, as they are valued for their rarity. Rock Cliff is now primarily a mercantile city, but embedded within it is a bloodied history befitting of its roots as a frontline fortress.

KARATE SURVIVOR IN ANOTHER WORLD

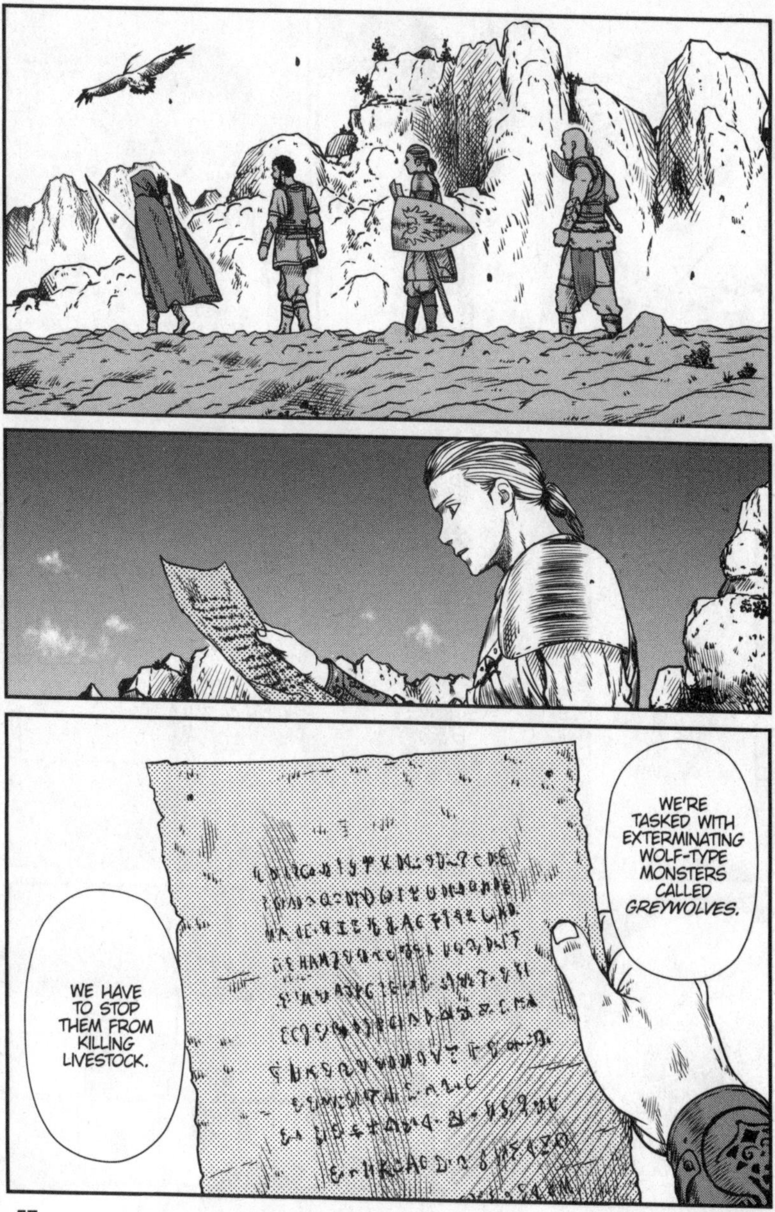
WE'RE TASKED WITH EXTERMINATING WOLF-TYPE MONSTERS CALLED GREYWOLVES.
WE HAVE TO STOP THEM FROM KILLING LIVESTOCK.

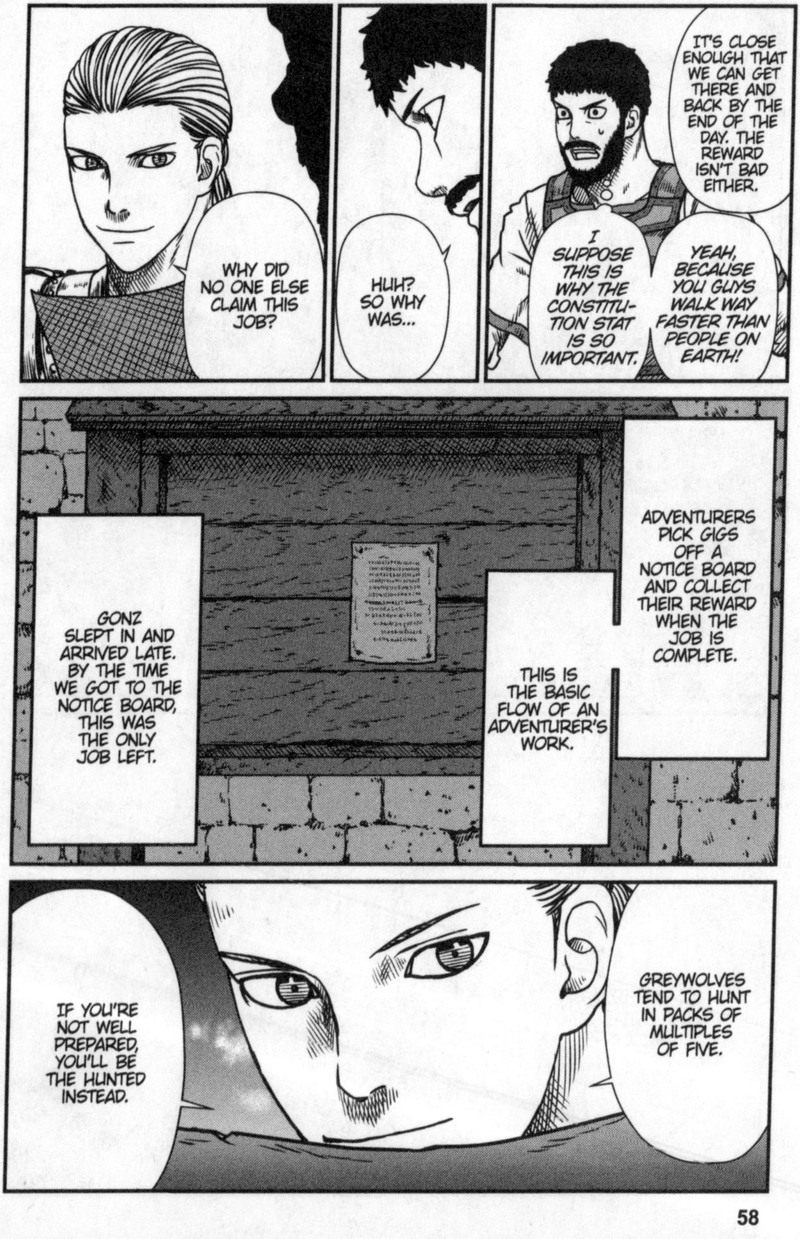
IT'S CLOSE ENOUGH THAT WE CAN GET THERE AND BACK BY THE END OF THE DAY. THE REWARD ISN'T BAD EITHER.
YEAH, BECAUSE YOU GUYS WALK WAY FASTER THAN PEOPLE ON EARTH!
I SUPPOSE THIS IS WHY THE CONSTITU-TION STAT IS SO IMPORTANT.
HUH? SO WHY WAS...
WHY DID NO ONE ELSE CLAIM THIS JOB?
ADVENTURERS PICK GIGS OFF A NOTICE BOARD AND COLLECT THEIR REWARD WHEN THE JOB IS COMPLETE.
THIS IS THE BASIC FLOW OF AN ADVENTURER'S WORK.
GONZ SLEPT IN AND ARRIVED LATE. BY THE TIME WE GOT TO THE NOTICE BOARD, THIS WAS THE ONLY JOB LEFT.
GREYWOLVES TEND TO HUNT IN PACKS OF MULTIPLES OF FIVE.
IF YOU'RE NOT WELL PREPARED, YOU'LL BE THE HUNTED INSTEAD.

THERE IT IS.

GULP...

SERIOUS-LY...?

EPISODE 9
MY FIRST SUBJUGATION REQUEST

THERE'S THE VILLAGE.

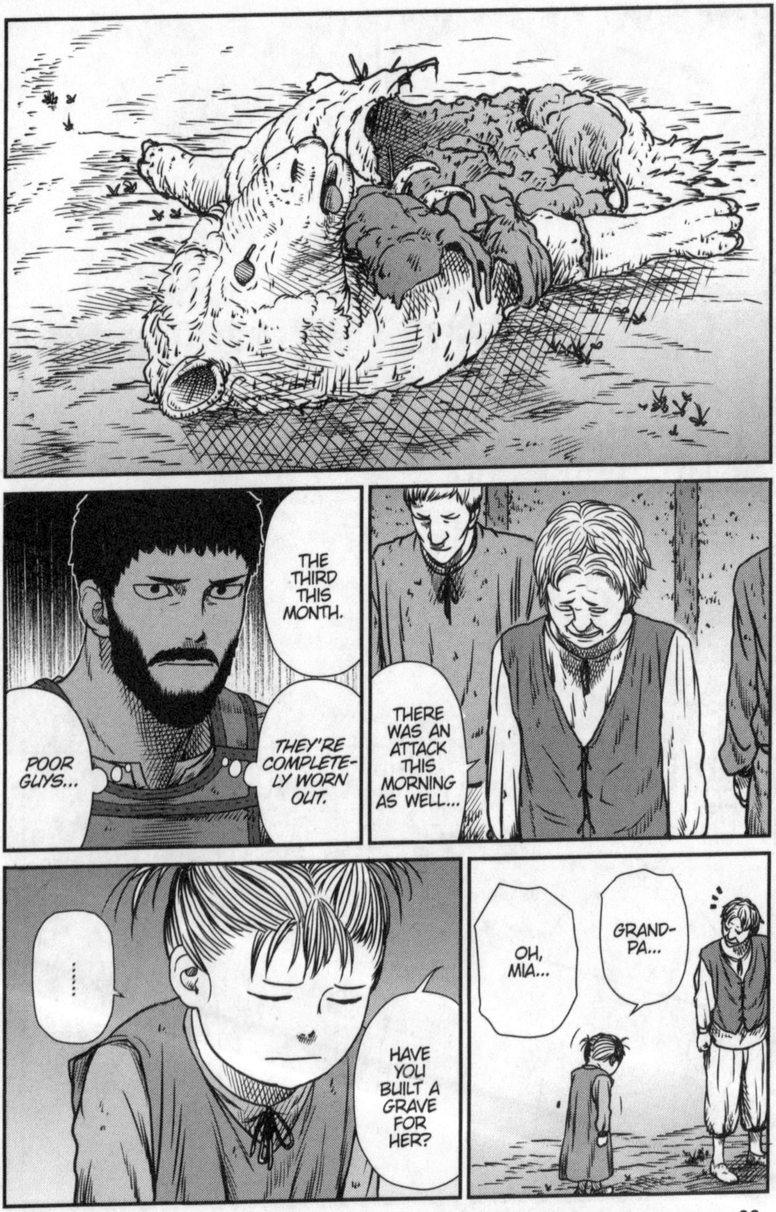
THERE WAS AN ATTACK THIS MORNING AS WELL...
THE THIRD THIS MONTH.
THEY'RE COMPLETELY WORN OUT.
POOR GUYS...
GRANDPA...
OH, MIA...
......
HAVE YOU BUILT A GRAVE FOR HER?

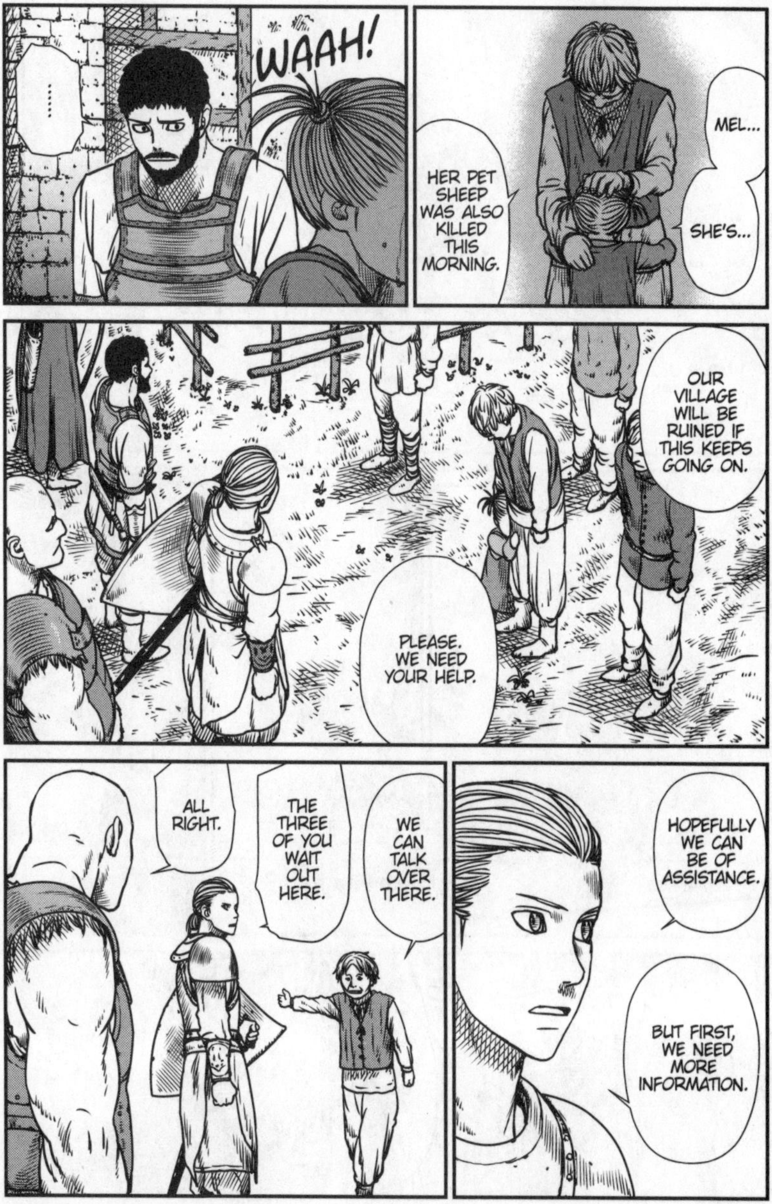
MEL...
SHE'S...
HER PET SHEEP WAS ALSO KILLED THIS MORNING.
WAAH!
......
OUR VILLAGE WILL BE RUINED IF THIS KEEPS GOING ON.
PLEASE. WE NEED YOUR HELP.
HOPEFULLY WE CAN BE OF ASSISTANCE.
BUT FIRST, WE NEED MORE INFORMATION.
WE CAN TALK OVER THERE.
THE THREE OF YOU WAIT OUT HERE.
ALL RIGHT.

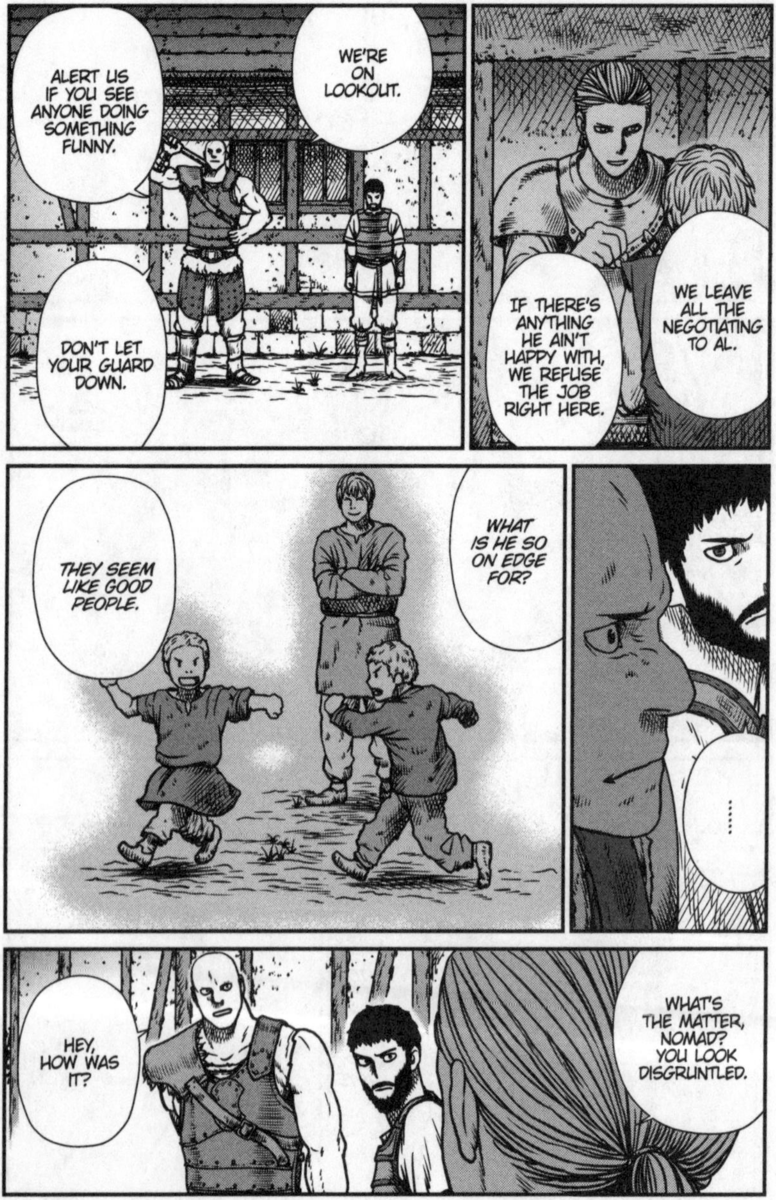
WE LEAVE ALL THE NEGOTIATING TO AL.
IF THERE'S ANYTHING HE AIN'T HAPPY WITH, WE REFUSE THE JOB RIGHT HERE.
WE'RE ON LOOKOUT.
ALERT US IF YOU SEE ANYONE DOING SOMETHING FUNNY.
DON'T LET YOUR GUARD DOWN.
……
WHAT IS HE SO ON EDGE FOR?
THEY SEEM LIKE GOOD PEOPLE.
WHAT'S THE MATTER, NOMAD? YOU LOOK DISGRUNTLED.
HEY, HOW WAS IT?

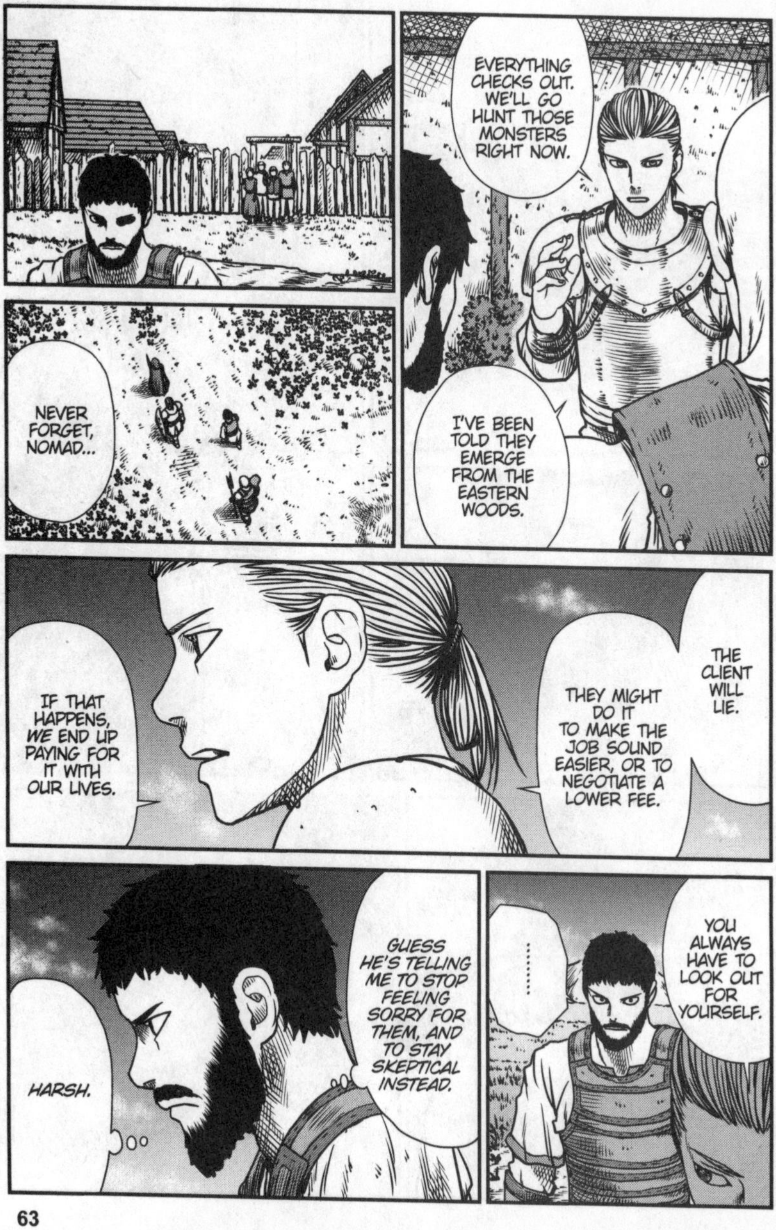
EVERYTHING CHECKS OUT. WE'LL GO HUNT THOSE MONSTERS RIGHT NOW.
I'VE BEEN TOLD THEY EMERGE FROM THE EASTERN WOODS.
NEVER FORGET, NOMAD...
THE CLIENT WILL LIE.
THEY MIGHT DO IT TO MAKE THE JOB SOUND EASIER, OR TO NEGOTIATE A LOWER FEE.
IF THAT HAPPENS, WE END UP PAYING FOR IT WITH OUR LIVES.
YOU ALWAYS HAVE TO LOOK OUT FOR YOURSELF.
......
GUESS HE'S TELLING ME TO STOP FEELING SORRY FOR THEM, AND TO STAY SKEPTICAL INSTEAD.
HARSH.

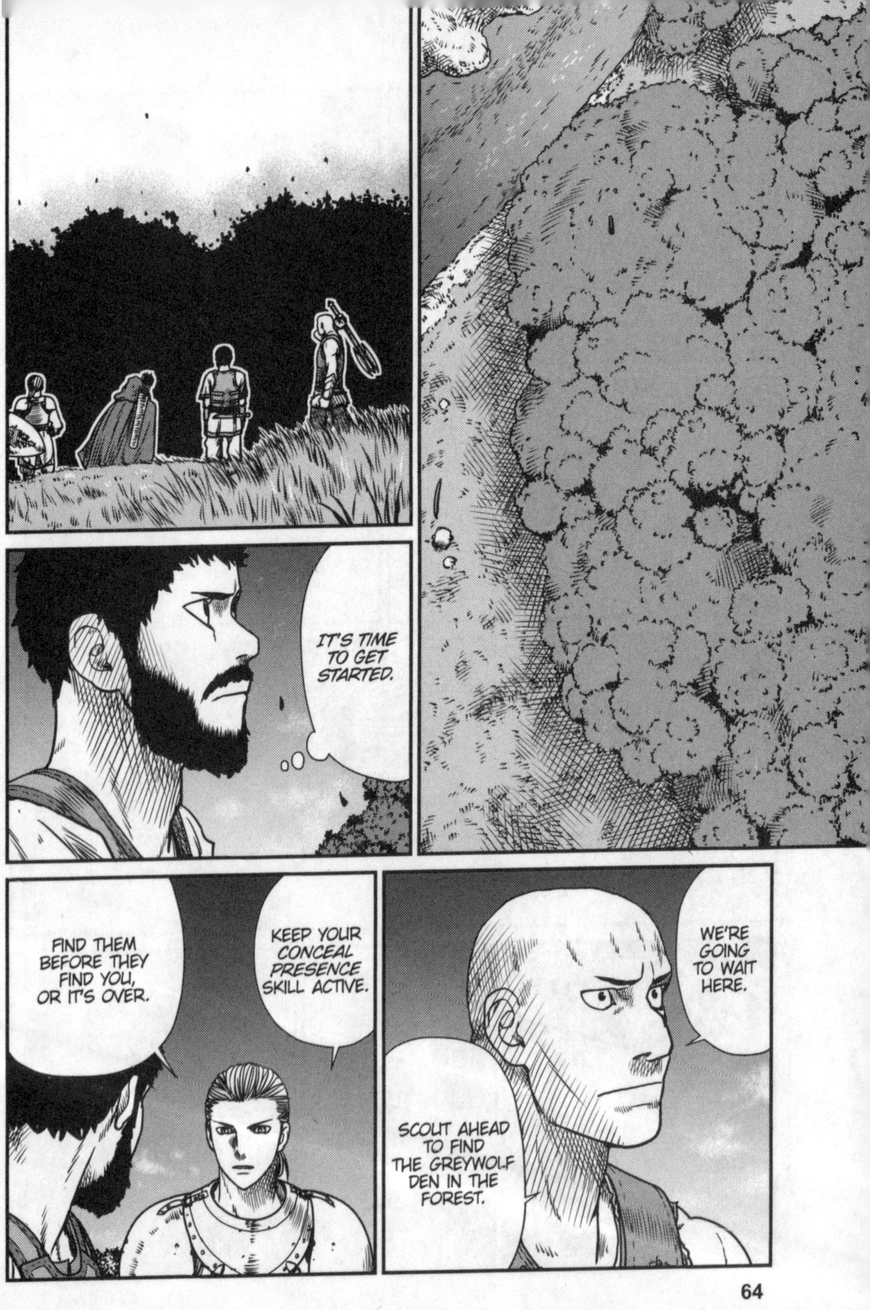
IT'S TIME TO GET STARTED.
WE'RE GOING TO WAIT HERE.
SCOUT AHEAD TO FIND THE GREYWOLF DEN IN THE FOREST.
KEEP YOUR CONCEAL PRESENCE SKILL ACTIVE.
FIND THEM BEFORE THEY FIND YOU, OR IT'S OVER.

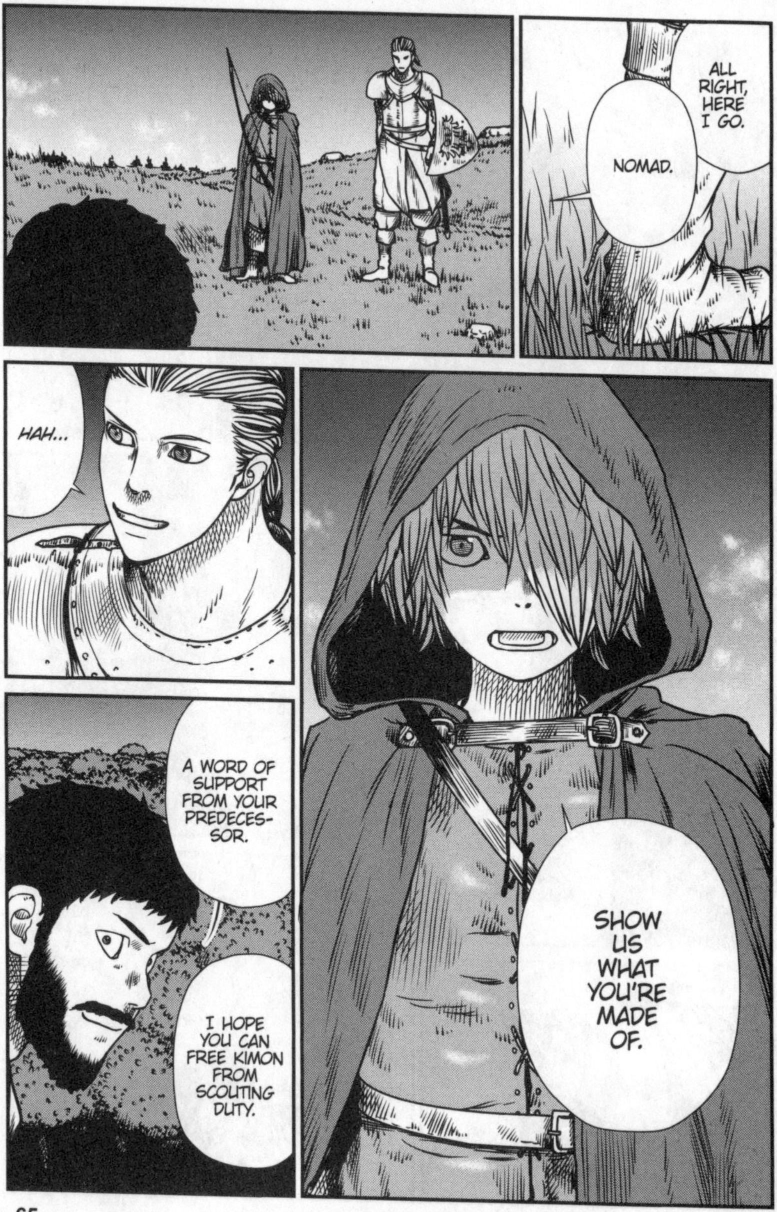
ALL RIGHT, HERE I GO.
NOMAD.
SHOW US WHAT YOU'RE MADE OF.
HAH...
A WORD OF SUPPORT FROM YOUR PREDECES-SOR.
I HOPE YOU CAN FREE KIMON FROM SCOUTING DUTY.

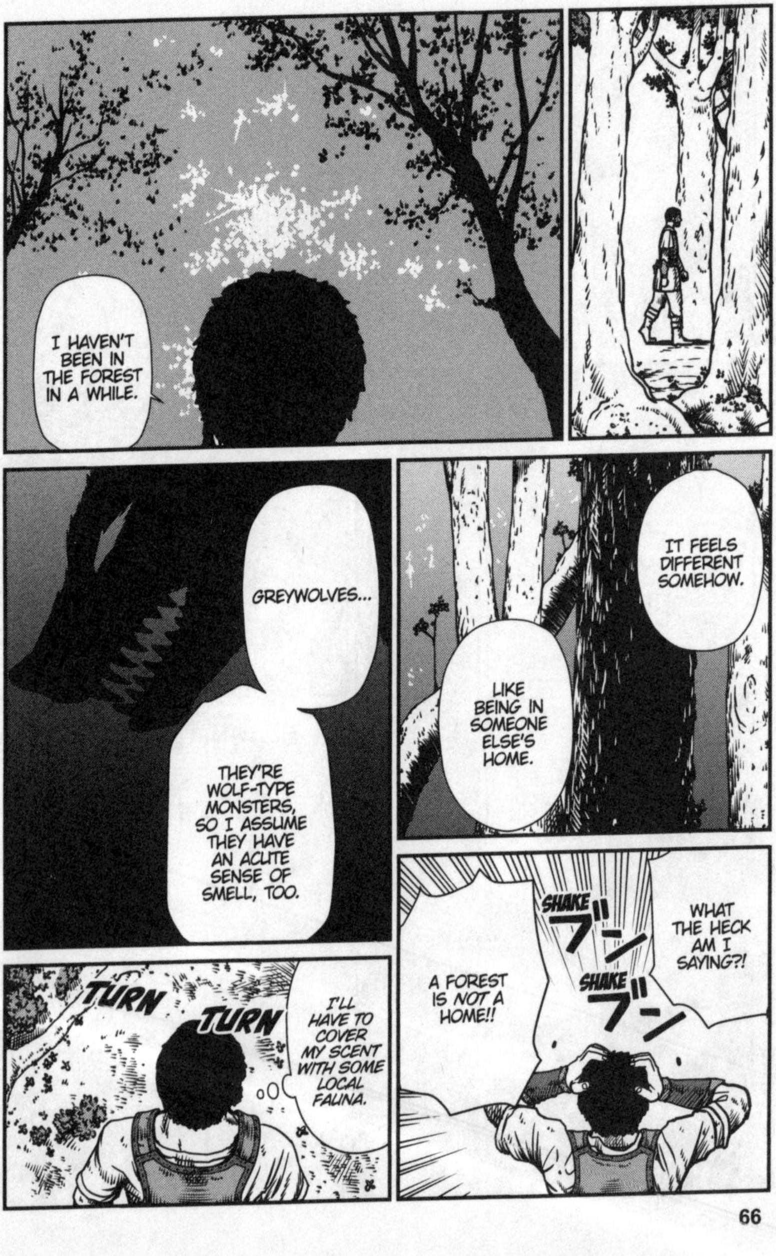
I HAVEN'T BEEN IN THE FOREST IN A WHILE.
IT FEELS DIFFERENT SOMEHOW.
LIKE BEING IN SOMEONE ELSE'S HOME.
SHAKE
SHAKE
WHAT THE HECK AM I SAYING?!
A FOREST IS NOT A HOME!!
GREYWOLVES...
THEY'RE WOLF-TYPE MONSTERS, SO I ASSUME THEY HAVE AN ACUTE SENSE OF SMELL, TOO.
TURN
TURN
I'LL HAVE TO COVER MY SCENT WITH SOME LOCAL FAUNA.

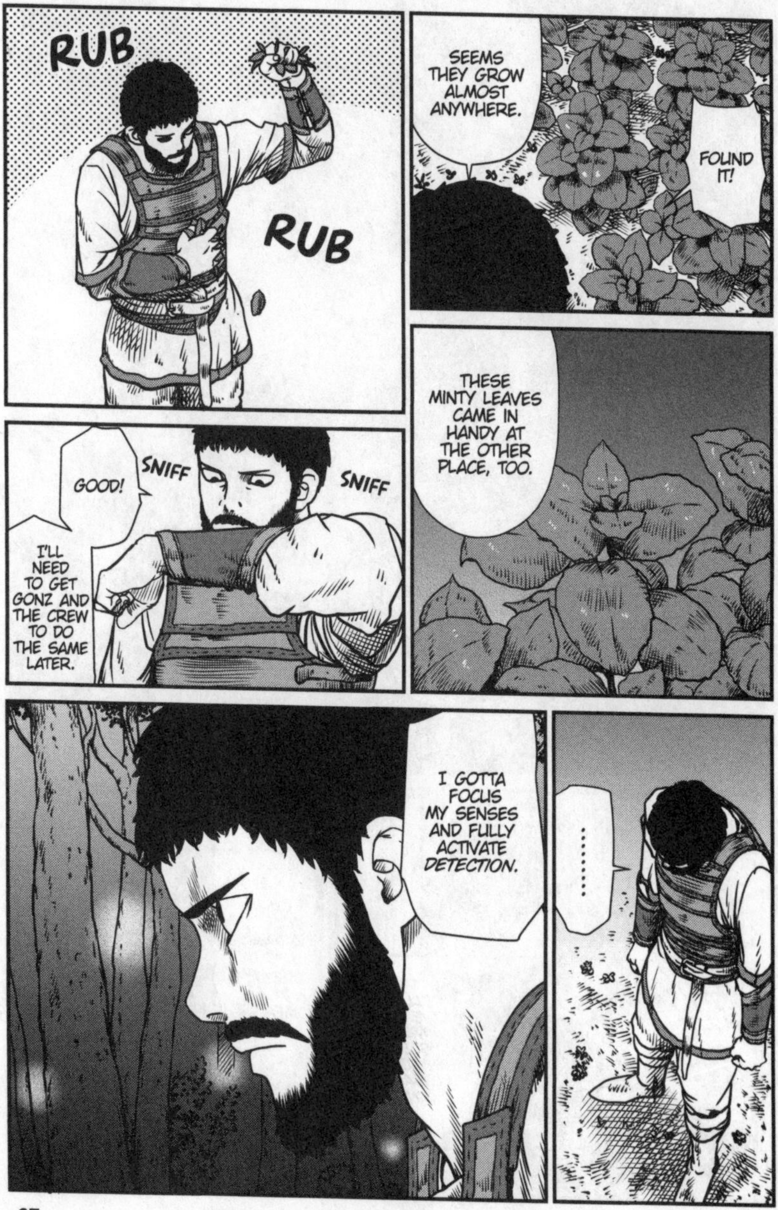
FOUND IT!
SEEMS THEY GROW ALMOST ANYWHERE.
RUB
RUB
THESE MINTY LEAVES CAME IN HANDY AT THE OTHER PLACE, TOO.
SNIFF
SNIFF
GOOD!
I'LL NEED TO GET GONZ AND THE CREW TO DO THE SAME LATER.
......
I GOTTA FOCUS MY SENSES AND FULLY ACTIVATE DETECTION.

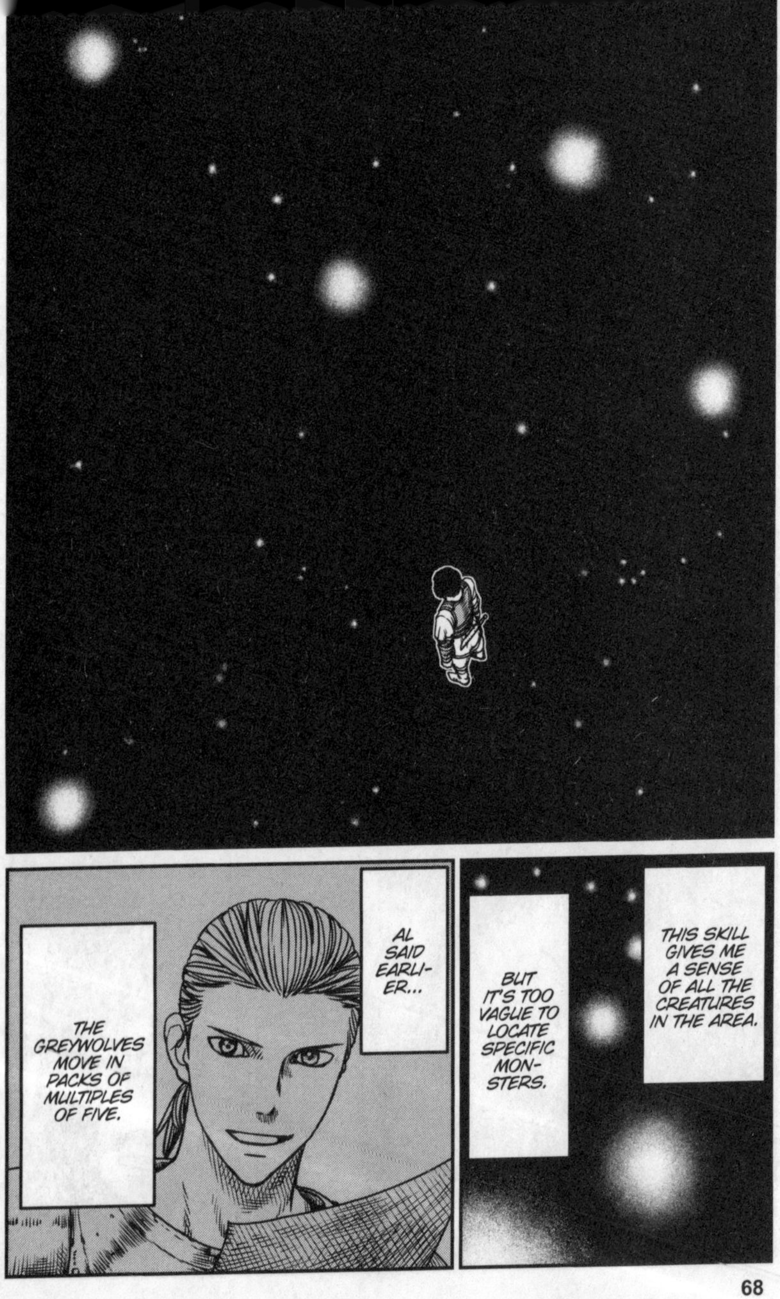
THIS SKILL GIVES ME A SENSE OF ALL THE CREATURES IN THE AREA.
BUT IT'S TOO VAGUE TO LOCATE SPECIFIC MON-STERS.
AL SAID EARLI-ER...
THE GREYWOLVES MOVE IN PACKS OF MULTIPLES OF FIVE.

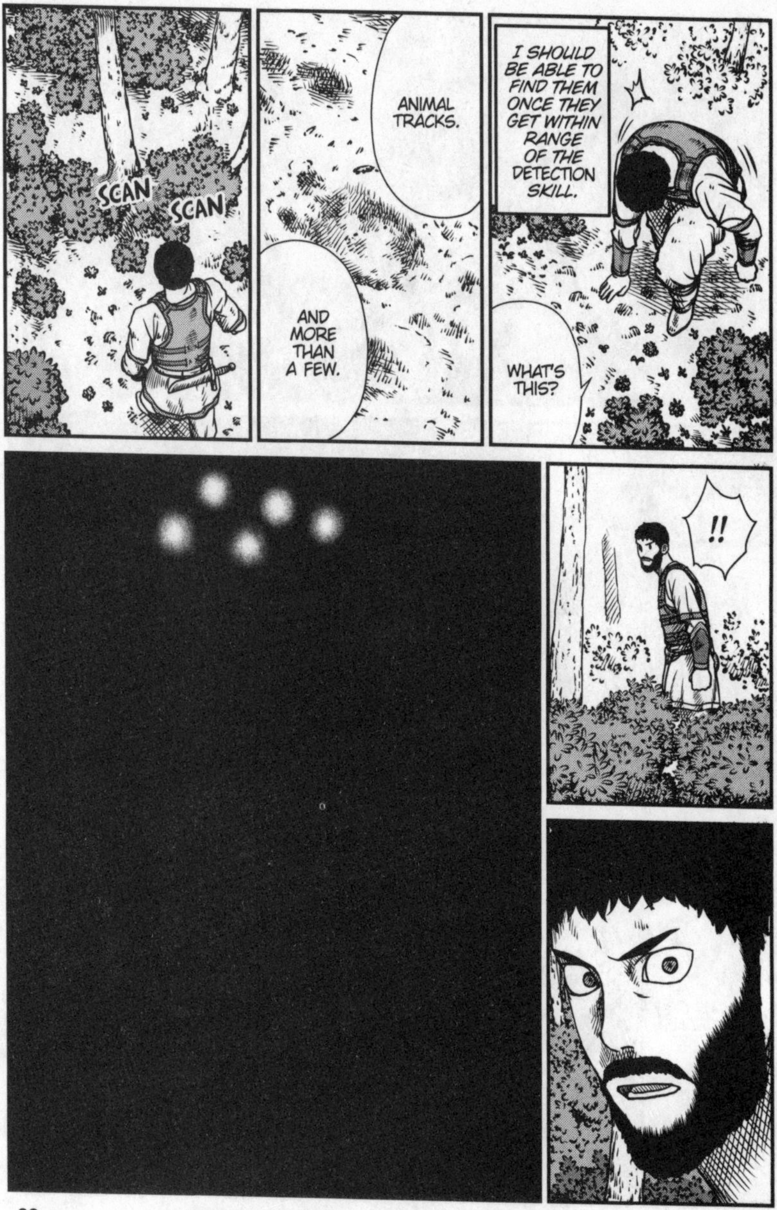
I SHOULD BE ABLE TO FIND THEM ONCE THEY GET WITHIN RANGE OF THE DETECTION SKILL.
WHAT'S THIS?
ANIMAL TRACKS.
AND MORE THAN A FEW.
SCAN
SCAN
!!

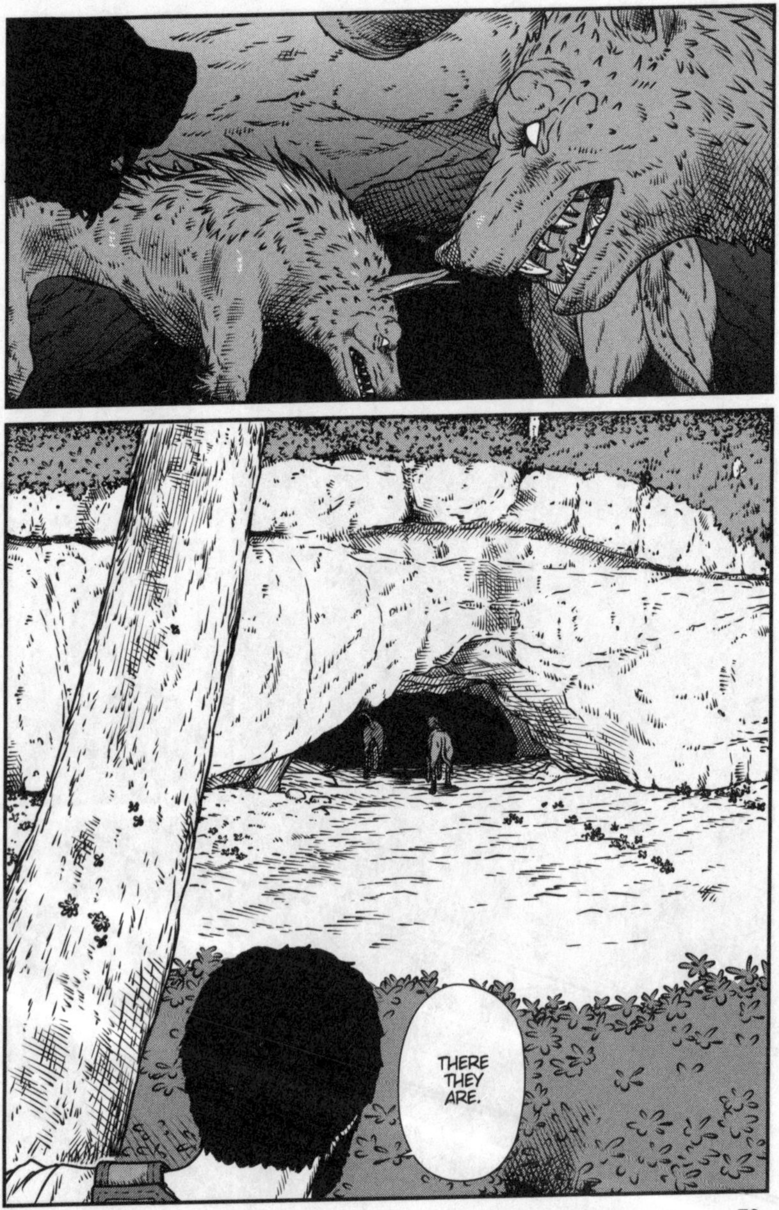
THERE THEY ARE.

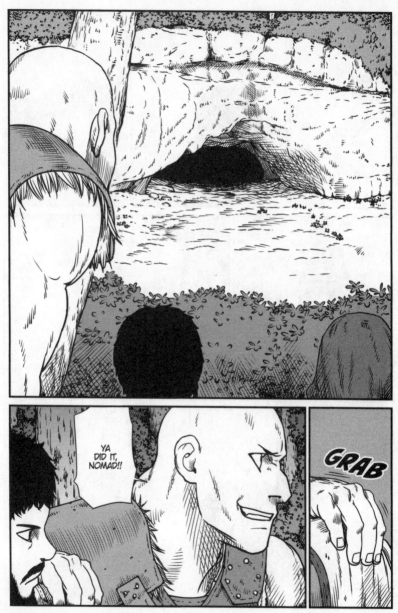

YA DID IT, NOMAD!!

GRAB

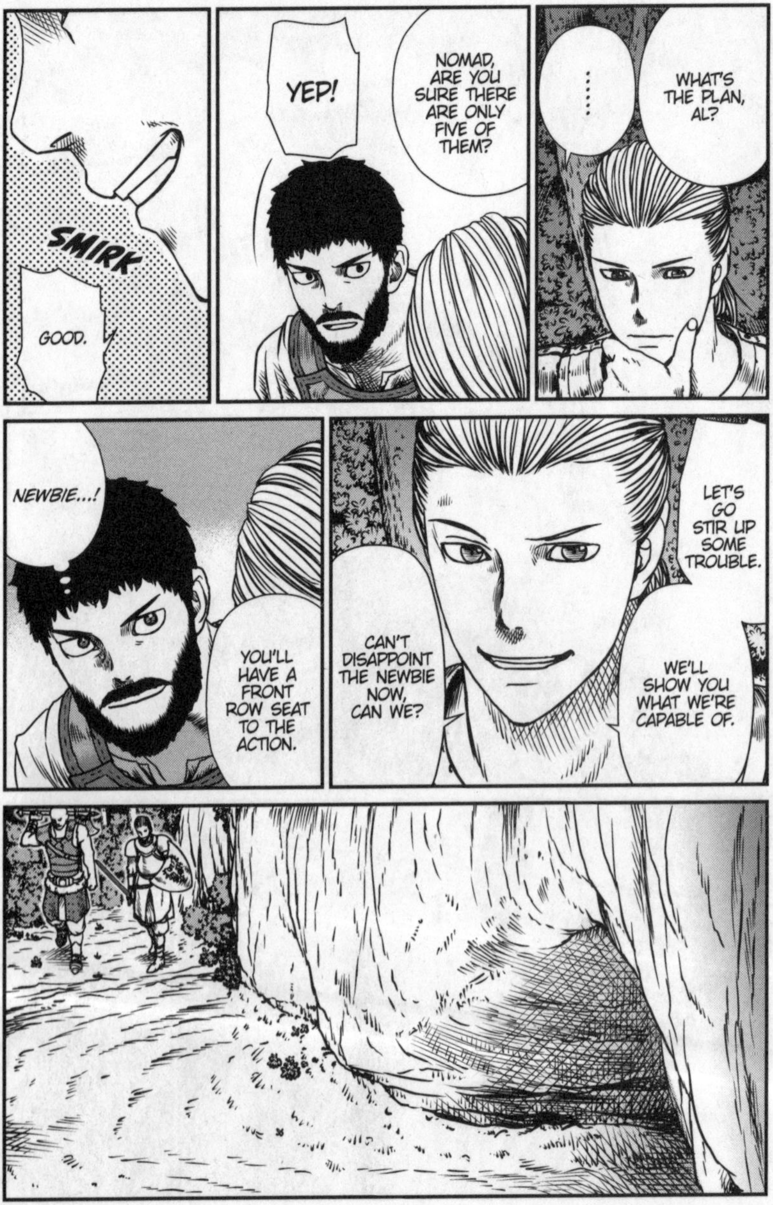

WHAT'S THE PLAN, AL?
......
NOMAD, ARE YOU SURE THERE ARE ONLY FIVE OF THEM?
YEP!
SMIRK
GOOD.
LET'S GO STIR UP SOME TROUBLE.
WE'LL SHOW YOU WHAT WE'RE CAPABLE OF.
CAN'T DISAPPOINT THE NEWBIE NOW, CAN WE?
NEWBIE...!
YOU'LL HAVE A FRONT ROW SEAT TO THE ACTION.

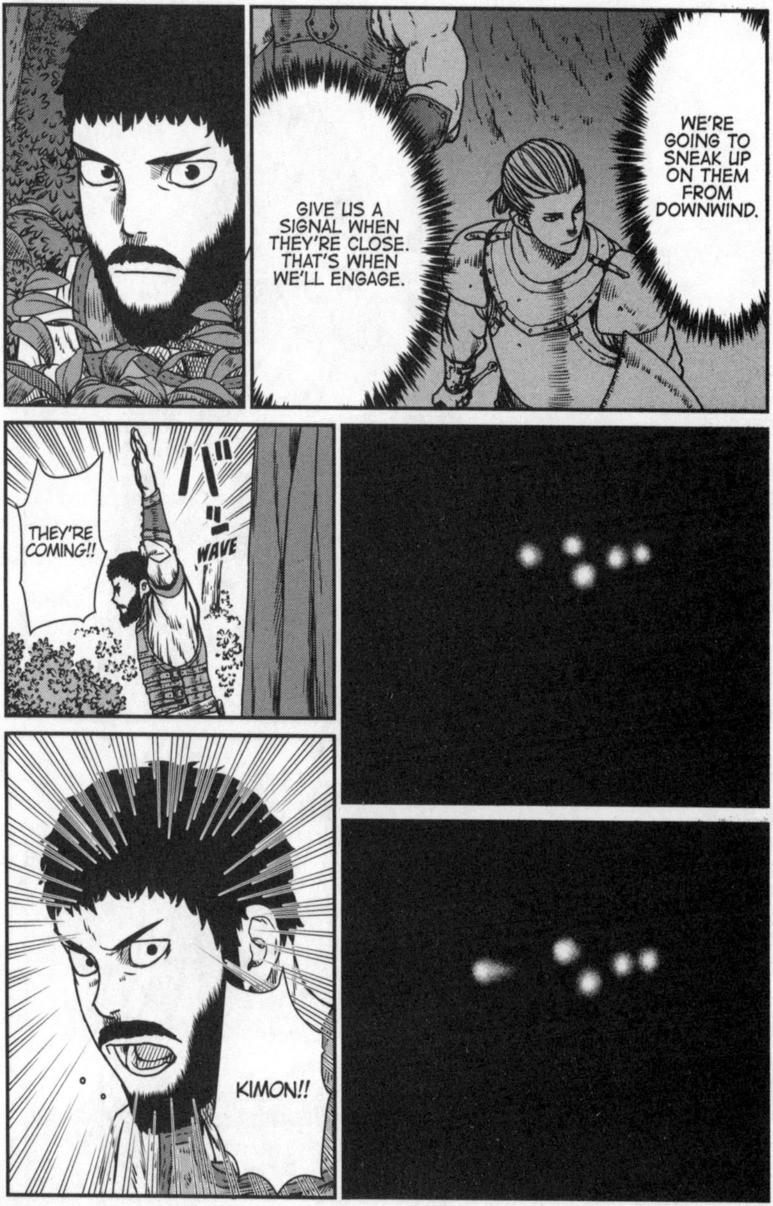
WE'RE GOING TO SNEAK UP ON THEM FROM DOWNWIND.
GIVE US A SIGNAL WHEN THEY'RE CLOSE. THAT'S WHEN WE'LL ENGAGE.
THEY'RE COMING!!
バッ
WAVE
KIMON!!

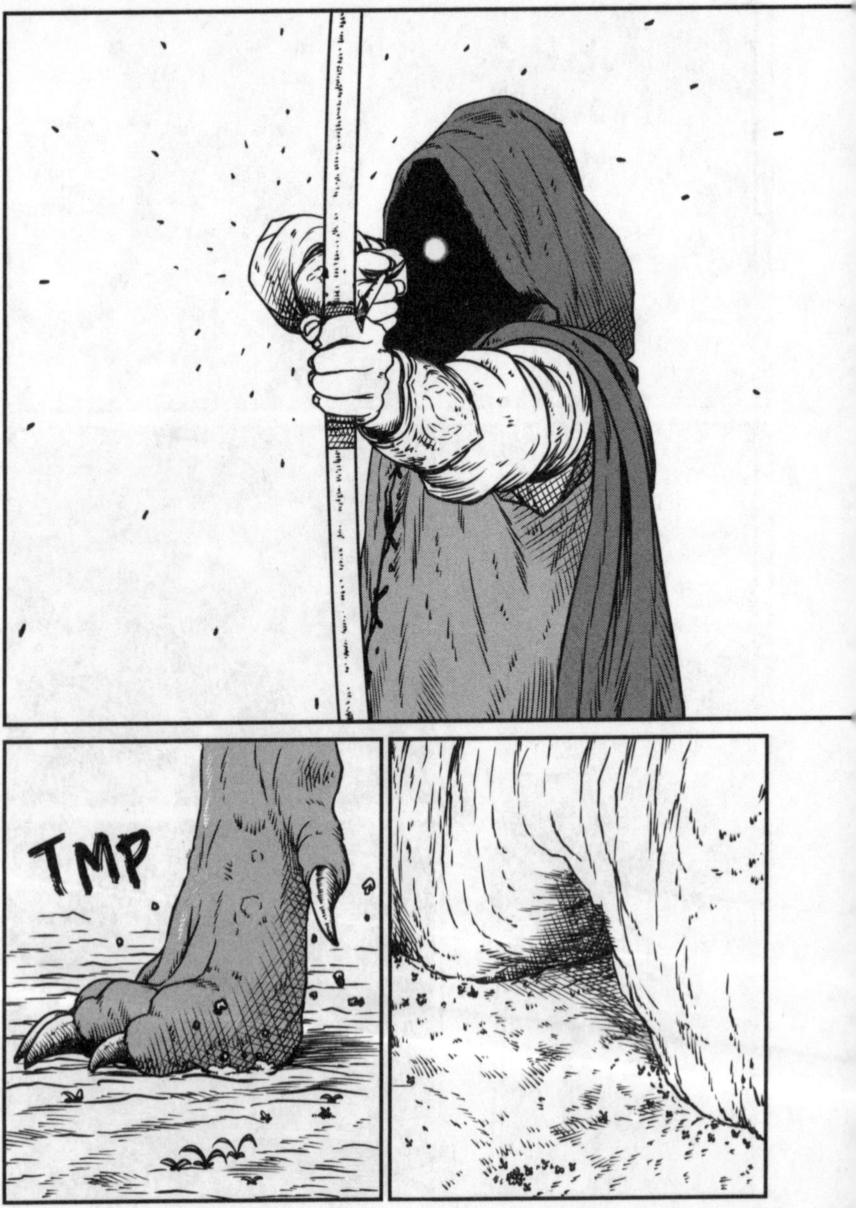
TMP

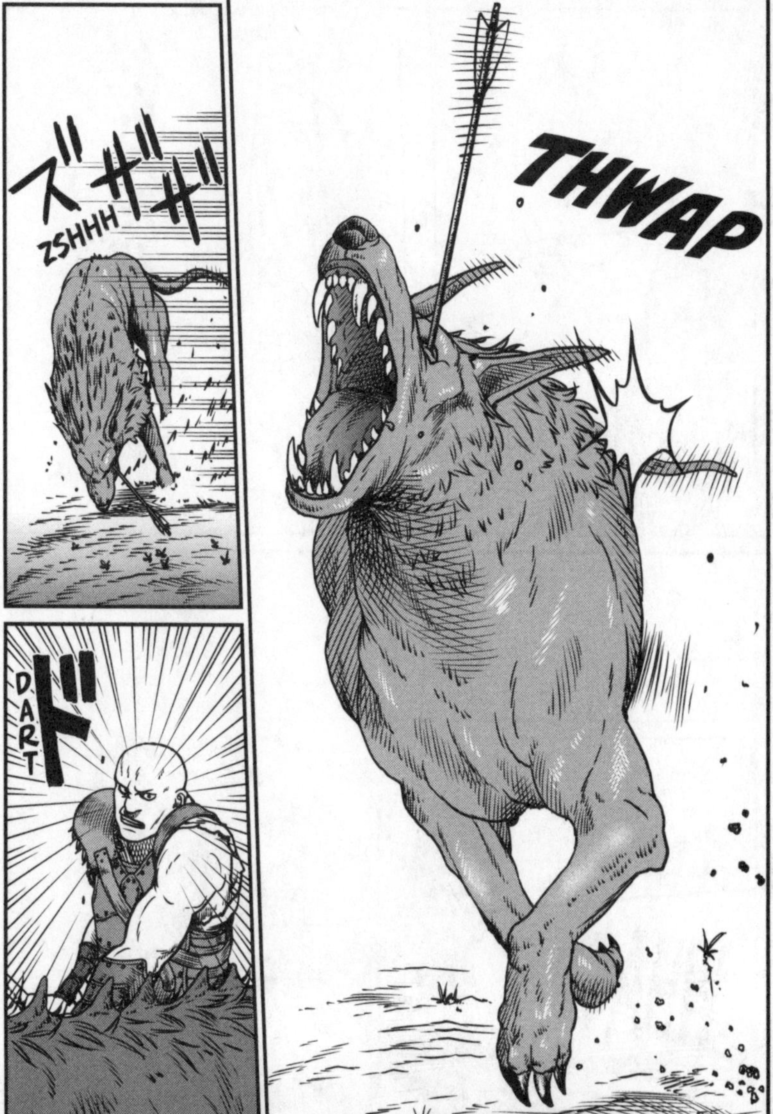
THWAP
ズザザ
ZSHHH
ド
DART

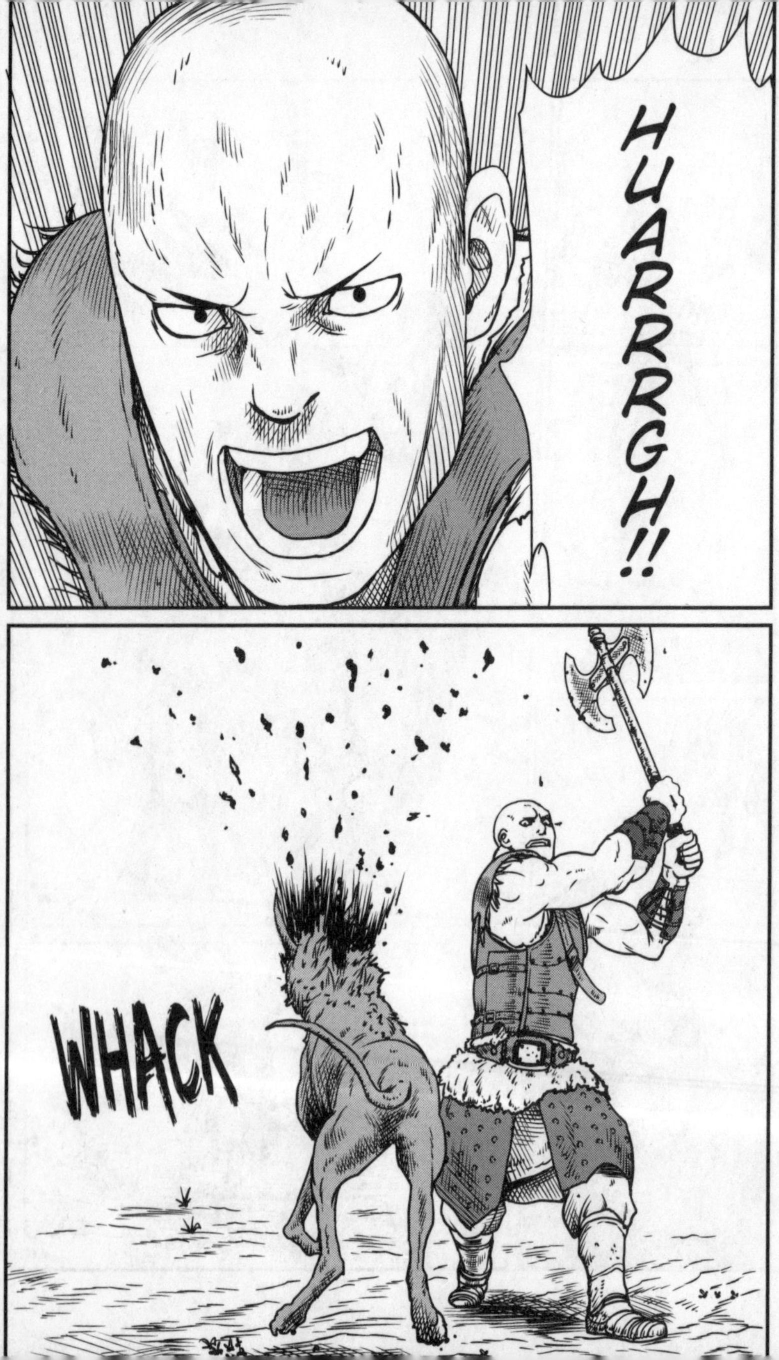
HUARRRGH!!
WHACK

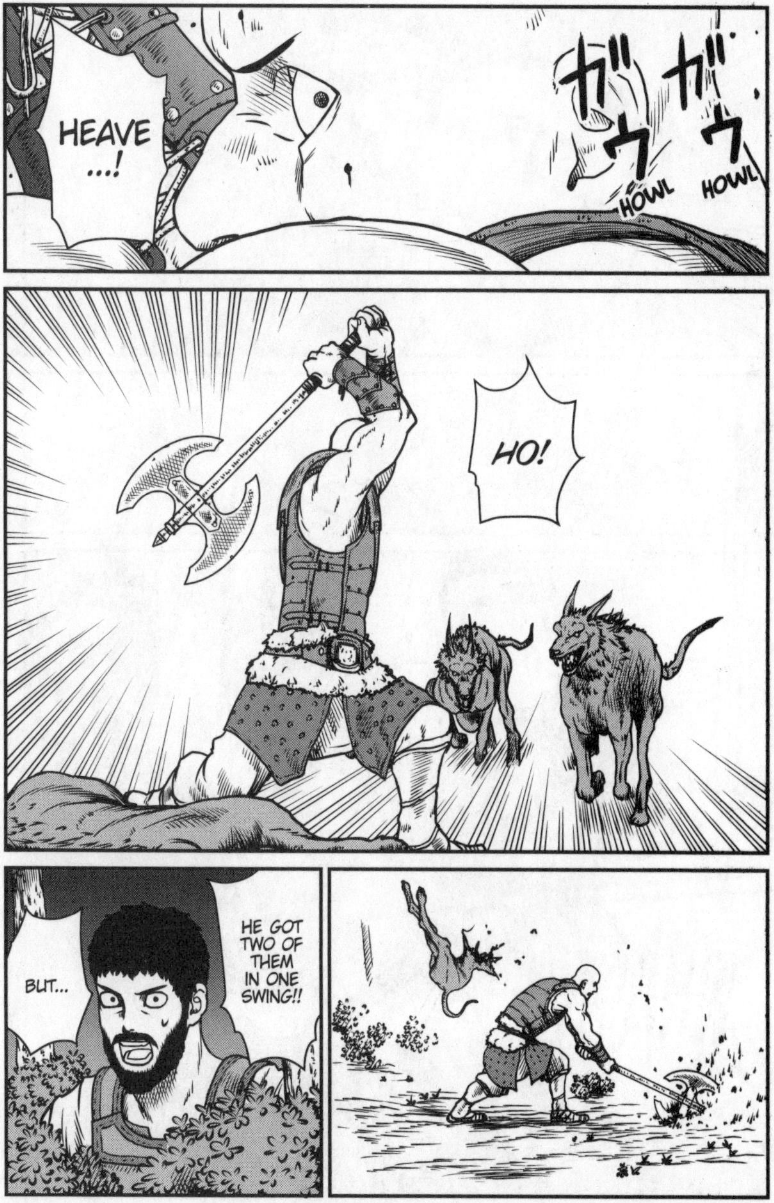
ガウ
HOWL
ガウ
HOWL
HEAVE ...!
HO!
HE GOT TWO OF THEM IN ONE SWING!!
BUT...

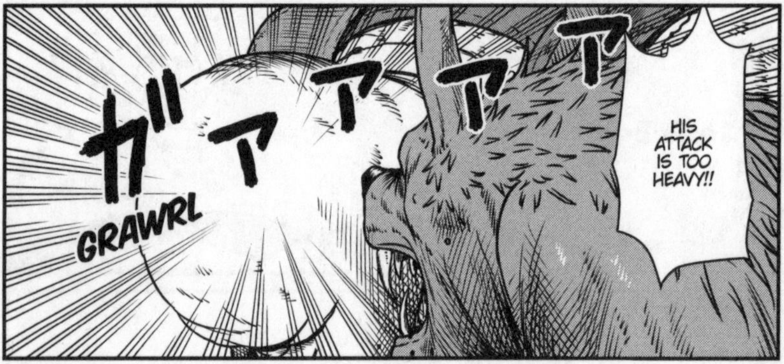
HIS ATTACK IS TOO HEAVY!!
ガアアアア
GRAWRL

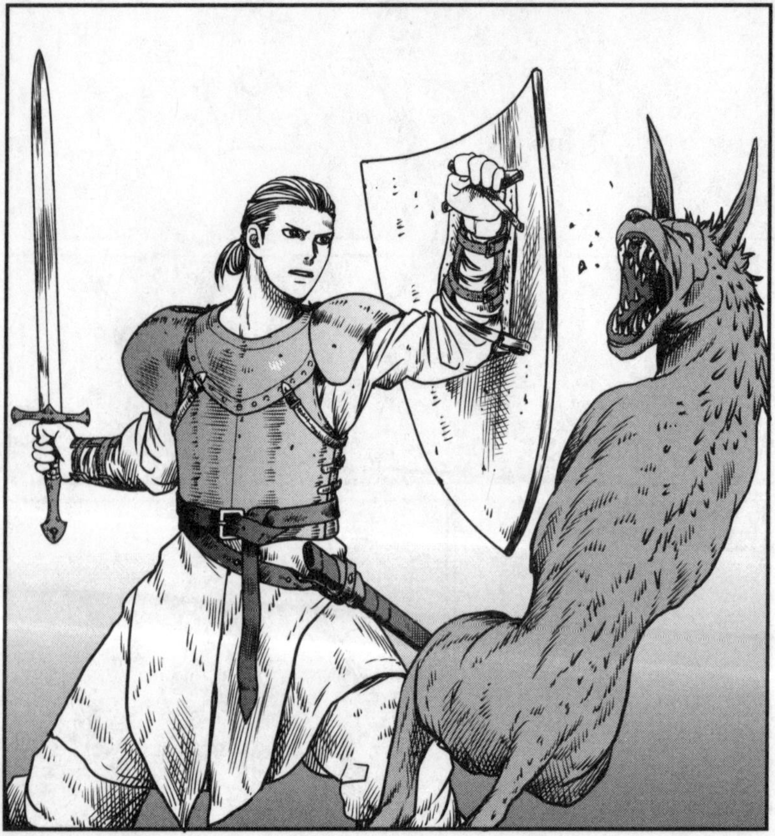

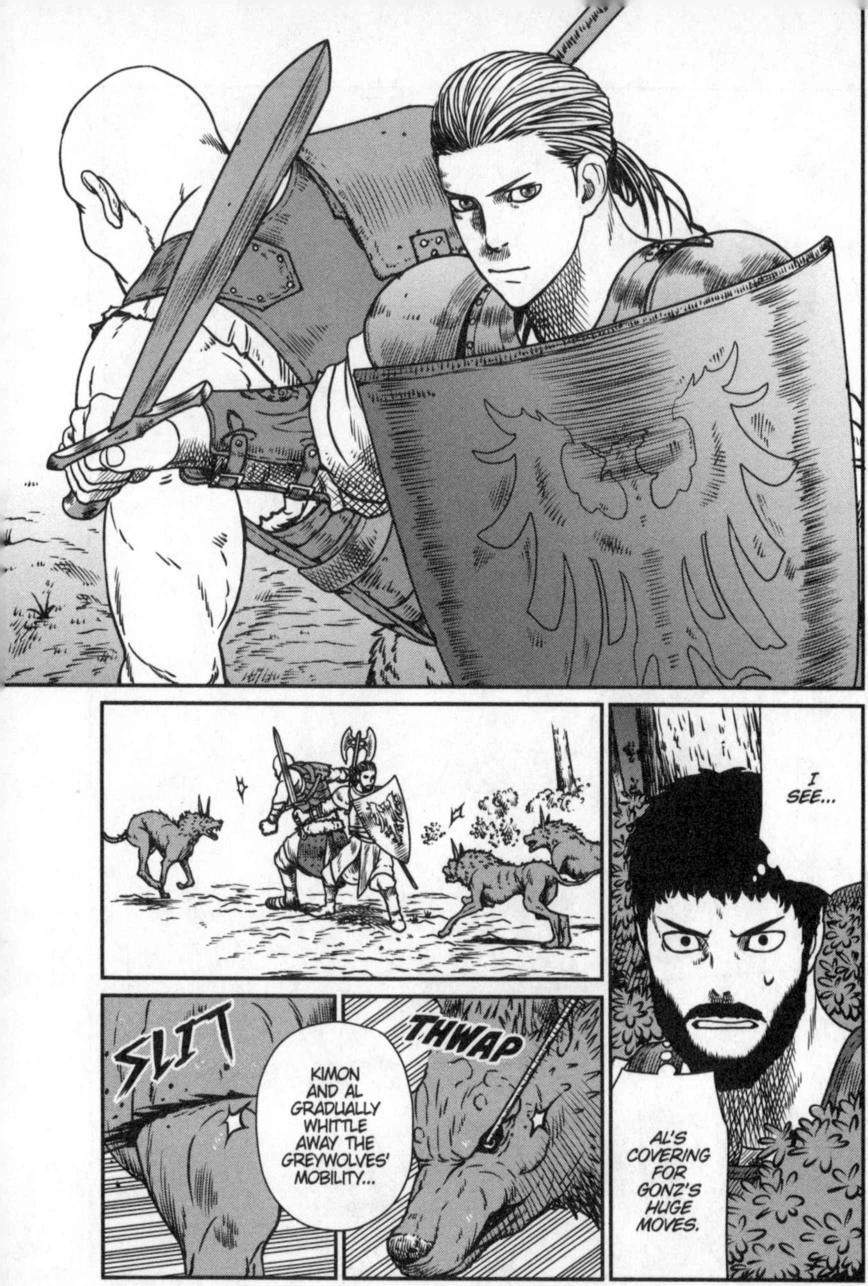
I SEE...
AL'S COVERING FOR GONZ'S HUGE MOVES.
THWAP
SLIT
KIMON AND AL GRADUALLY WHITTLE AWAY THE GREYWOLVES' MOBILITY...

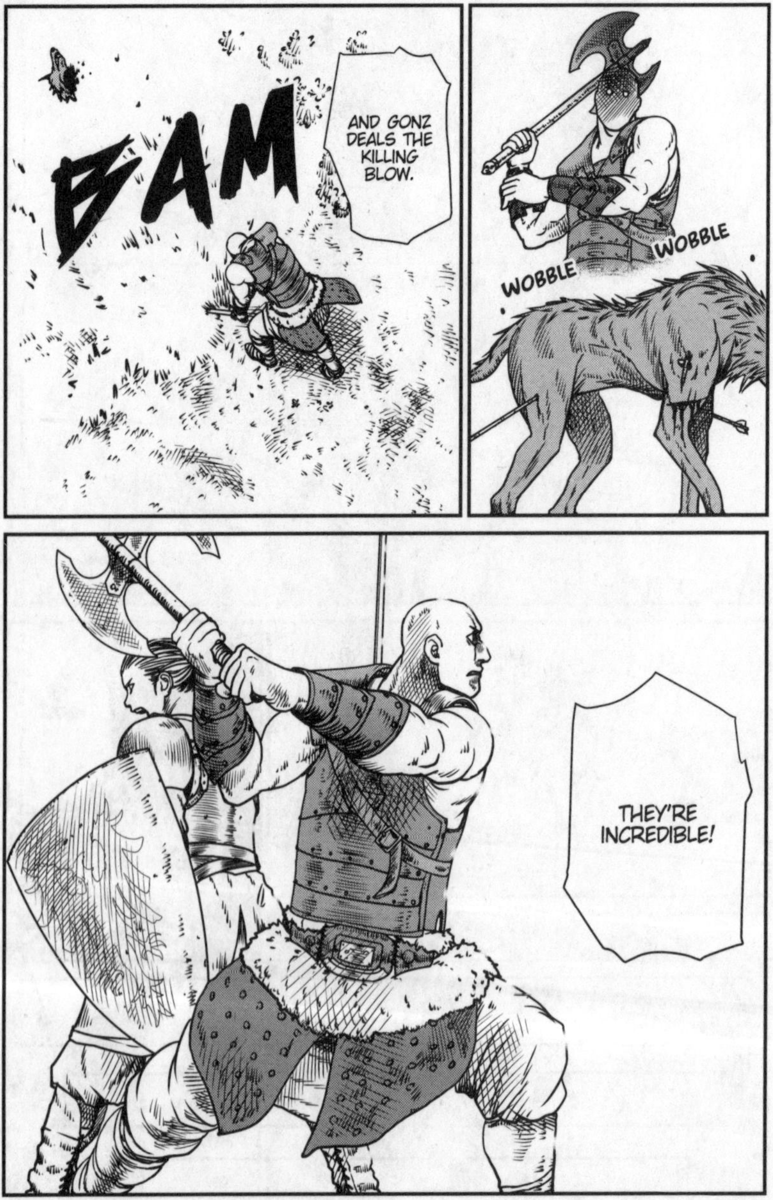
WOBBLE
WOBBLE
AND GONZ DEALS THE KILLING BLOW.
BAM
THEY'RE INCREDIBLE!

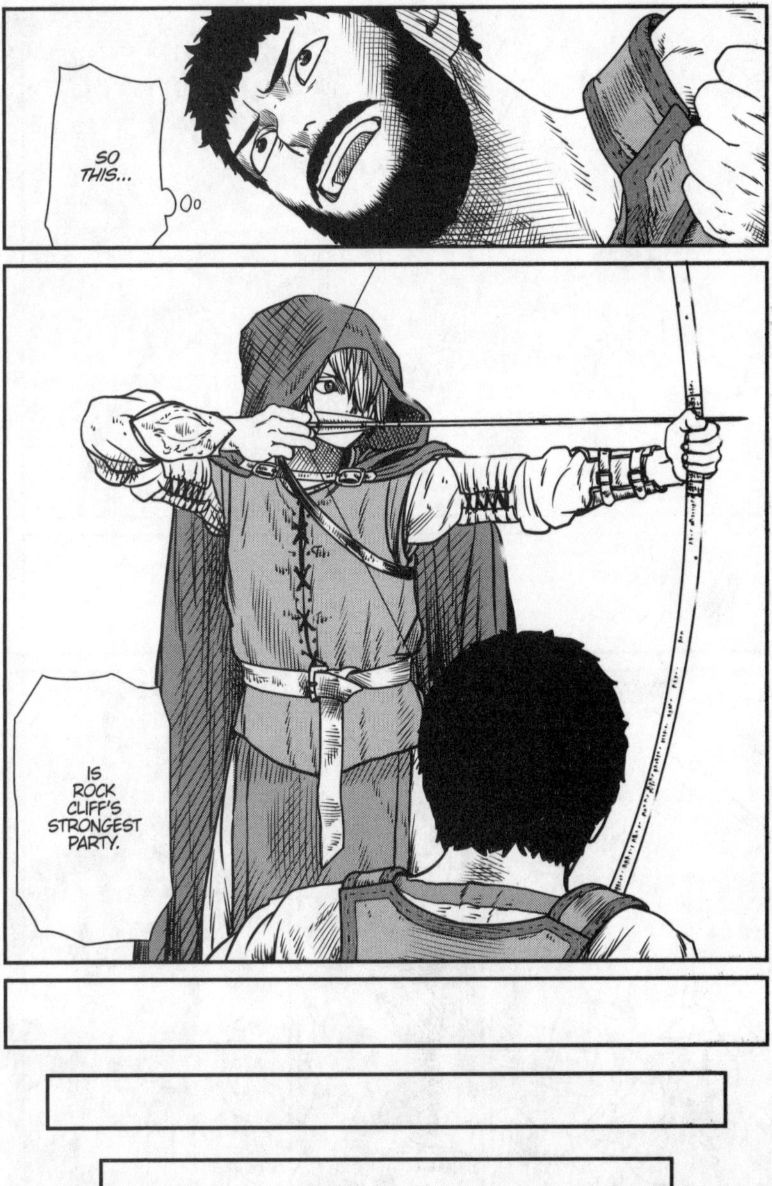
SO THIS...
IS ROCK CLIFF'S STRONGEST PARTY.

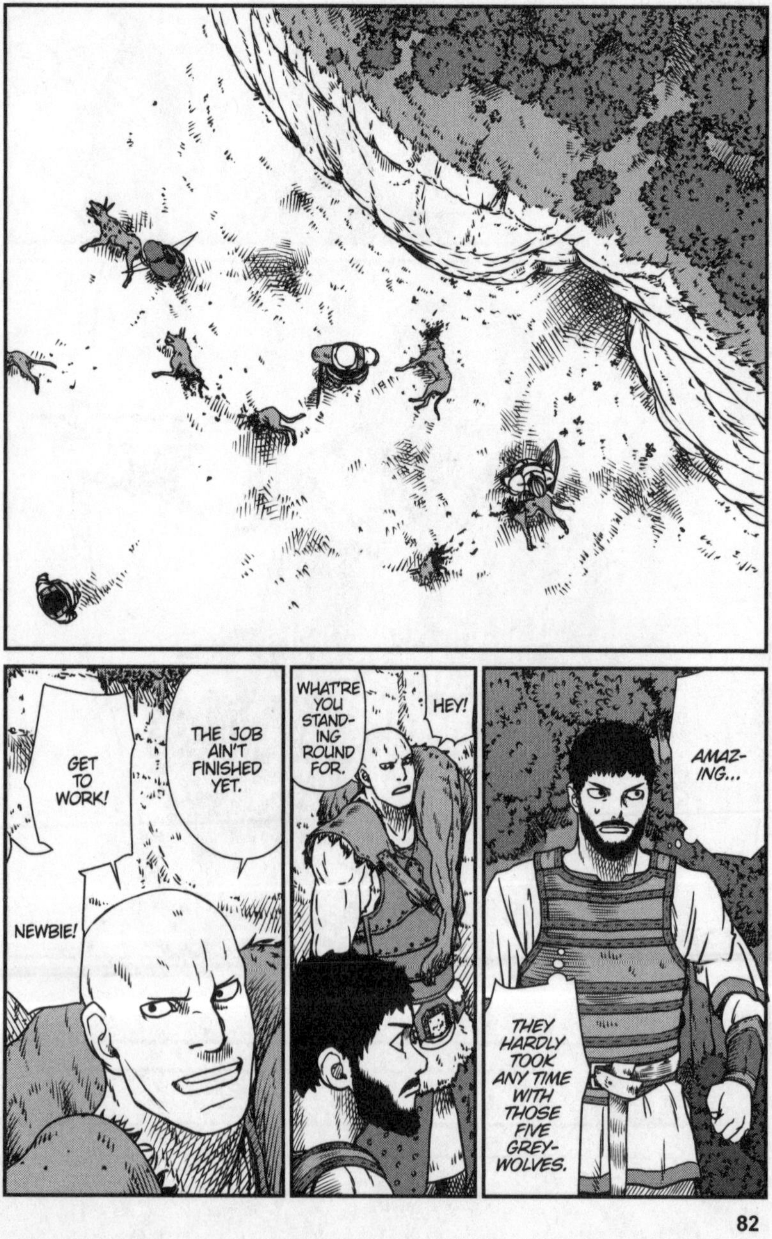
AMAZ-ING...
THEY HARDLY TOOK ANY TIME WITH THOSE FIVE GREY-WOLVES.
HEY!
WHAT'RE YOU STANDING ROUND FOR.
THE JOB AIN'T FINISHED YET.
GET TO WORK!
NEWBIE!

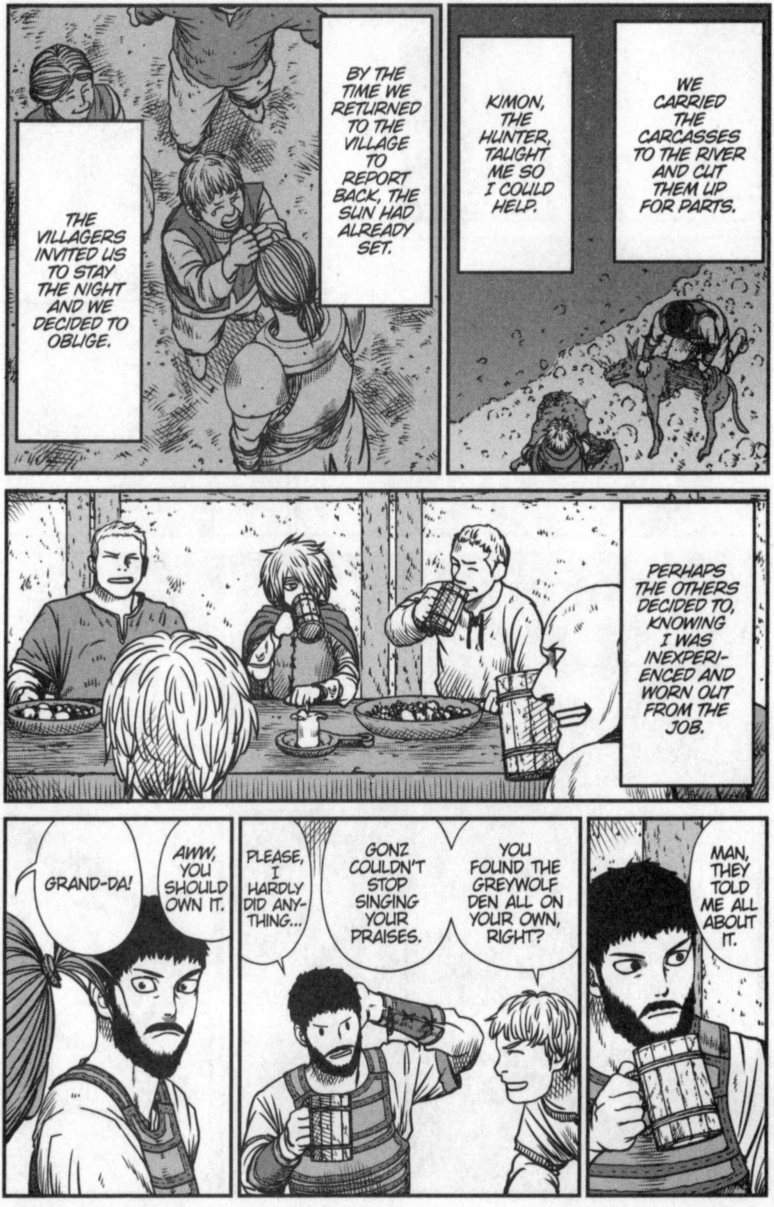
WE CARRIED THE CARCASSES TO THE RIVER AND CUT THEM UP FOR PARTS.
KIMON, THE HUNTER, TAUGHT ME SO I COULD HELP.
BY THE TIME WE RETURNED TO THE VILLAGE TO REPORT BACK, THE SUN HAD ALREADY SET.
THE VILLAGERS INVITED US TO STAY THE NIGHT AND WE DECIDED TO OBLIGE.
PERHAPS THE OTHERS DECIDED TO, KNOWING I WAS INEXPERI-ENCED AND WORN OUT FROM THE JOB.
MAN, THEY TOLD ME ALL ABOUT IT.
YOU FOUND THE GREYWOLF DEN ALL ON YOUR OWN, RIGHT?
GONZ COULDN'T STOP SINGING YOUR PRAISES.
PLEASE, I HARDLY DID ANY-THING...
AWW, YOU SHOULD OWN IT.
GRAND-DA!

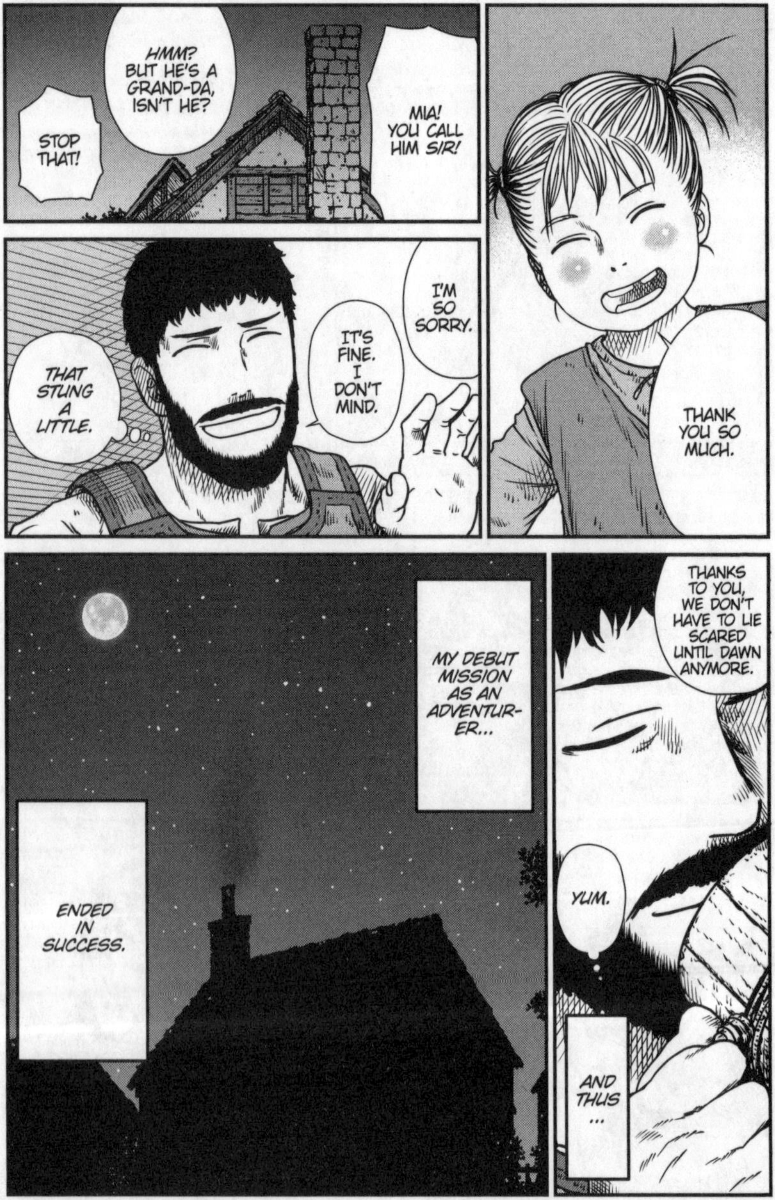
THANK YOU SO MUCH.
MIA! YOU CALL HIM SIR!
HMM? BUT HE'S A GRAND-DA, ISN'T HE?
STOP THAT!
I'M SO SORRY.
IT'S FINE. I DON'T MIND.
THAT STUNG A LITTLE.
THANKS TO YOU, WE DON'T HAVE TO LIE SCARED UNTIL DAWN ANYMORE.
YUM.
AND THUS...
MY DEBUT MISSION AS AN ADVENTURER...
ENDED IN SUCCESS.

SPECIAL COLUMN BY AUTHOR, YAZIN

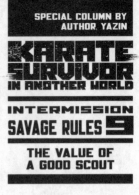

KARATE SURVIVOR IN ANOTHER WORLD

INTERMISSION
SAVAGE RULES 9
THE VALUE OF A GOOD SCOUT

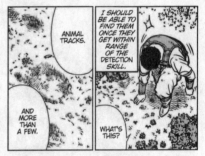

The importance of scouts cannot be underestimated. They may seem inconsequential, but a good scout can easily turn the tide of battle. Knowing the precise location of the enemy allows you to avoid ambushes and lay your own traps for the enemy. The tactical advantage of landing the first strike is immense. A skilled scout that can prevent the enemy from gaining the initiative and can prepare ambushes for them essentially decides the outcome of a skirmish.

During the wars against the various Native tribes, the United States Army recruited a band of highly skilled scouts to combat the indigenous people. The U.S. military struggled with frequent ambushes by the Natives, so they hired people from the Apache tribe to act as their scouts.

There are many tribes among the Native peoples of America, and the Apache were not opposed to fighting against rival tribes. The Apache were feared for their scouting expertise and respected for their relentless persistence in tracking and running their quarry down. The U.S. Army needed skilled scouts so urgently that they were keen to recruit Apache to help take out rival tribes.

Exploration and the tracking of game requires a high level of observational skill and experience. Animals and people leave traces behind that offer valuable information. Footprints can tell you the target's numbers, weight, and physical build. Their dung can inform you of their diet. The dryness of the dung can tell you how long ago they were in the area.

However, these traces are not always recoverable. They can be erased by rain, or the target may traverse environments that do not retain the spoor for long.

Once their tracks have disappeared, the scout must predict their actions from knowledge and experience of the quarry, watching carefully until their trail can be found again.

Native Americans sometimes included a spiritual element to their technique by attempting to embody the spirit of their quarry. By attempting to put themselves in the mind of their targets and mimicking their movements, thereby reducing the target's cautiousness and increasing their own chances of success. This was perhaps a form of self-hypnosis designed to help them more perfectly profile their quarry.

I SHOULD BE ABLE TO FIND THEM ONCE THEY GET WITHIN RANGE OF THE DETECTION SKILL.
WHAT'S THIS?
ANIMAL TRACKS.
AND MORE THAN A FEW.

Native tracking techniques were so comprehensive it is said expert Native scouts could intuit not only the target's weight and build, but also their gender, behavior, and emotional state by tracks alone.

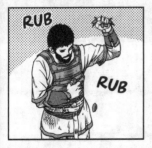

RUB
RUB

Sun Tzu once famously said, "If you know the enemy and know yourself, you need not fear the result of a hundred battles."

A good scout could comprehensively analyze the enemy via the tracks they left behind. If a scout could remain levelheaded as well, they would then be able to claim those hundred battles.

KARATE SURVIVOR IN ANOTHER WORLD

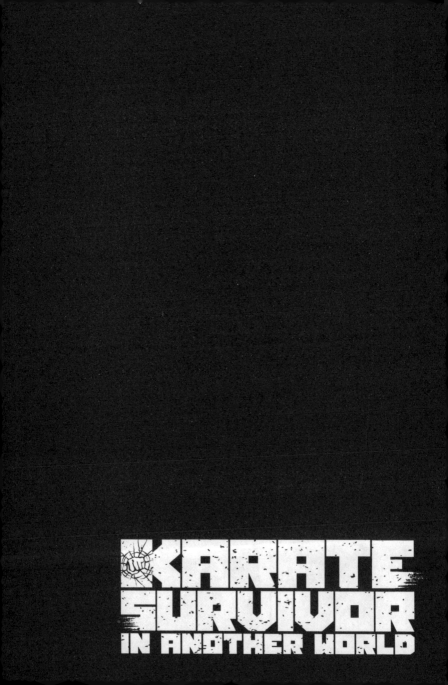

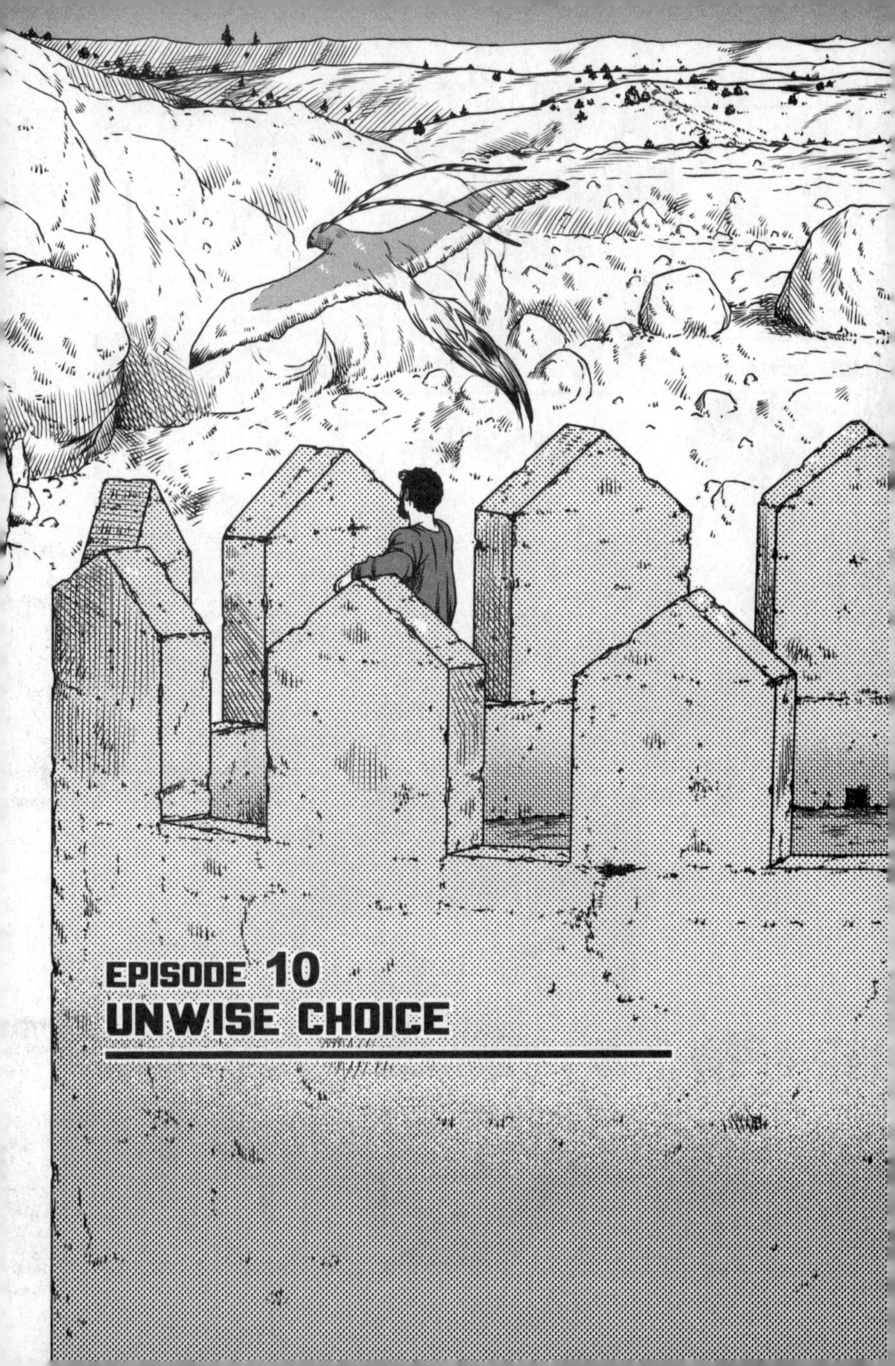
EPISODE 10
UNWISE CHOICE

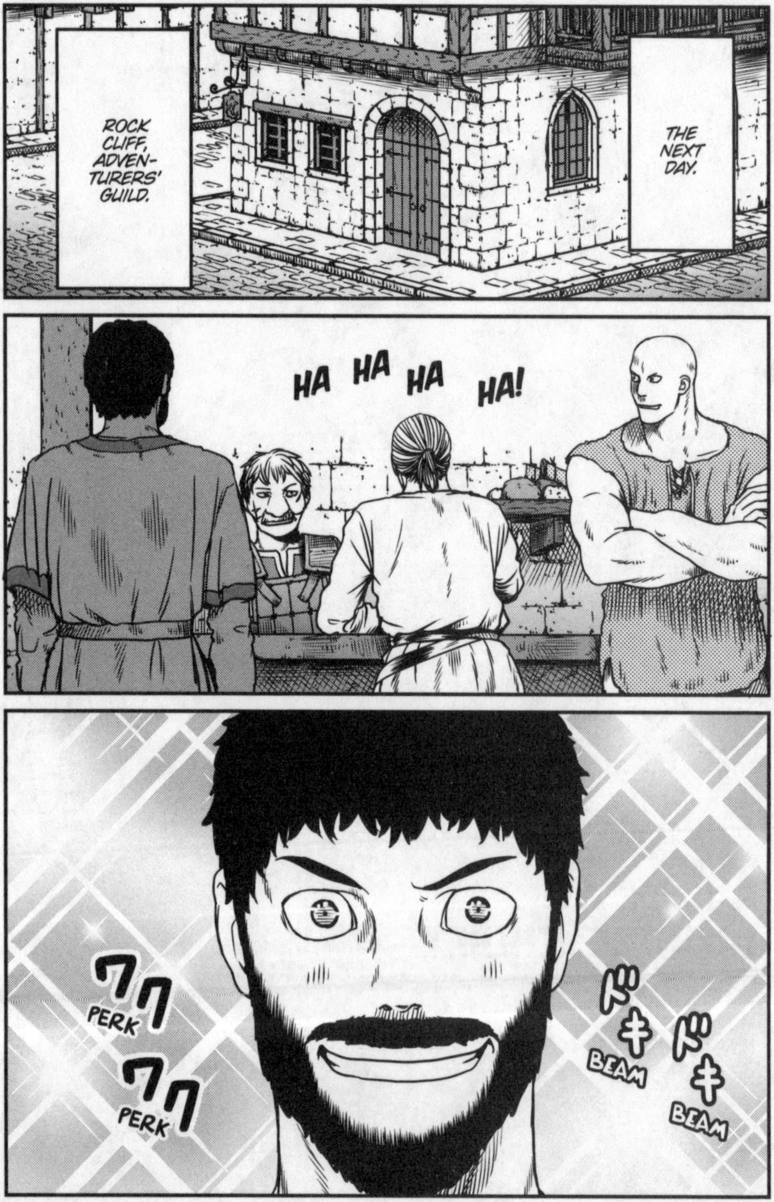
THE NEXT DAY.
ROCK CLIFF, ADVEN-TURERS' GUILD.
HA HA HA HA!
ドキ BEAM
ドキ BEAM
ワク PERK
ワク PERK

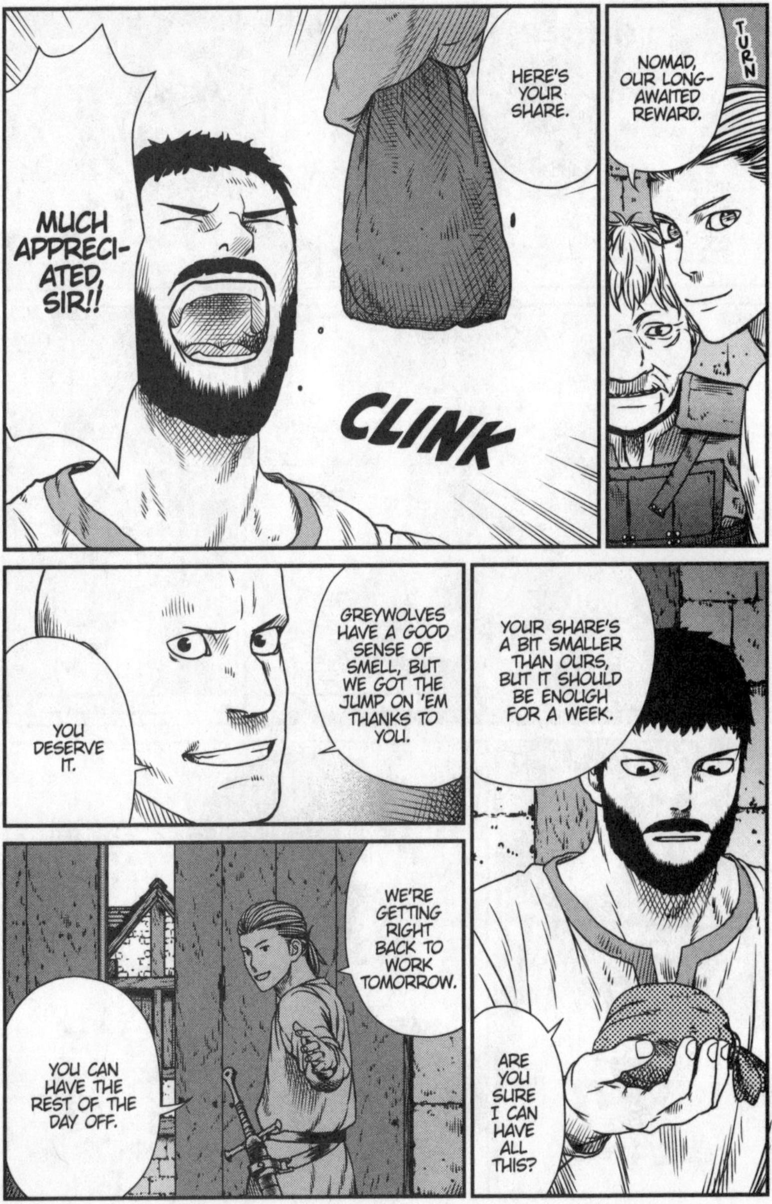
TURN
NOMAD, OUR LONG-AWAITED REWARD.
HERE'S YOUR SHARE.
MUCH APPRECIATED, SIR!!
CLINK
YOUR SHARE'S A BIT SMALLER THAN OURS, BUT IT SHOULD BE ENOUGH FOR A WEEK.
ARE YOU SURE I CAN HAVE ALL THIS?
GREYWOLVES HAVE A GOOD SENSE OF SMELL, BUT WE GOT THE JUMP ON 'EM THANKS TO YOU.
YOU DESERVE IT.
WE'RE GETTING RIGHT BACK TO WORK TOMORROW.
YOU CAN HAVE THE REST OF THE DAY OFF.

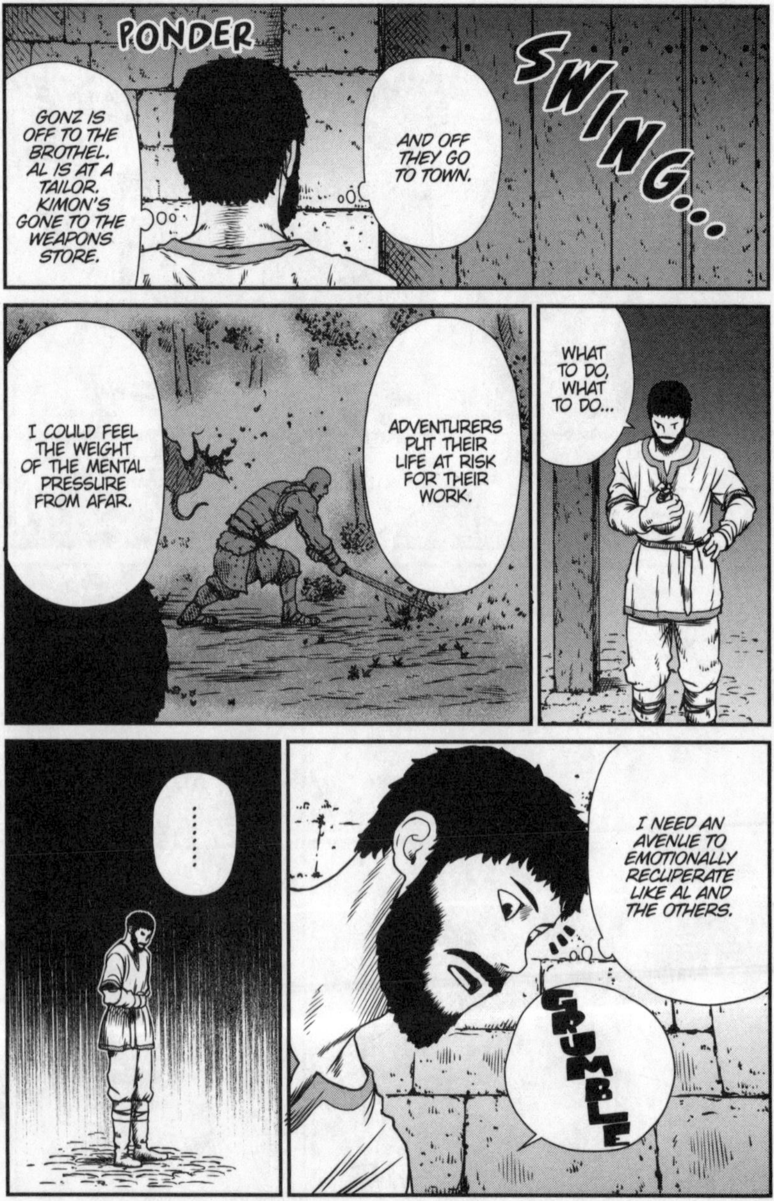
SWING...
AND OFF THEY GO TO TOWN.
PONDER
GONZ IS OFF TO THE BROTHEL. AL IS AT A TAILOR. KIMON'S GONE TO THE WEAPONS STORE.
WHAT TO DO, WHAT TO DO...
ADVENTURERS PUT THEIR LIFE AT RISK FOR THEIR WORK.
I COULD FEEL THE WEIGHT OF THE MENTAL PRESSURE FROM AFAR.
I NEED AN AVENUE TO EMOTIONALLY RECUPERATE LIKE AL AND THE OTHERS.
GRUMBLE
......

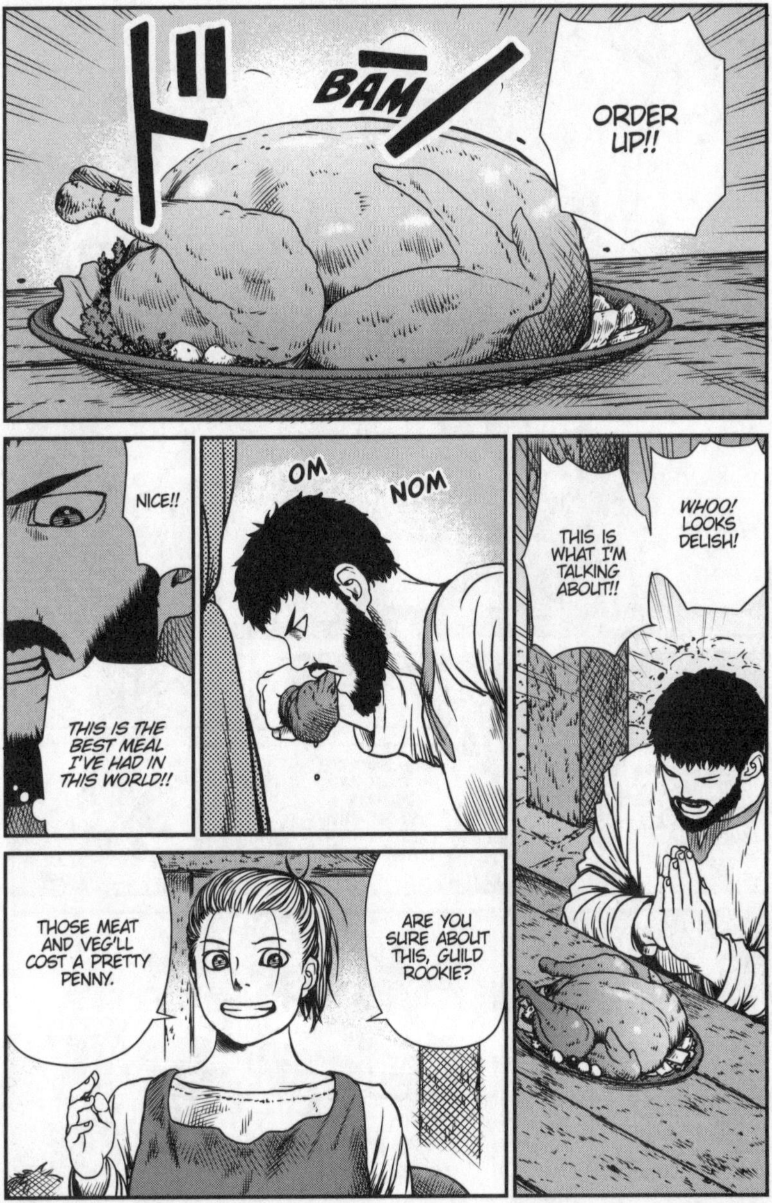
ド
BĀM
ORDER UP!!
WHOO! LOOKS DELISH!
THIS IS WHAT I'M TALKING ABOUT!!
OM
NOM
NICE!!
THIS IS THE BEST MEAL I'VE HAD IN THIS WORLD!!
ARE YOU SURE ABOUT THIS, GUILD ROOKIE?
THOSE MEAT AND VEG'LL COST A PRETTY PENNY.

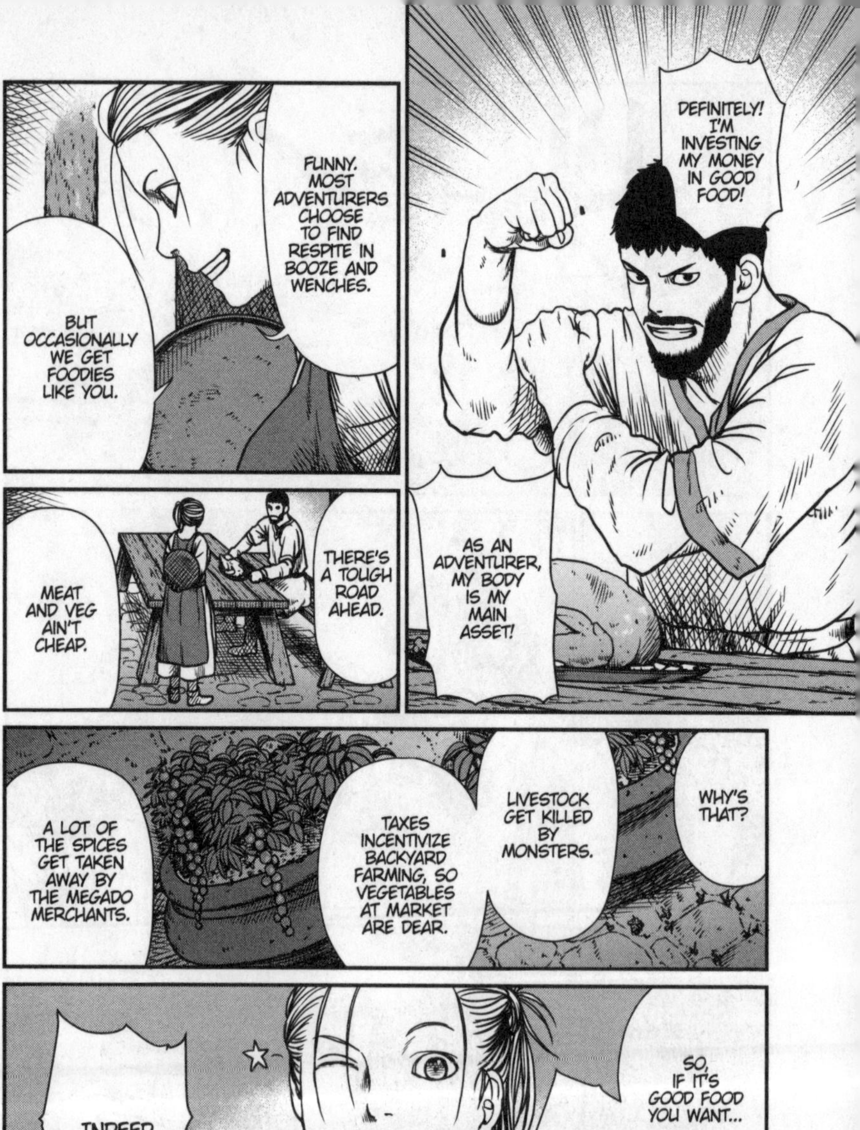
DEFINITELY! I'M INVESTING MY MONEY IN GOOD FOOD!
AS AN ADVENTURER, MY BODY IS MY MAIN ASSET!
FUNNY. MOST ADVENTURERS CHOOSE TO FIND RESPITE IN BOOZE AND WENCHES.
BUT OCCASIONALLY WE GET FOODIES LIKE YOU.
THERE'S A TOUGH ROAD AHEAD.
MEAT AND VEG AIN'T CHEAP.
WHY'S THAT?
LIVESTOCK GET KILLED BY MONSTERS.
TAXES INCENTIVIZE BACKYARD FARMING, SO VEGETABLES AT MARKET ARE DEAR.
A LOT OF THE SPICES GET TAKEN AWAY BY THE MEGADO MERCHANTS.
SO, IF IT'S GOOD FOOD YOU WANT...
YOU BEST KEEP EARNING THAT MOOLA!
INDEED, I WILL!

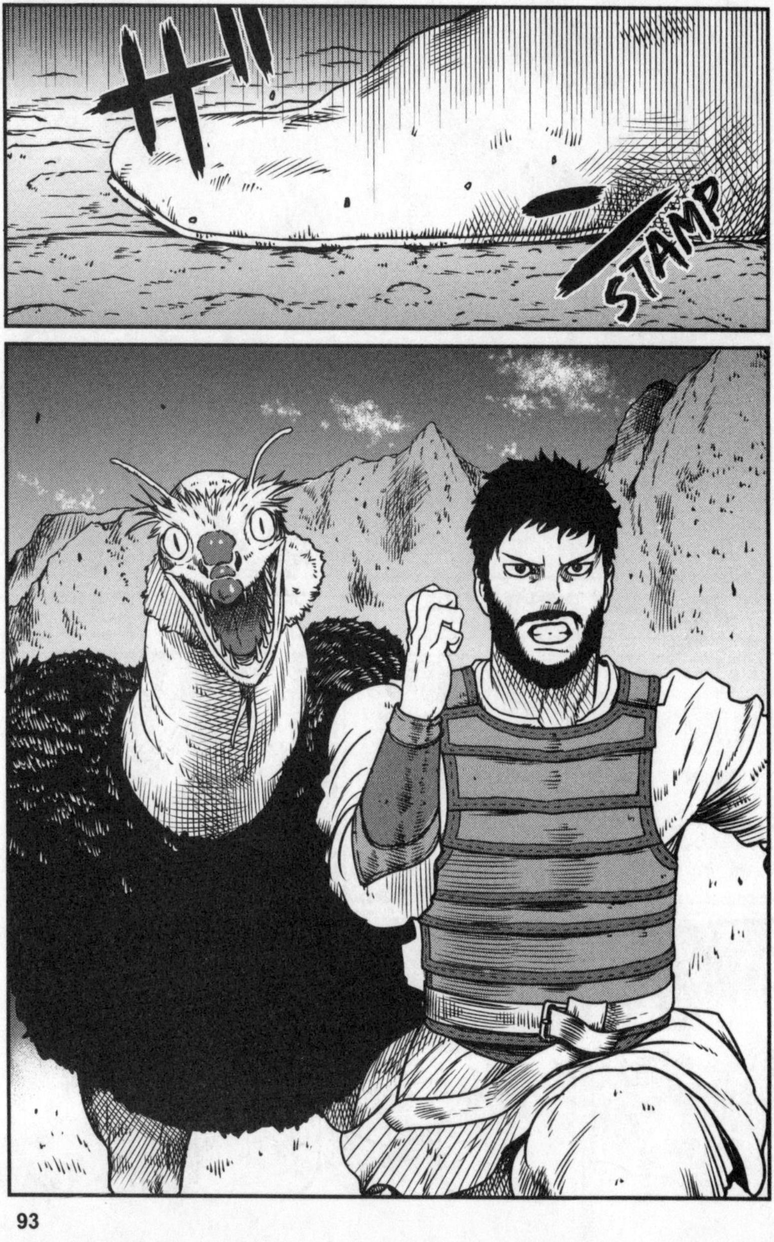
STAMP

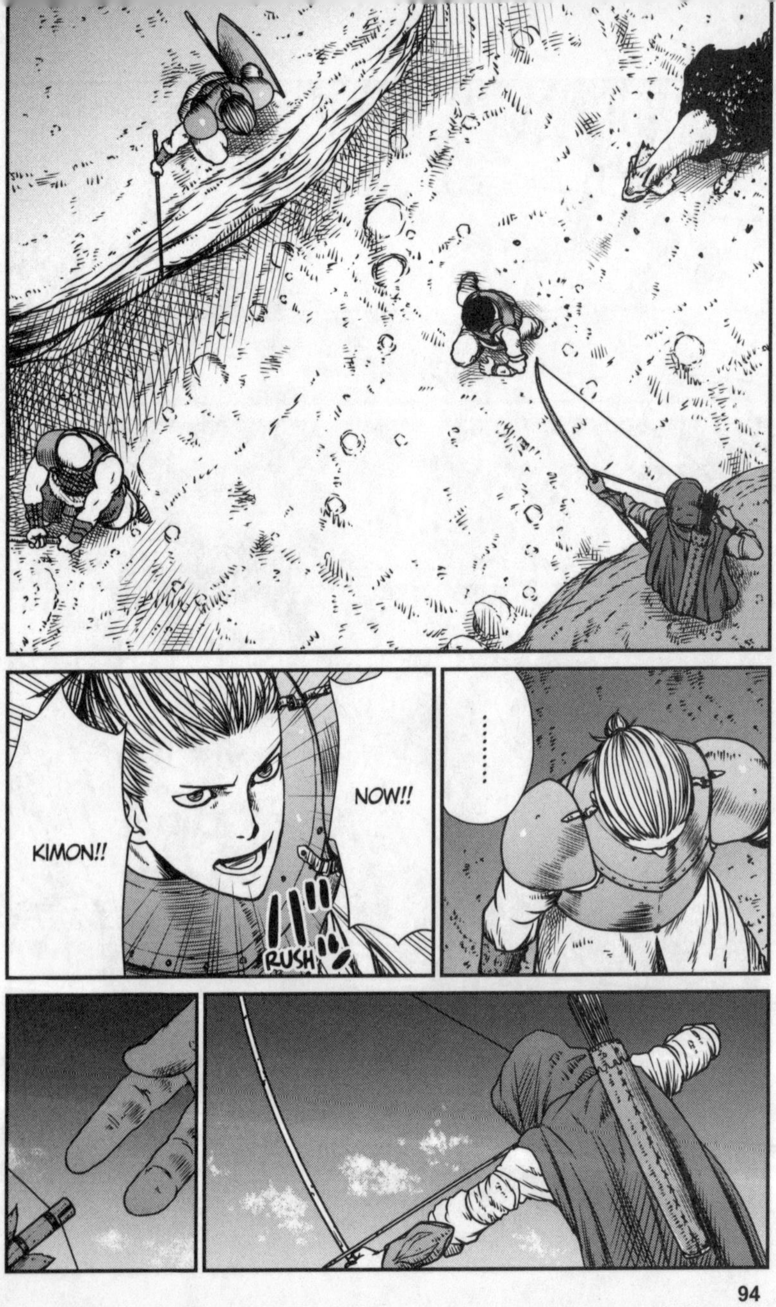
......
NOW!!
KIMON!!
RUSH

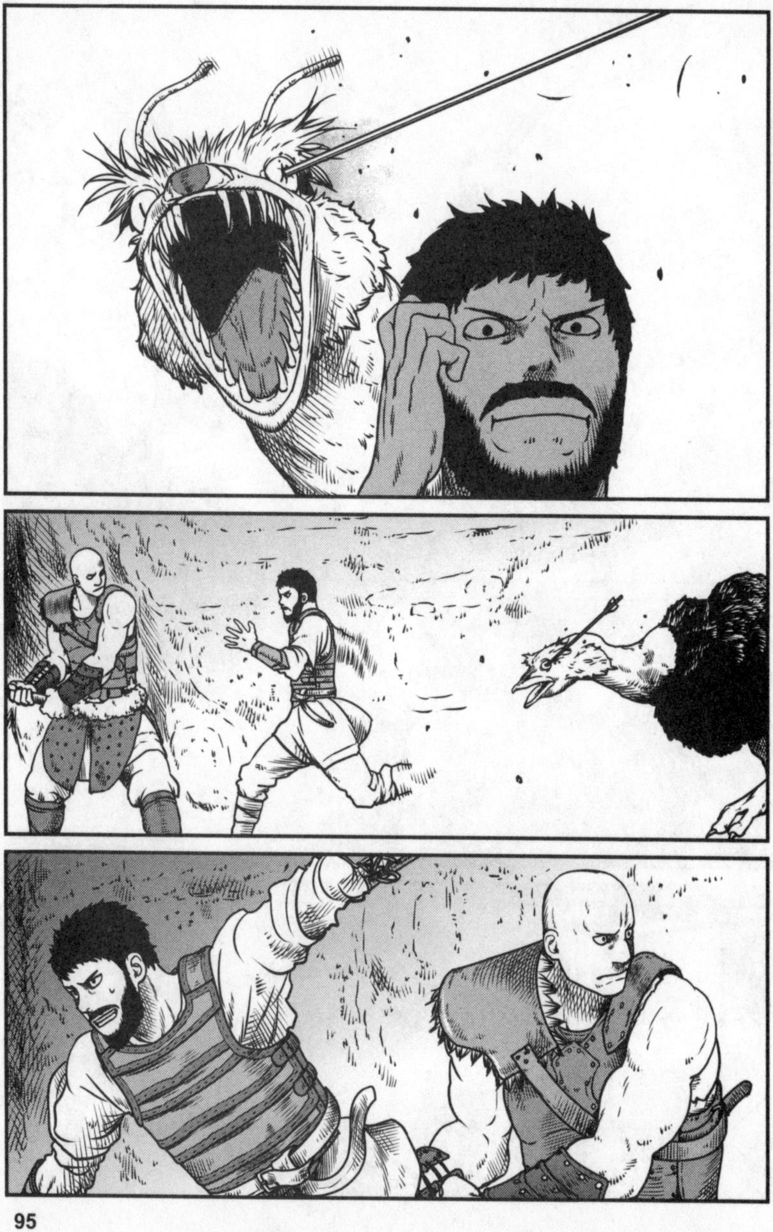

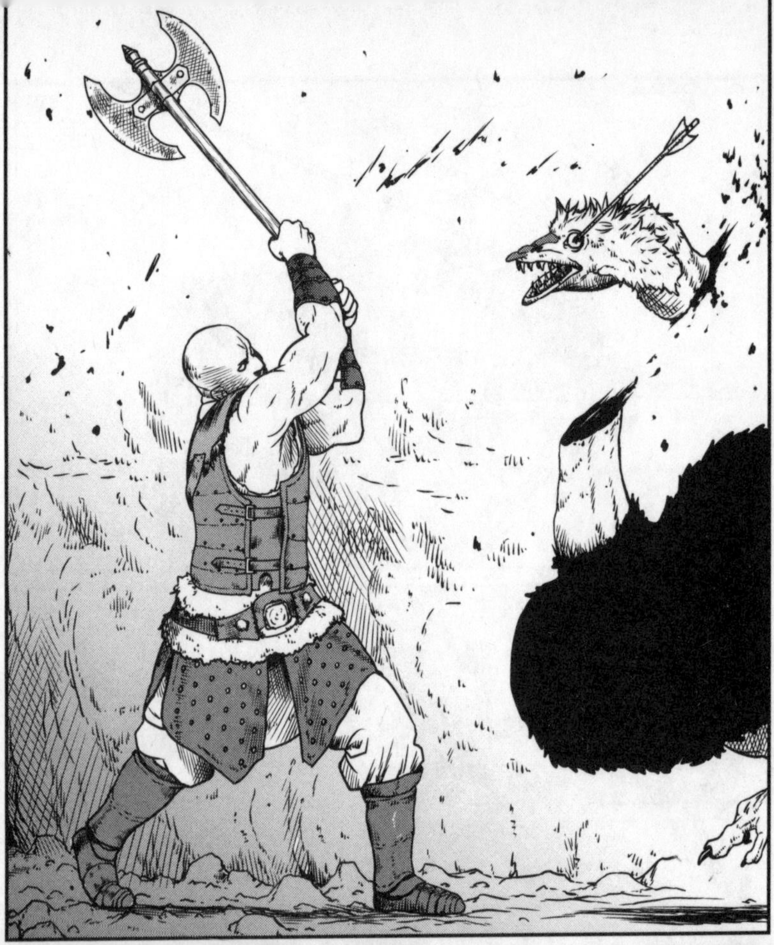

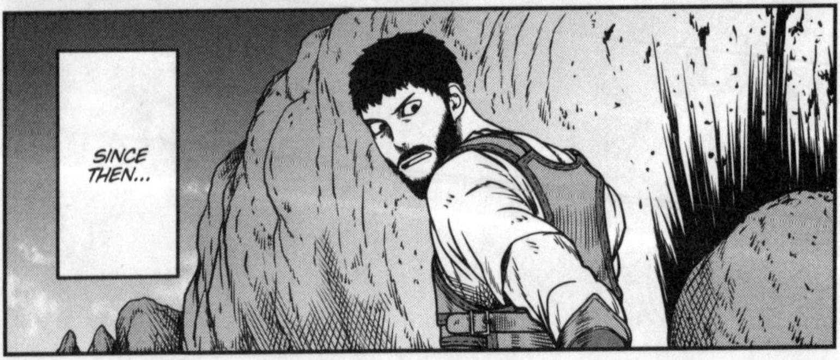
SINCE THEN...

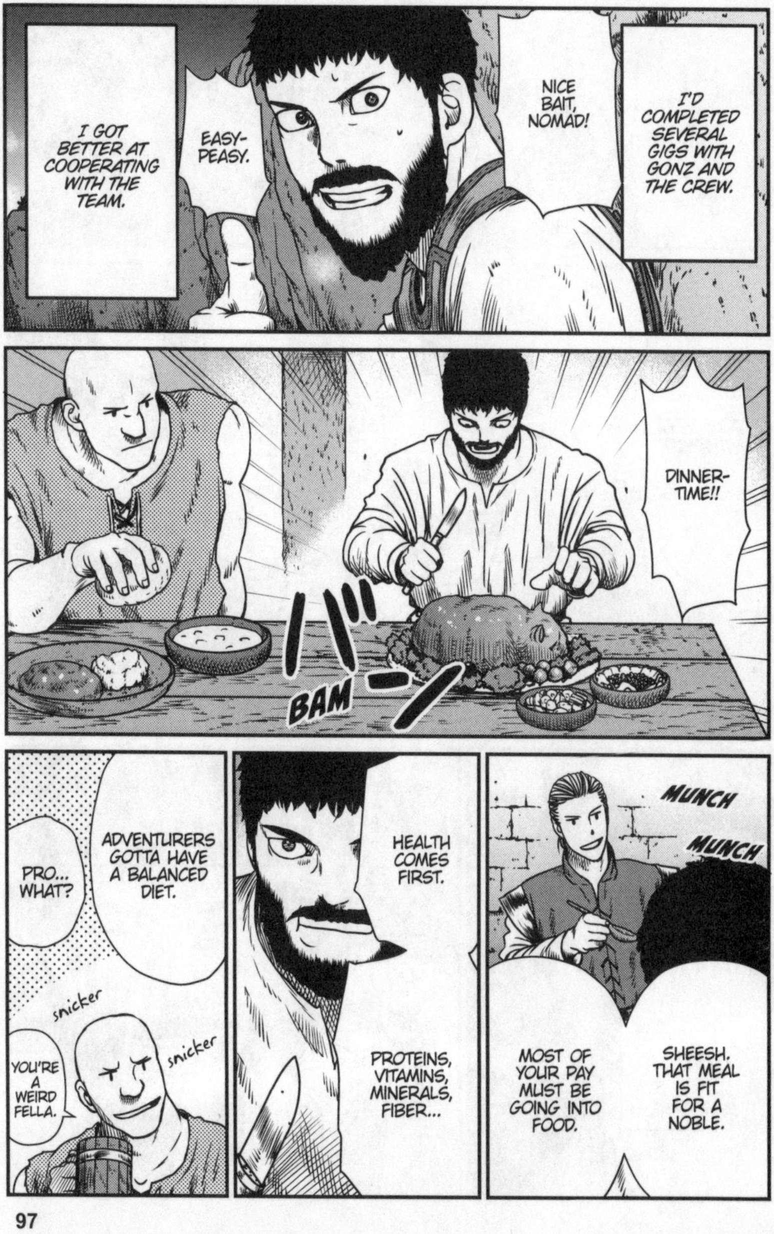
I'D COMPLETED SEVERAL GIGS WITH GONZ AND THE CREW.
NICE BAIT, NOMAD!
EASY-PEASY.
I GOT BETTER AT COOPERATING WITH THE TEAM.
DINNER-TIME!!
BAM
MUNCH
MUNCH
SHEESH. THAT MEAL IS FIT FOR A NOBLE.
MOST OF YOUR PAY MUST BE GOING INTO FOOD.
HEALTH COMES FIRST.
PROTEINS, VITAMINS, MINERALS, FIBER...
ADVENTURERS GOTTA HAVE A BALANCED DIET.
PRO... WHAT?
snicker
snicker
YOU'RE A WEIRD FELLA.

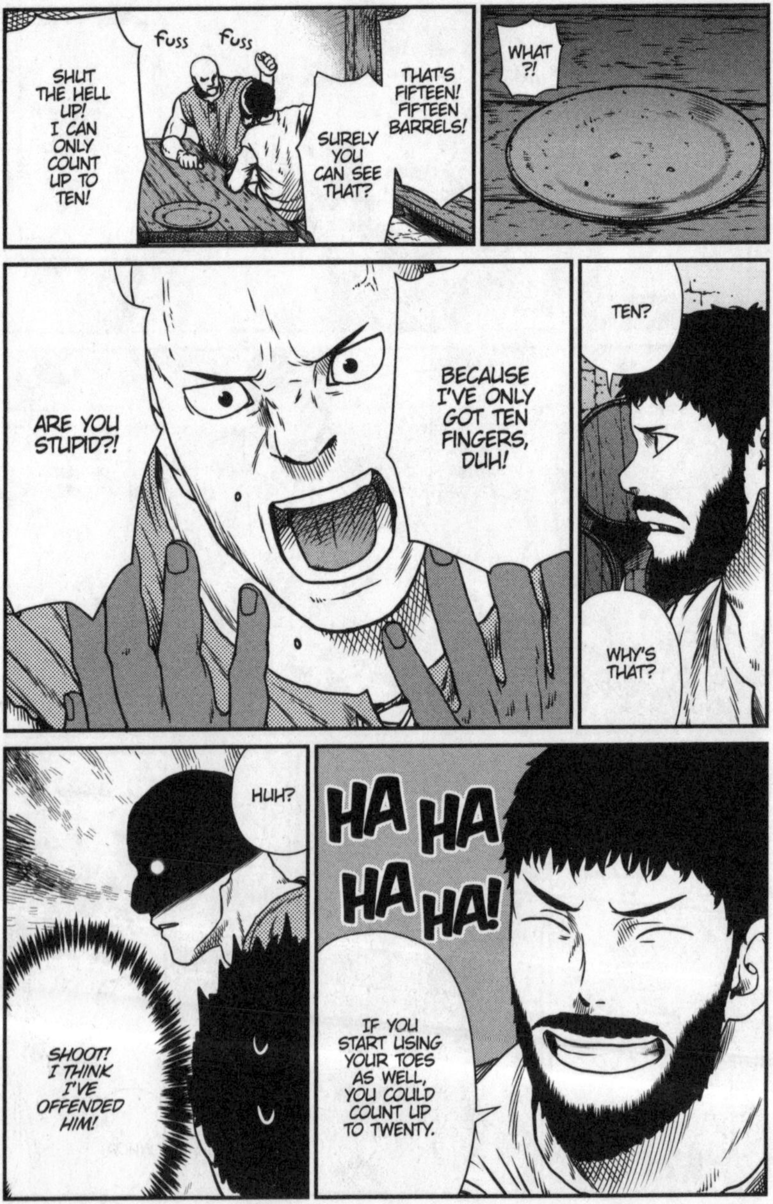
WHAT ?!
THAT'S FIFTEEN! FIFTEEN BARRELS!
SURELY YOU CAN SEE THAT?
fuss fuss
SHUT THE HELL UP! I CAN ONLY COUNT UP TO TEN!
TEN?
WHY'S THAT?
BECAUSE I'VE ONLY GOT TEN FINGERS, DUH!
ARE YOU STUPID?!
HA HA HA HA!
IF YOU START USING YOUR TOES AS WELL, YOU COULD COUNT UP TO TWENTY.
HUH?
SHOOT! I THINK I'VE OFFENDED HIM!

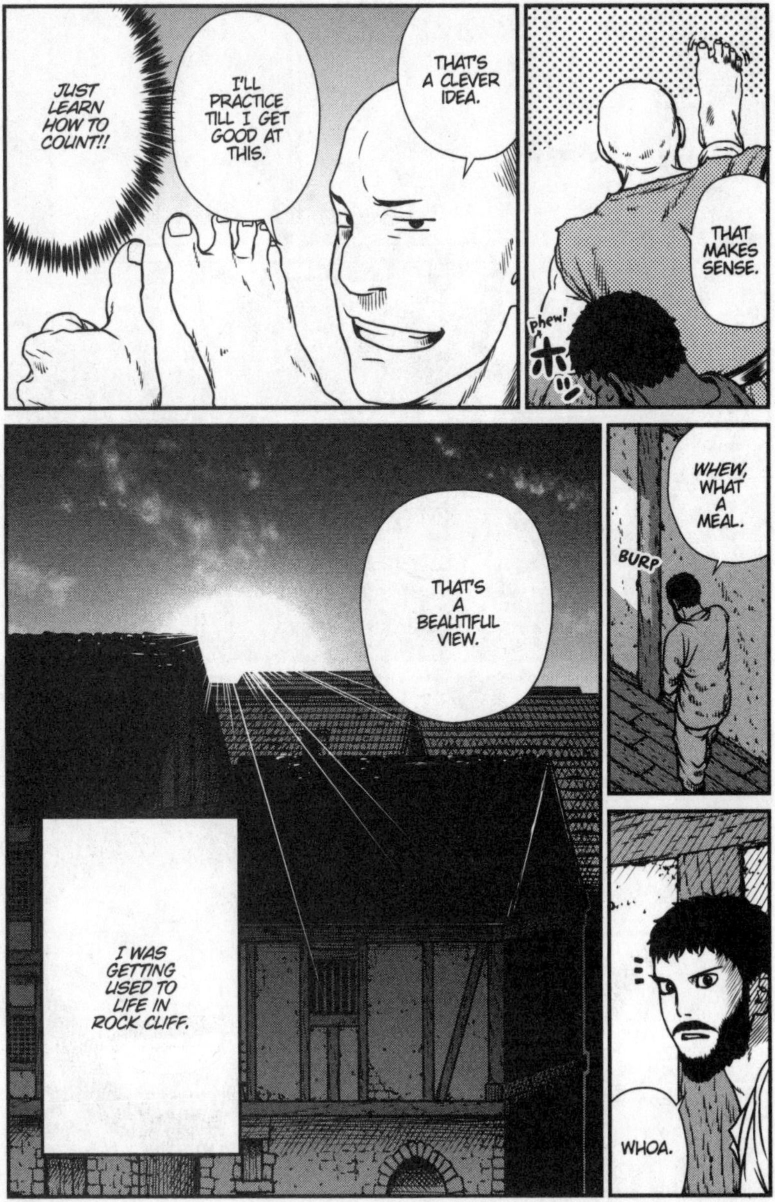
THAT MAKES SENSE.
phew!
ホッ
THAT'S A CLEVER IDEA.
I'LL PRACTICE TILL I GET GOOD AT THIS.
JUST LEARN HOW TO COUNT!!
WHEW, WHAT A MEAL.
BURP
WHOA.
THAT'S A BEAUTIFUL VIEW.
I WAS GETTING USED TO LIFE IN ROCK CLIFF.

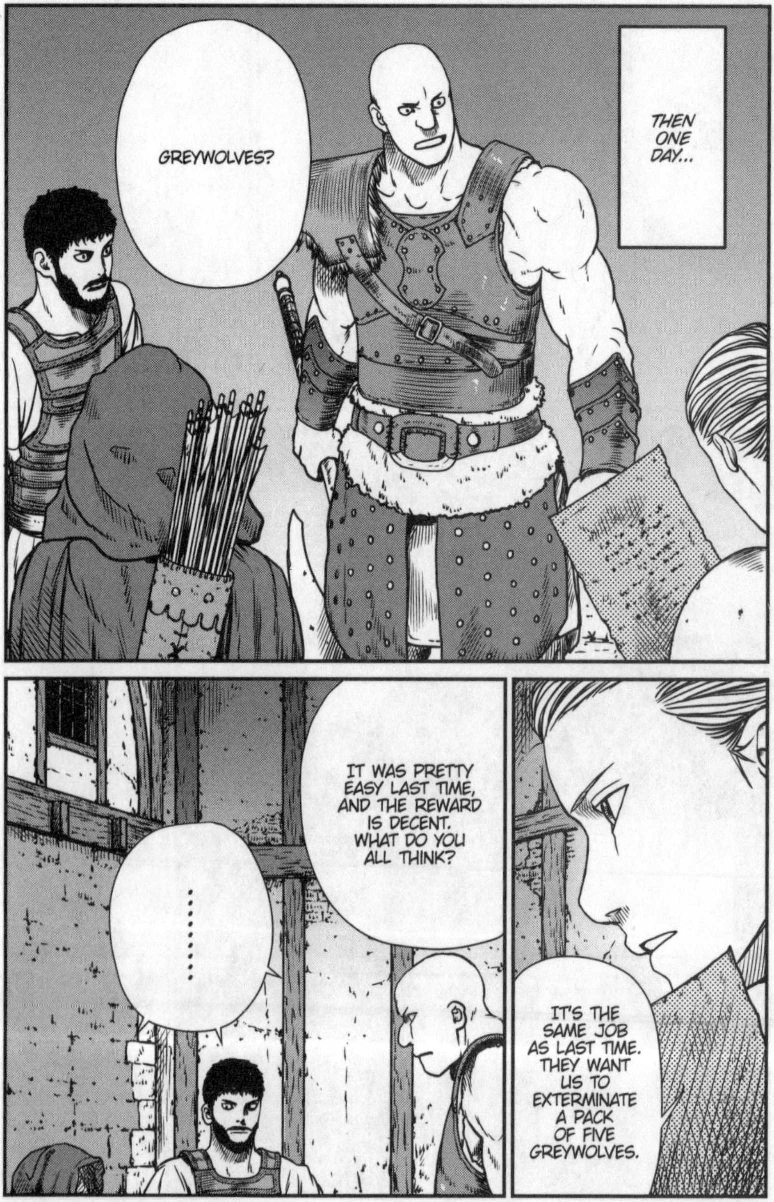
THEN ONE DAY...
GREYWOLVES?
IT'S THE SAME JOB AS LAST TIME. THEY WANT US TO EXTERMINATE A PACK OF FIVE GREYWOLVES.
IT WAS PRETTY EASY LAST TIME, AND THE REWARD IS DECENT. WHAT DO YOU ALL THINK?
......

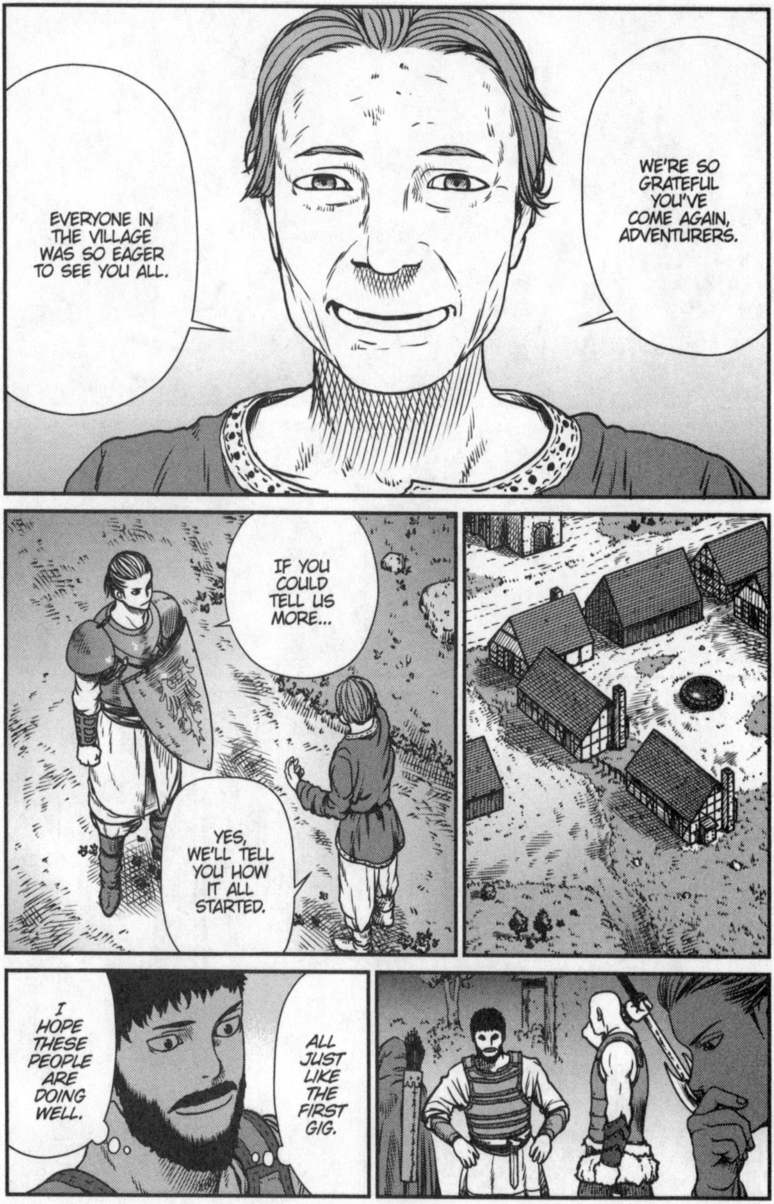
WE'RE SO GRATEFUL YOU'VE COME AGAIN, ADVENTURERS.
EVERYONE IN THE VILLAGE WAS SO EAGER TO SEE YOU ALL.
IF YOU COULD TELL US MORE...
YES, WE'LL TELL YOU HOW IT ALL STARTED.
ALL JUST LIKE THE FIRST GIG.
I HOPE THESE PEOPLE ARE DOING WELL.

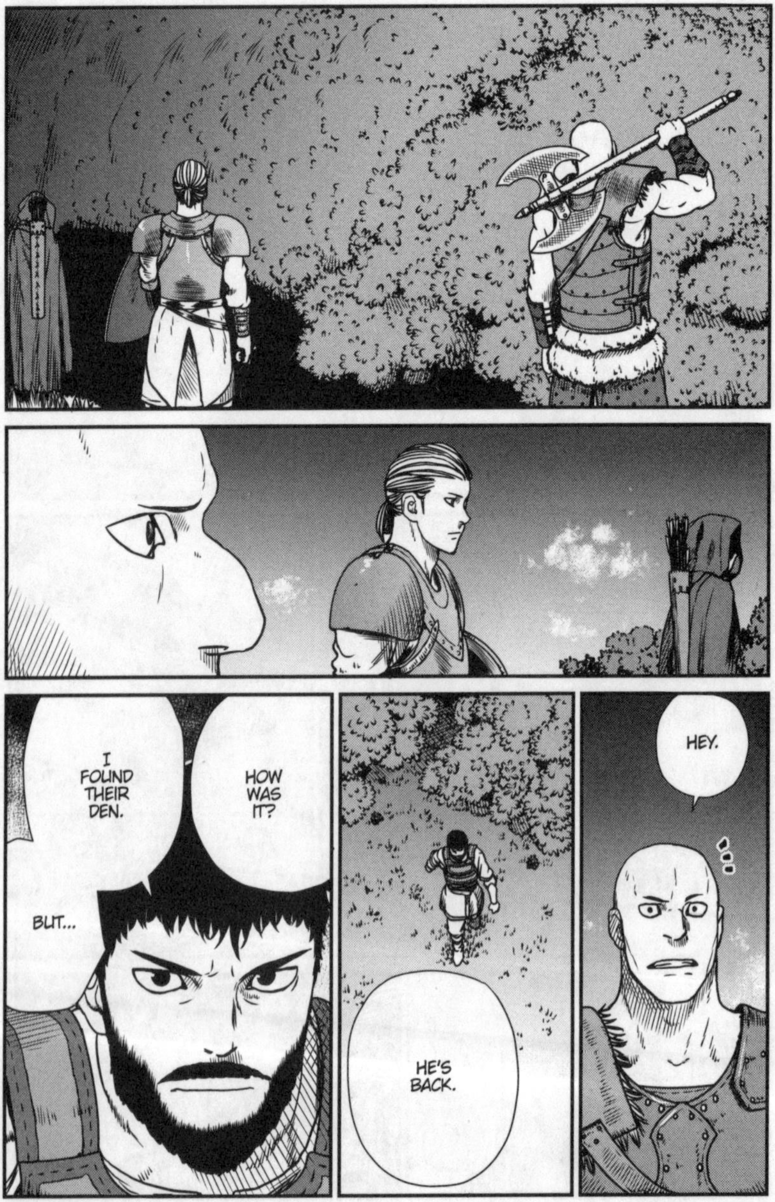
HEY.
HE'S BACK.
HOW WAS IT?
I FOUND THEIR DEN.
BUT...

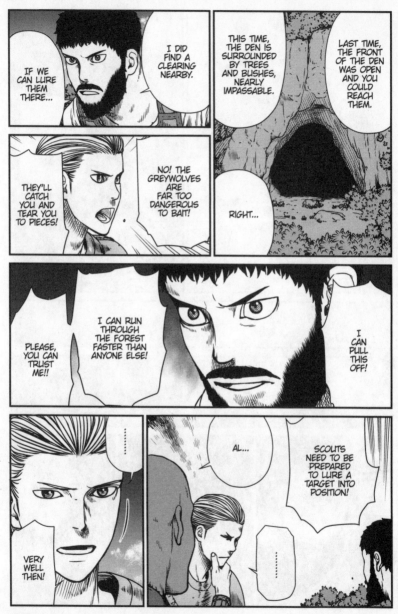

LAST TIME, THE FRONT OF THE DEN WAS OPEN AND YOU COULD REACH THEM.
THIS TIME, THE DEN IS SURROUNDED BY TREES AND BUSHES, NEARLY IMPASSABLE.
RIGHT...
I DID FIND A CLEARING NEARBY.
IF WE CAN LURE THEM THERE...
NO! THE GREYWOLVES ARE FAR TOO DANGEROUS TO BAIT!
THEY'LL CATCH YOU AND TEAR YOU TO PIECES!
I CAN PULL THIS OFF!
I CAN RUN THROUGH THE FOREST FASTER THAN ANYONE ELSE!
PLEASE, YOU CAN TRUST ME!!
SCOUTS NEED TO BE PREPARED TO LURE A TARGET INTO POSITION!
AL...
......
......
VERY WELL THEN!

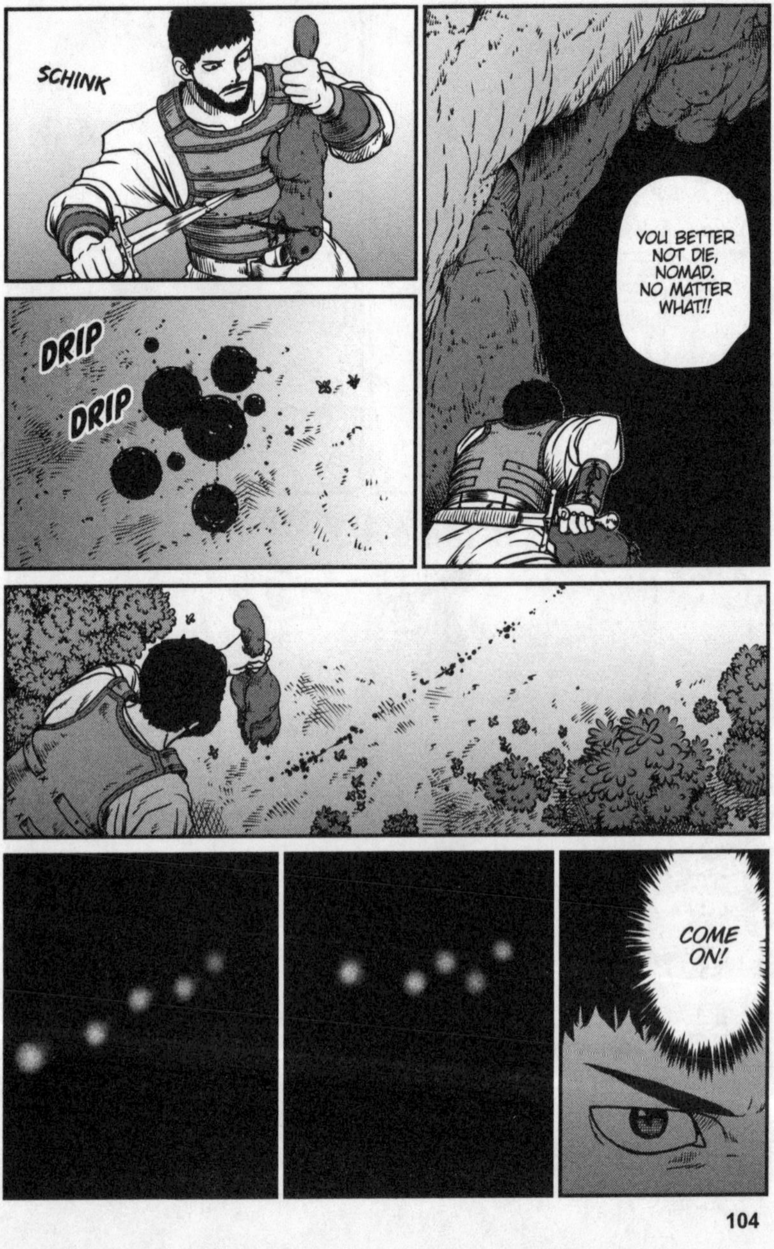
YOU BETTER NOT DIE, NOMAD. NO MATTER WHAT!!
SCHINK
DRIP
DRIP
COME ON!

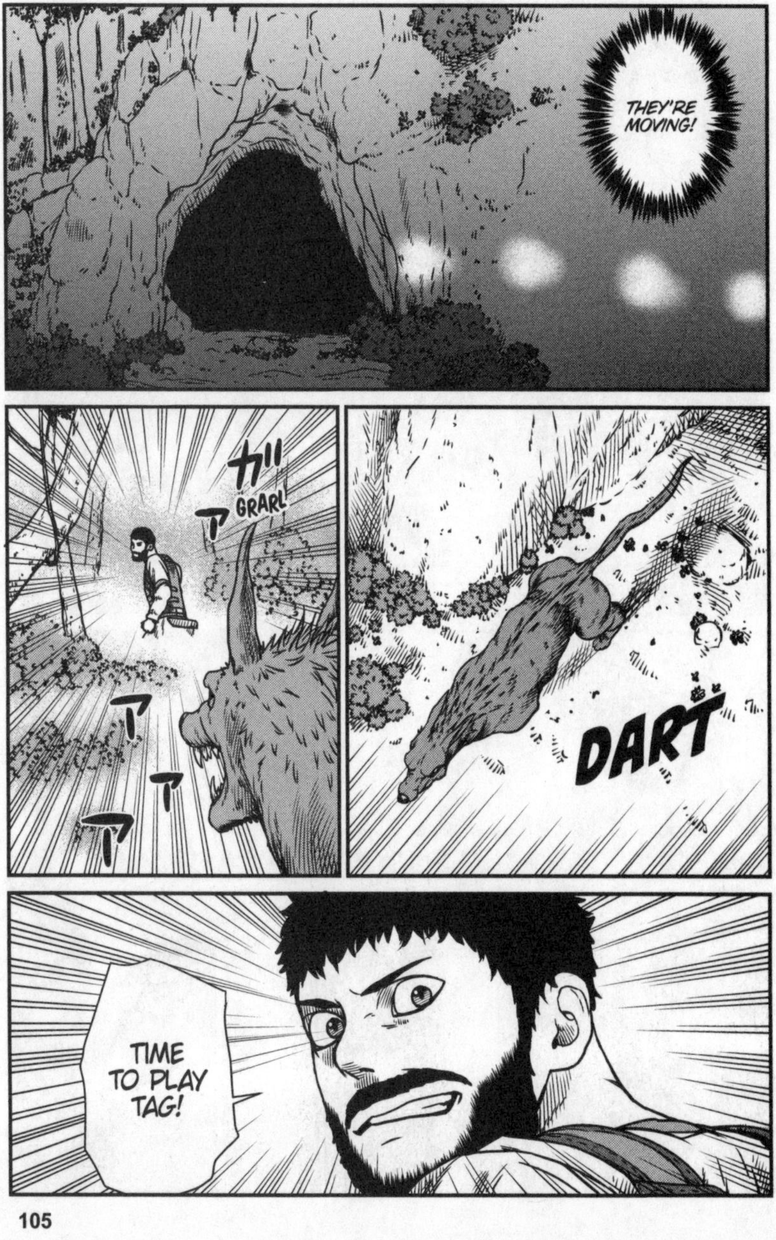
THEY'RE MOVING!
DART
ガッ
GRARL!
ア
ア
ア
ア
TIME TO PLAY TAG!

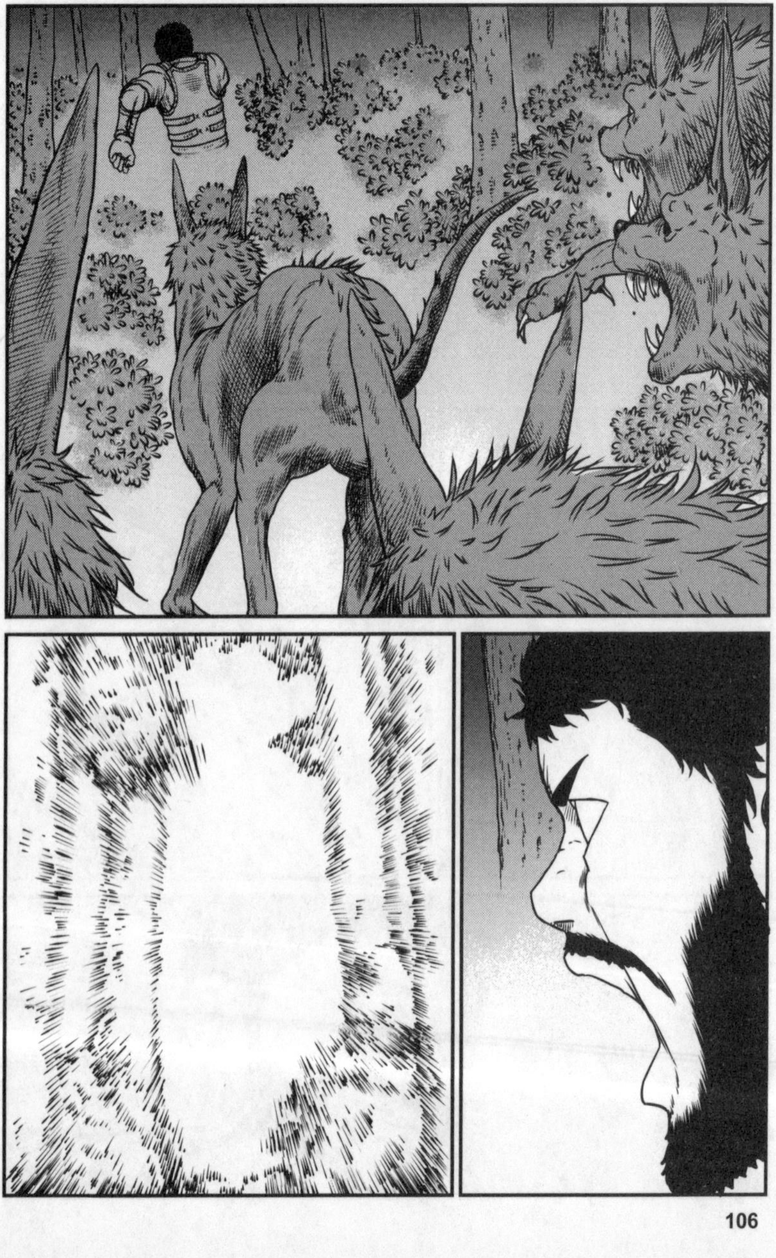

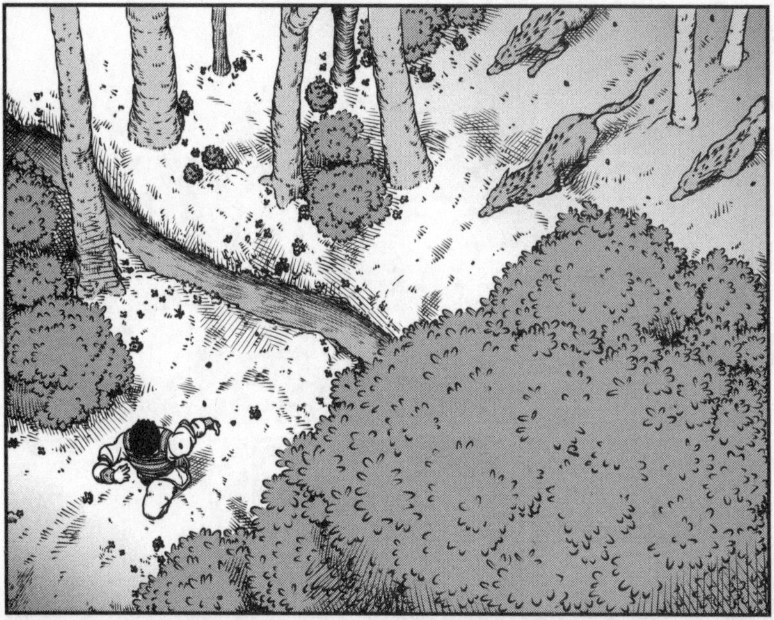
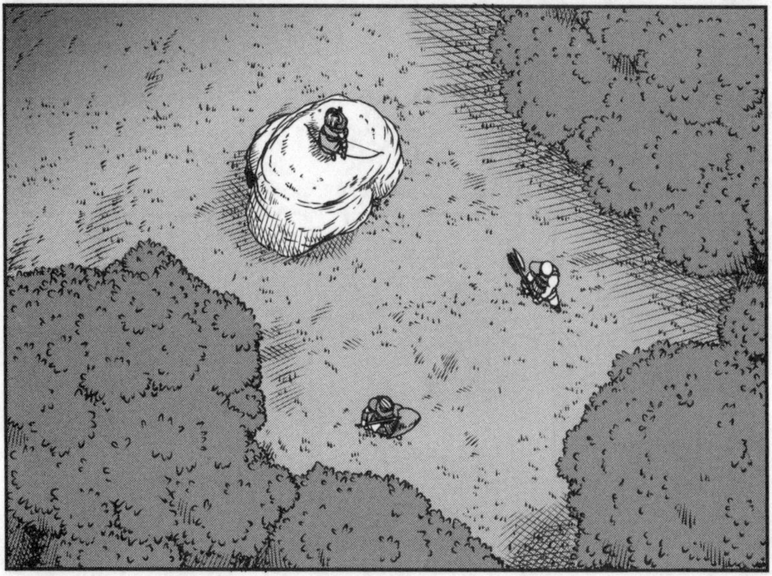

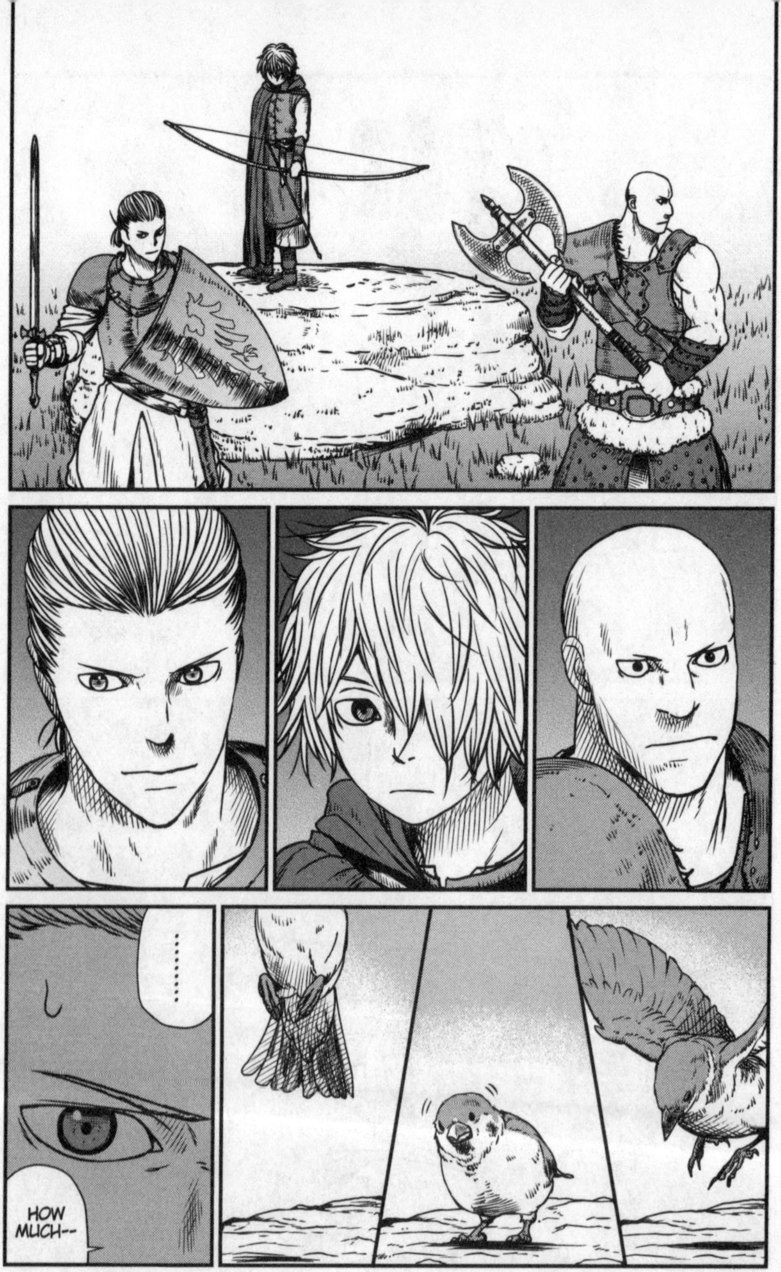

....
HOW MUCH--

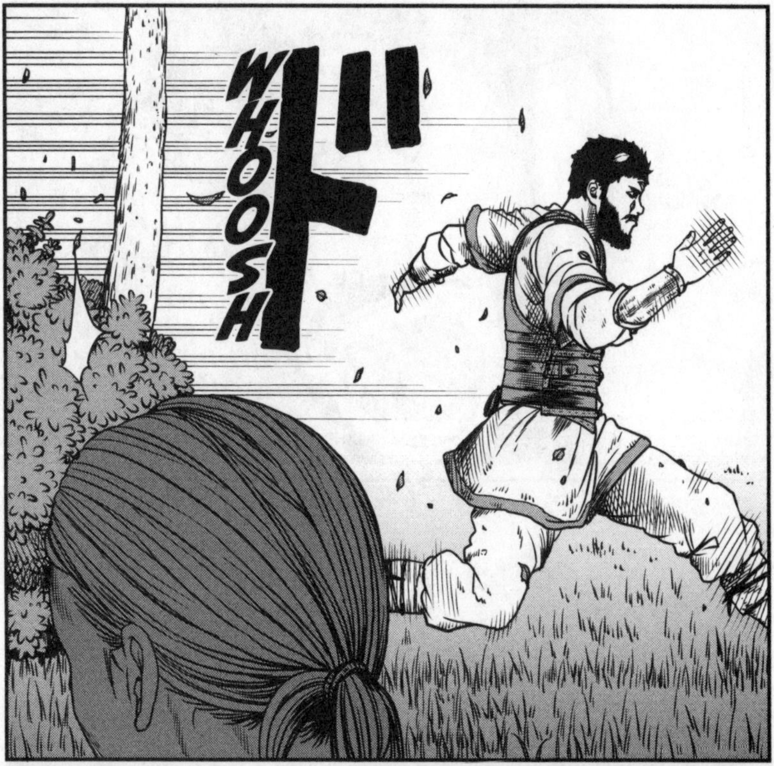
ド
WHOOSH
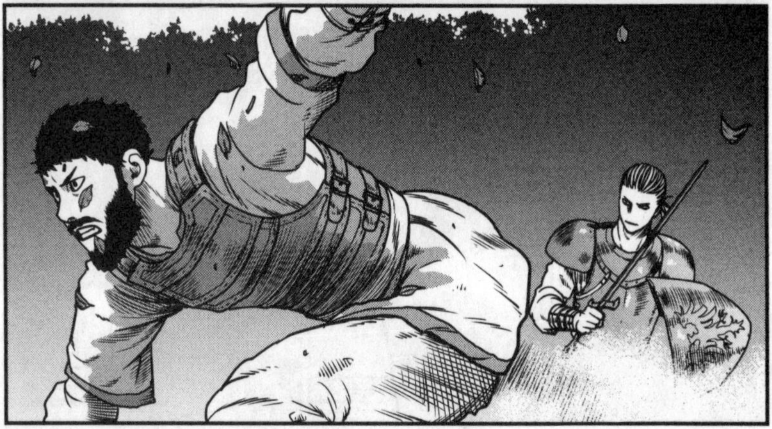

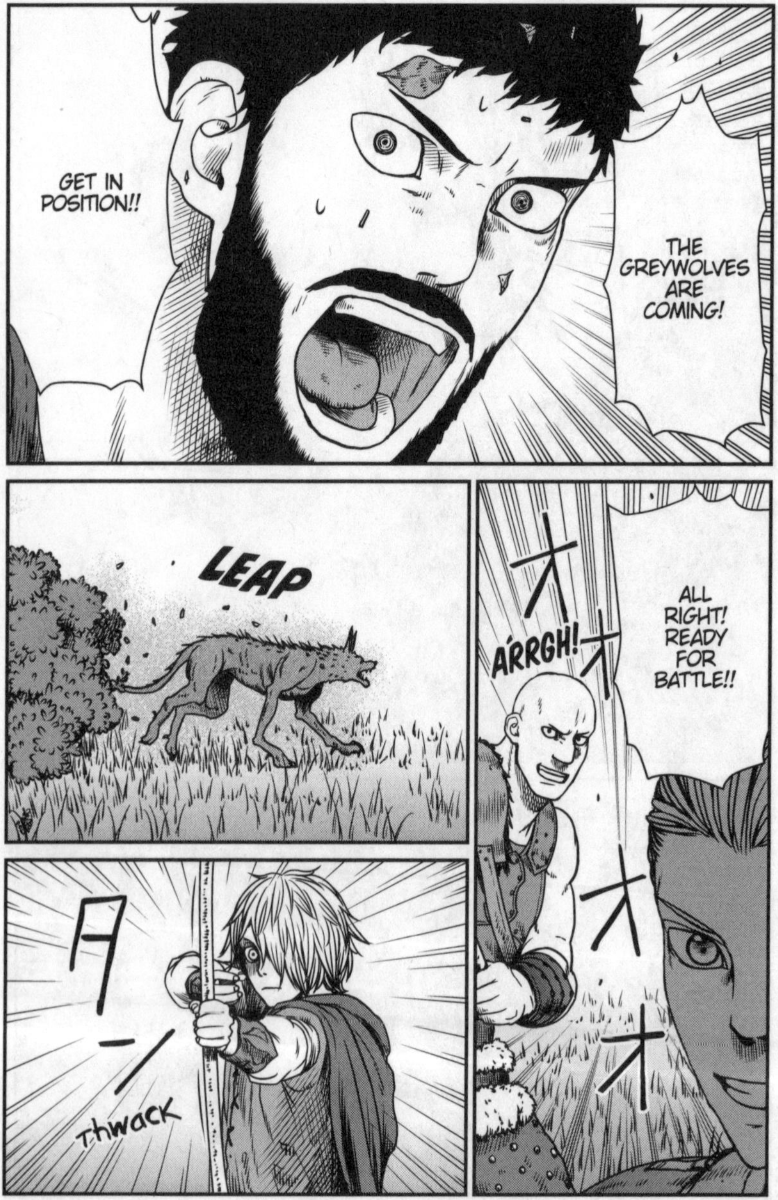
THE GREYWOLVES ARE COMING!
GET IN POSITION!!
ALL RIGHT! READY FOR BATTLE!!
オオオオ
ARRGH!
LEAP
ターン
THWACK

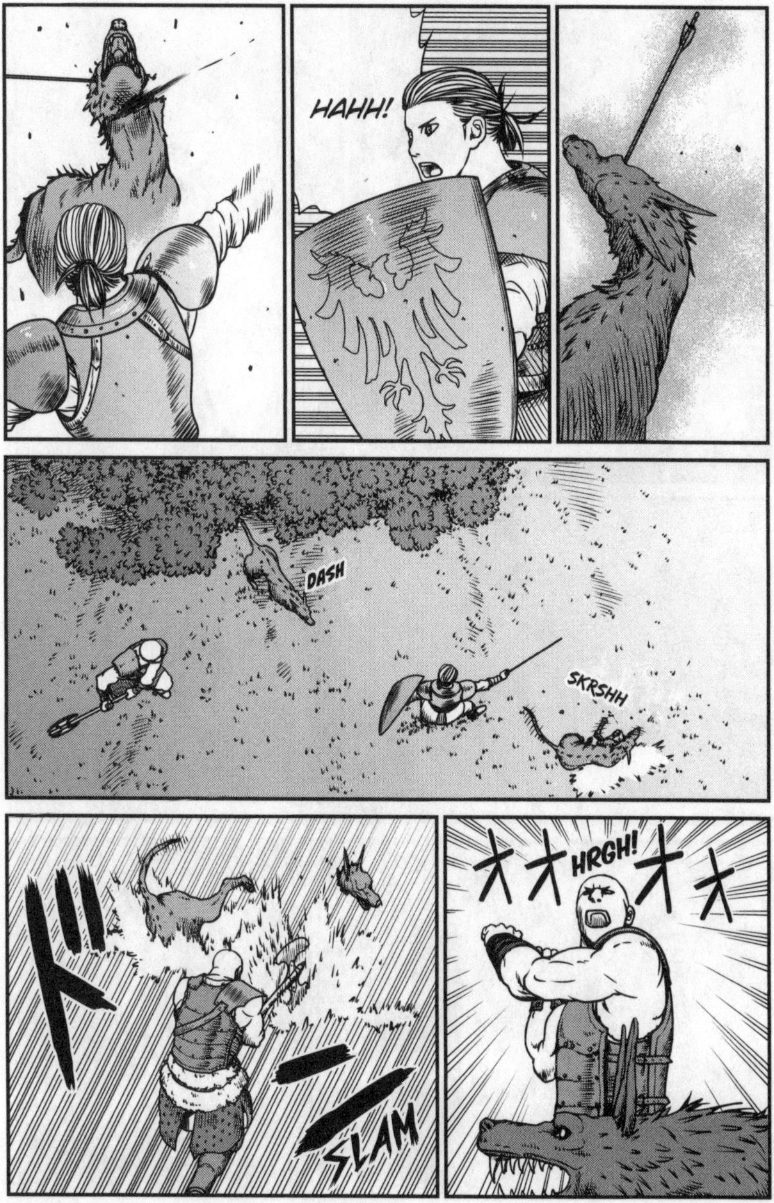
HAHH!
DASH
SKRSHH
HRGH!
SLAM

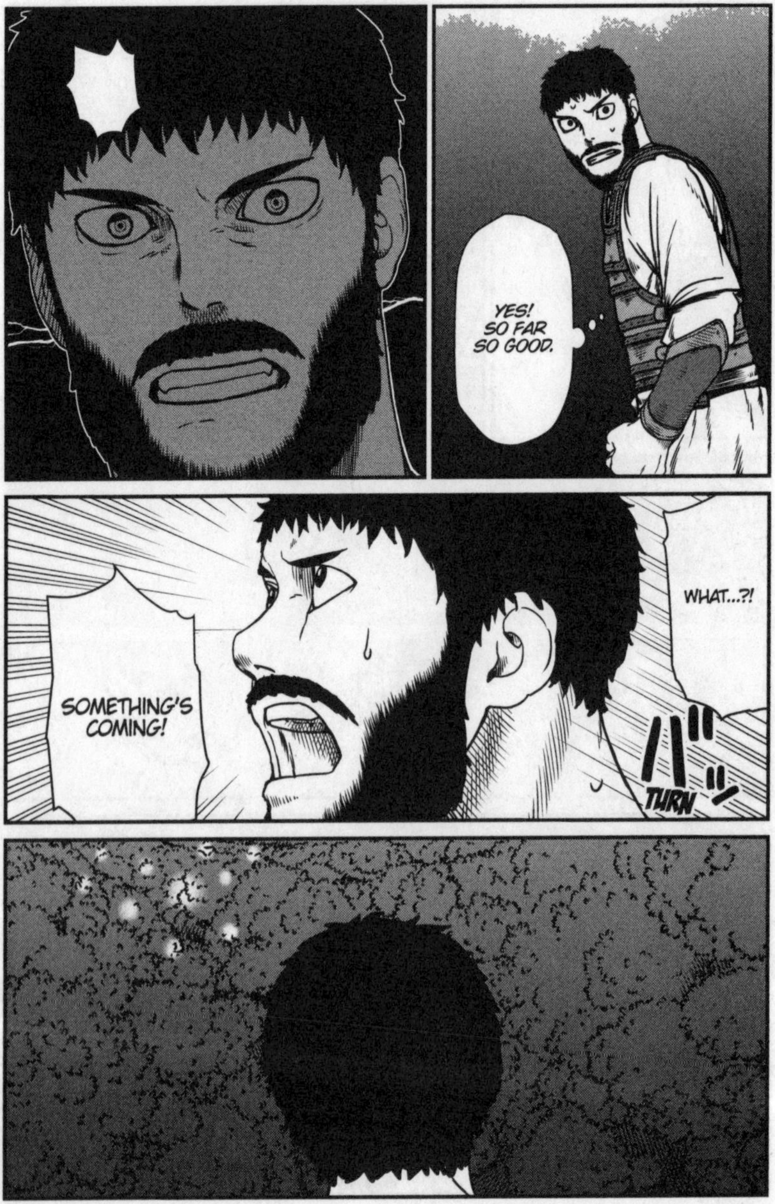
YES! SO FAR SO GOOD.
WHAT...?!
TURN
SOMETHING'S COMING!

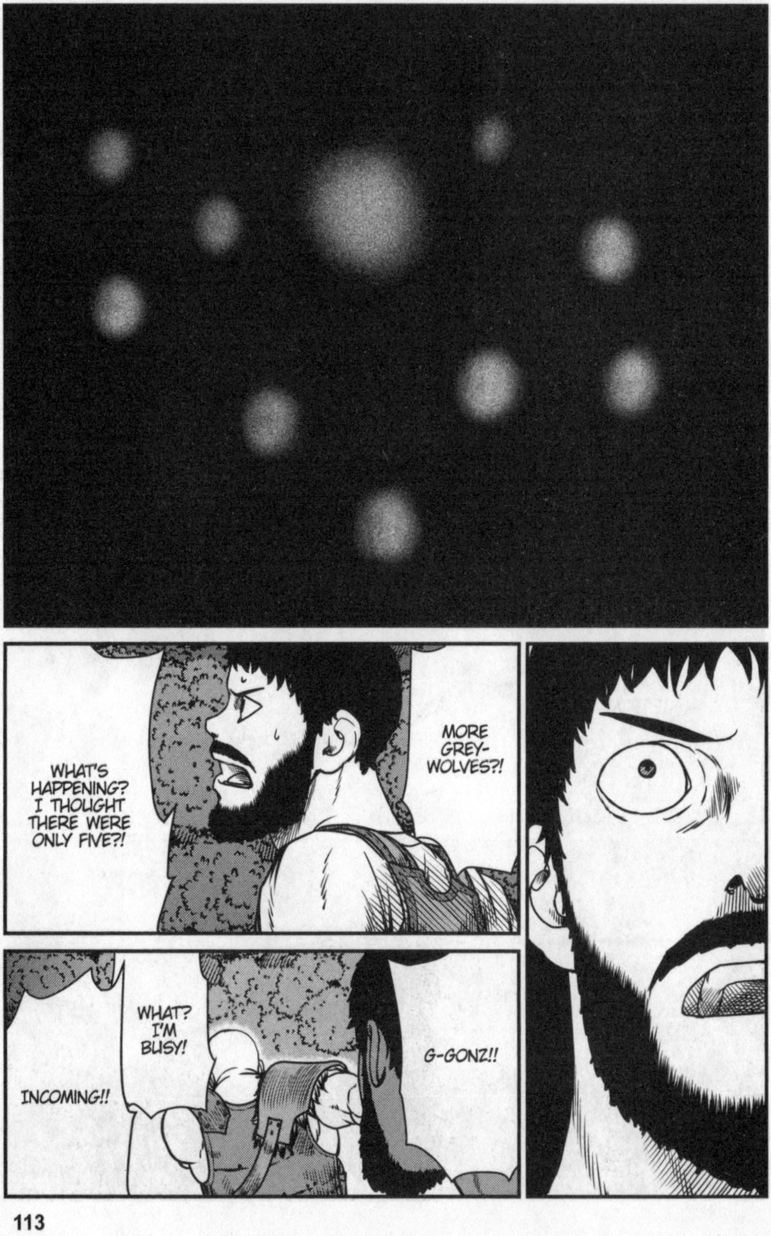
MORE GREY-WOLVES?!
WHAT'S HAPPENING? I THOUGHT THERE WERE ONLY FIVE?!
G-GONZ!!
WHAT? I'M BUSY!
INCOMING!!

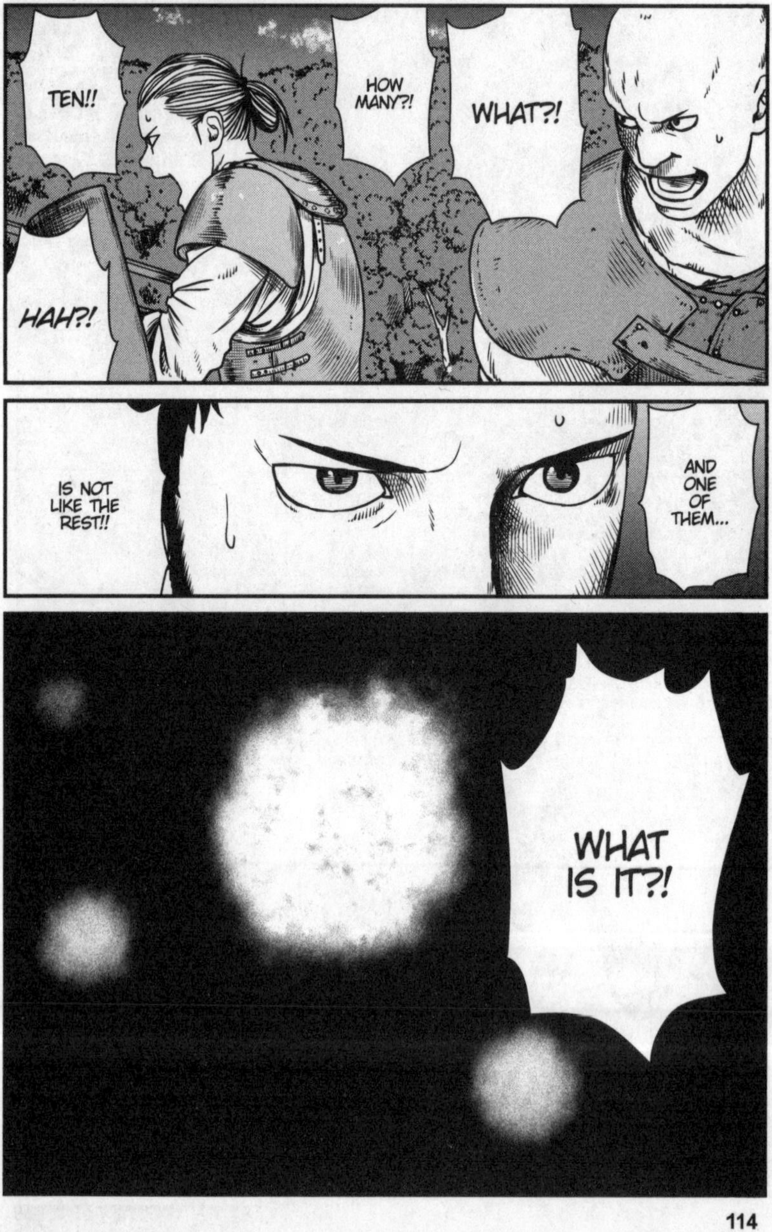
WHAT?!
HOW MANY?!
TEN!!
HAH?!
AND ONE OF THEM...
IS NOT LIKE THE REST!!
WHAT IS IT?!

SPECIAL COLUMN BY AUTHOR. YAZIN

KARATE SURVIVOR IN ANOTHER WORLD

INTERMISSION

SAVAGE RULES 10

FOOD IN THE OTHER WORLD

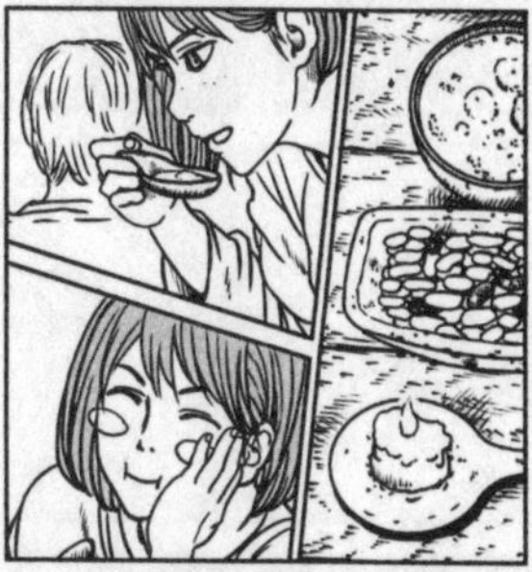

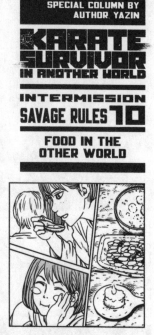

Needless to say, food important. Humans die when malnourished or undernourished. Survival without food is impossible.

However, food is not only a vehicle to replenish nutrients, but also a way to enrich people's lives and reduce stress. This has been true throughout history and all worlds.

The world Nomad is sent to is equivalent to the medieval/early modern civilization of earth. The medieval diet is perhaps associated with skinny peasants feeding on thin soup and bread. Peasants suffer from poor harvests and heavy taxes, and people inhabiting the slums live in squalor. There may be some truth to these depictions. People have often died of starvation under governments with no welfare provisions.

However, in truth, the average citizen was able to enjoy a reasonably good diet. It mainly consisted of bread and oatmeal. Soups were surprisingly well-balanced, made with lentils, chickpeas, turnips, carrots, and cabbages with a variety of other beans and vegetables. Whole wheat bread was standard in those days and has seen a resurgence recently for its nutritious value. Oatmeal is rich in fiber and minerals, including calcium and vitamin B1.

Flavors were not limited to salt, either. Although spices such as pepper and saffron were expensive and not available for commoners, cheap vinegar, wine, garlic, and other herbs were used to garnish their meals.

Options for nobles and the wealthy were just as diverse as ours in the modern day, including spices, nuts, honey, sugar, cheese, dairy, eggs, and both fresh and processed meat and fish. A cookbook by a medieval chef records recipes that eventually formed the basis of modern dishes.

Unfortunately, in the world Nomad is sent to, monsters limit the amount of farmable land. Consequently, wheat has been adopted as the main crop, and is rotated with turnips and other vegetables. Fresh leafy vegetables are difficult to grow and are expensive in the city. Monster meat can be eaten but cannot be consistently farmed like livestock. Thus, the nutritiously balanced meal that Nomad is after costs a significant sum.

If I may go off-topic for a bit, on Project Gutenberg, you can download *The Forme of Cury*, written by King Richard II's head chef. Perhaps you can give some of the recipes a try. It might help immerse you into the world of this story.

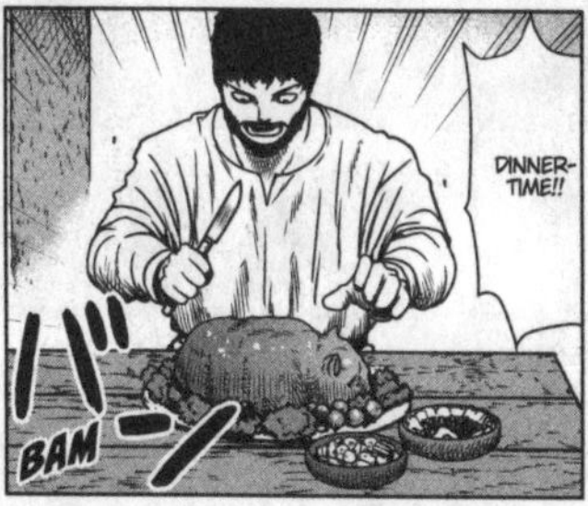
DINNER-TIME!!
BAM

KARATE SURVIVOR IN ANOTHER WORLD

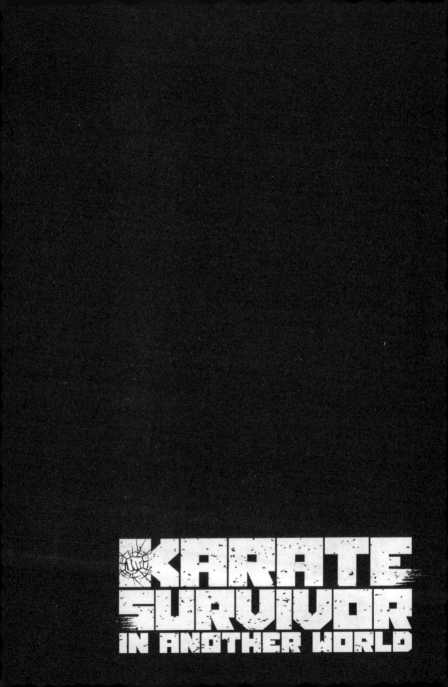

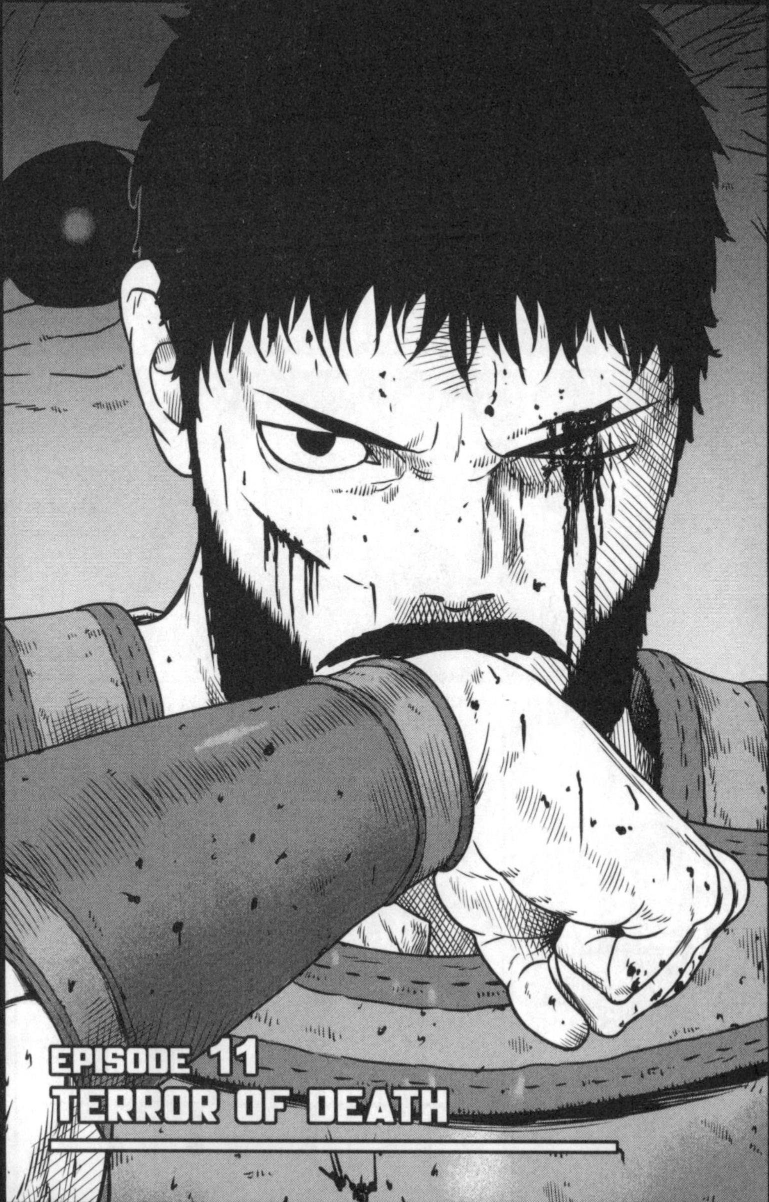
EPISODE 11
TERROR OF DEATH

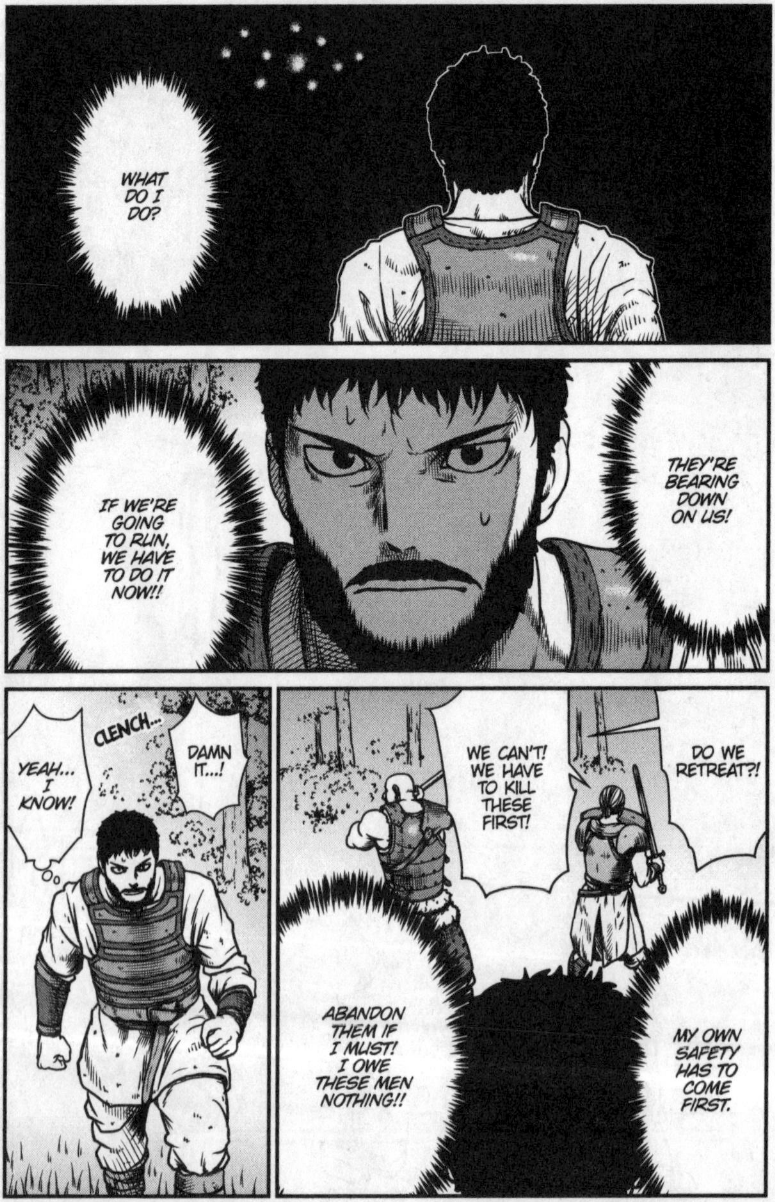
WHAT DO I DO?
THEY'RE BEARING DOWN ON US!
IF WE'RE GOING TO RUN, WE HAVE TO DO IT NOW!!
DO WE RETREAT?!
WE CAN'T! WE HAVE TO KILL THESE FIRST!
MY OWN SAFETY HAS TO COME FIRST.
ABANDON THEM IF I MUST! I OWE THESE MEN NOTHING!!
DAMN IT...!
CLENCH...
YEAH... I KNOW!

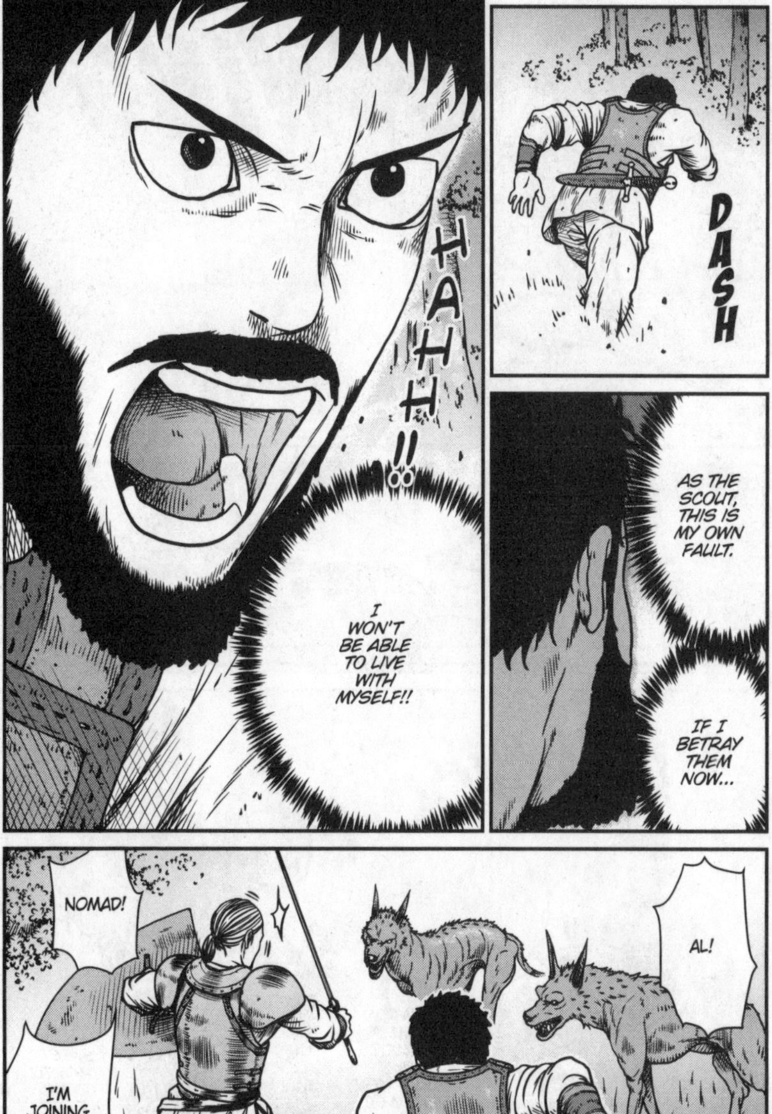
DASH
AS THE SCOUT, THIS IS MY OWN FAULT.
IF I BETRAY THEM NOW...
HAHH!!
I WON'T BE ABLE TO LIVE WITH MYSELF!!
AL!
NOMAD!
I'M JOINING IN!!

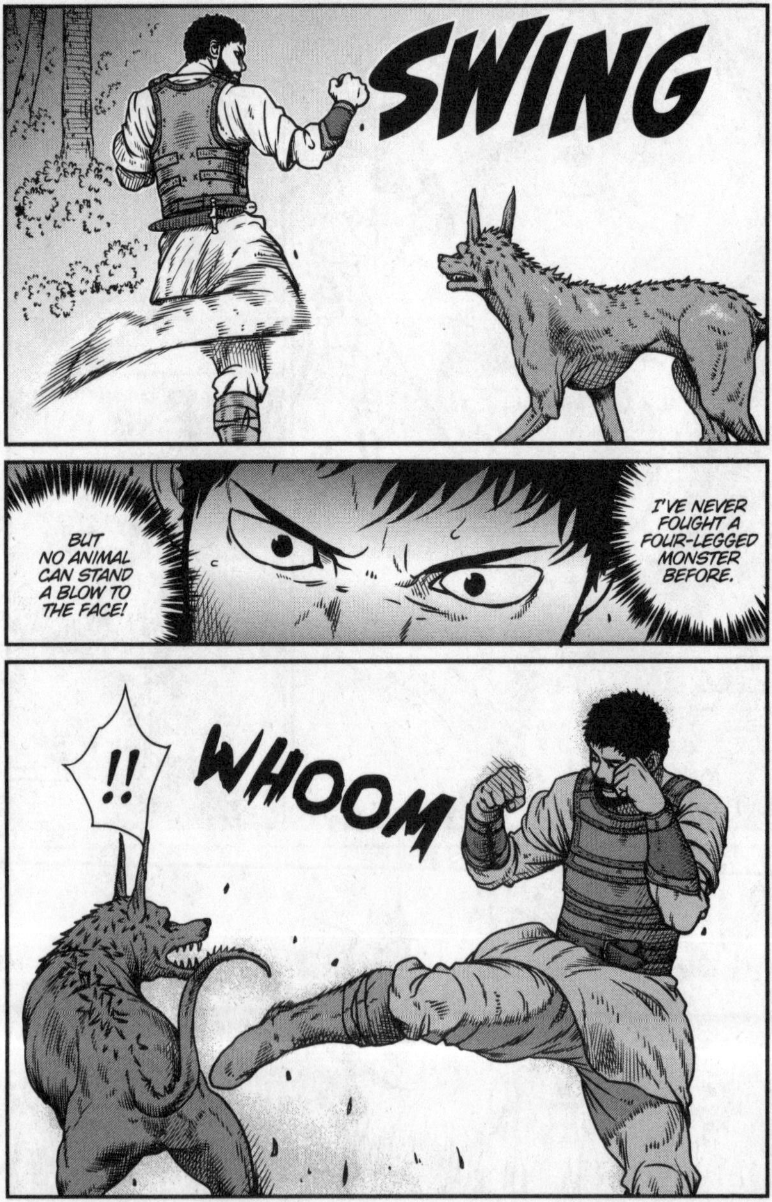
SWING
I'VE NEVER FOUGHT A FOUR-LEGGED MONSTER BEFORE.
BUT NO ANIMAL CAN STAND A BLOW TO THE FACE!
WHOOM
!!

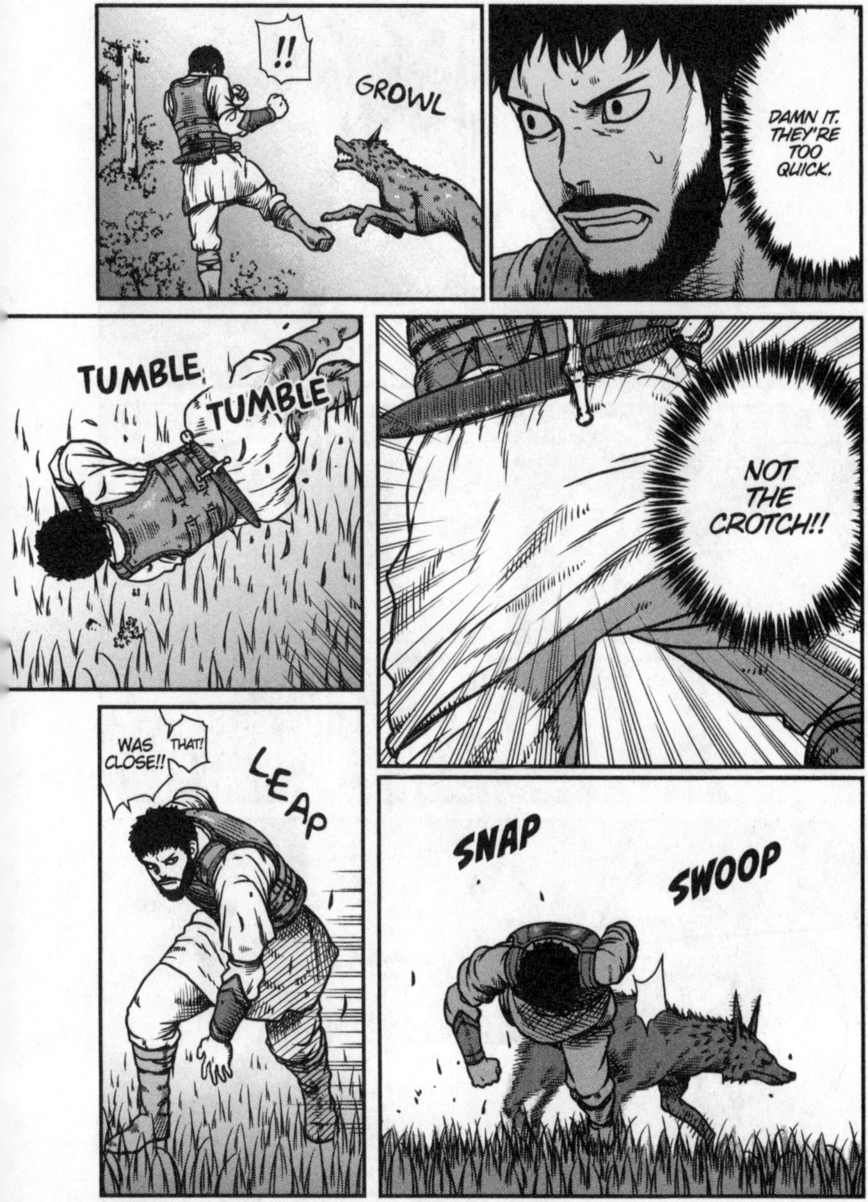
DAMN IT. THEY'RE TOO QUICK.
!!
GROWL
NOT THE CROTCH!!
TUMBLE
TUMBLE
SNAP
SWOOP
THAT! WAS CLOSE!!
LEAP

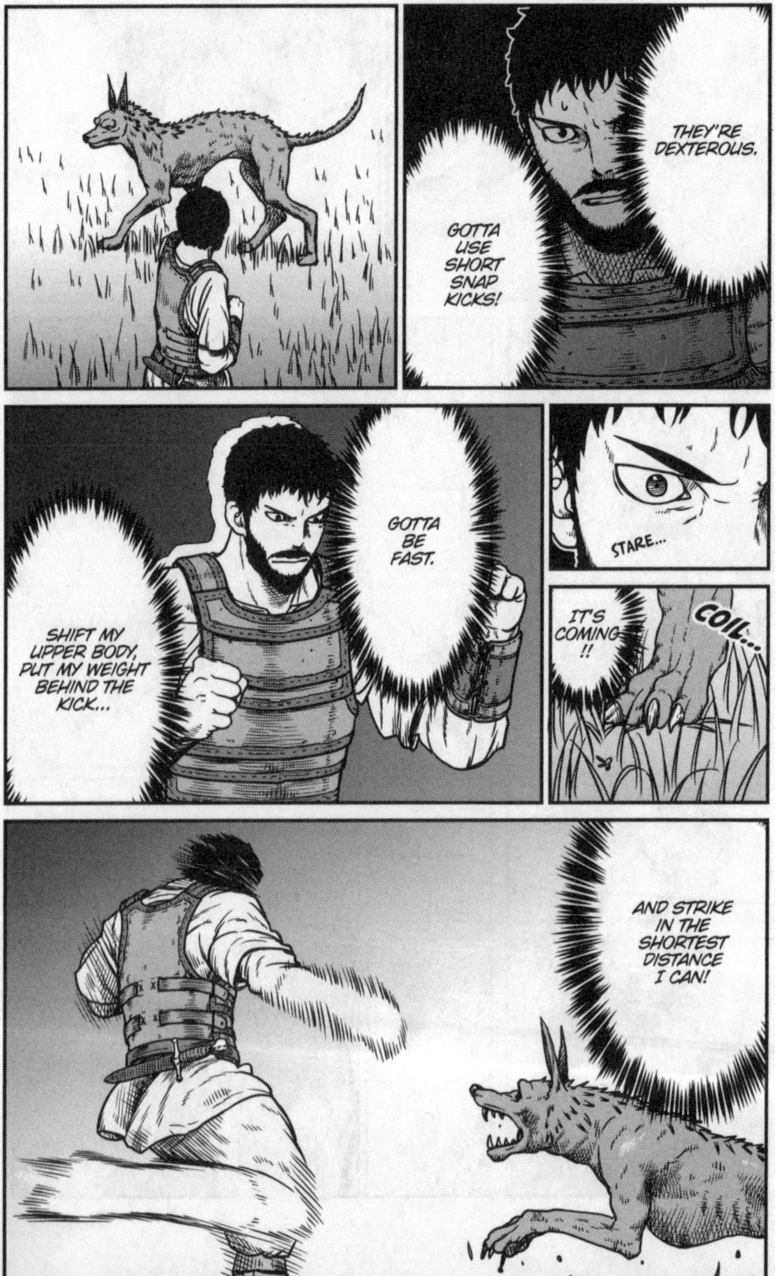
THEY'RE DEXTEROUS.
GOTTA USE SHORT SNAP KICKS!
STARE...
IT'S COMING!!
COIL...
GOTTA BE FAST.
SHIFT MY UPPER BODY, PUT MY WEIGHT BEHIND THE KICK...
AND STRIKE IN THE SHORTEST DISTANCE I CAN!

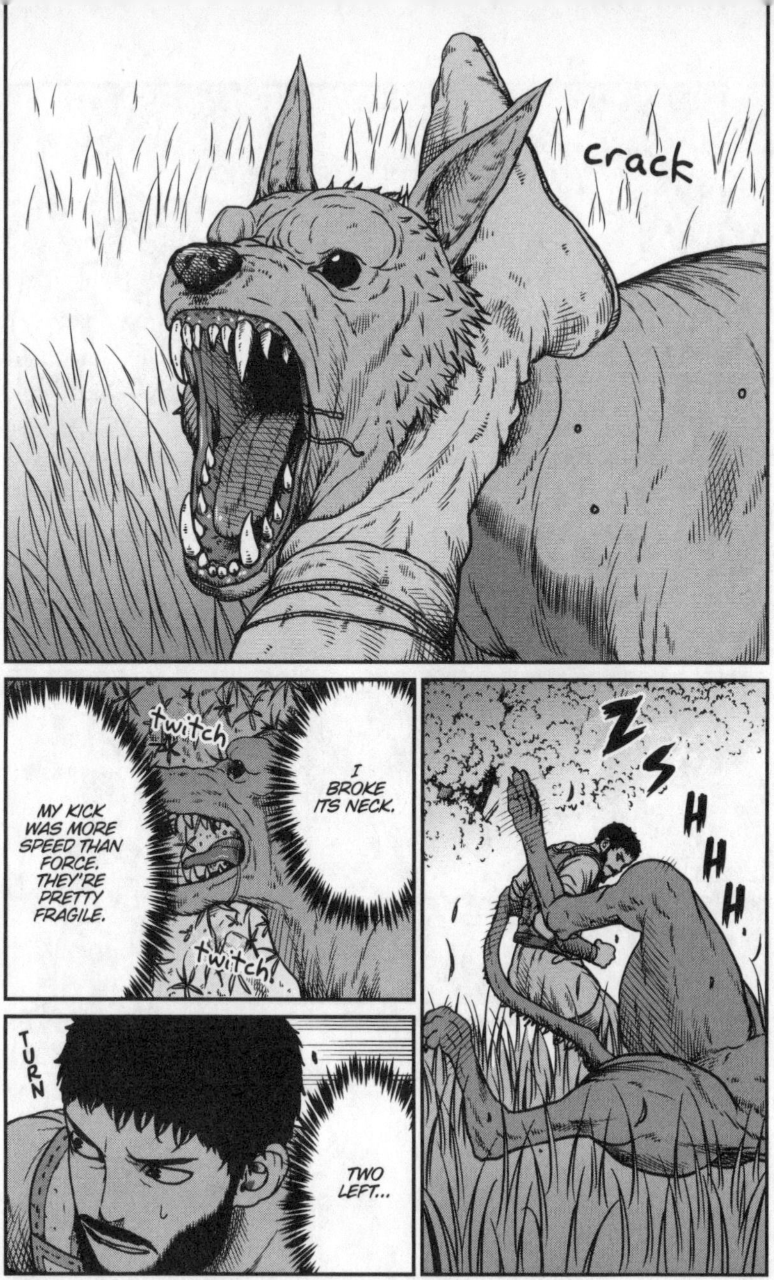
crack
ZSHHHH.
twitch
I BROKE ITS NECK.
MY KICK WAS MORE SPEED THAN FORCE. THEY'RE PRETTY FRAGILE.
twitch
TURN
TWO LEFT...

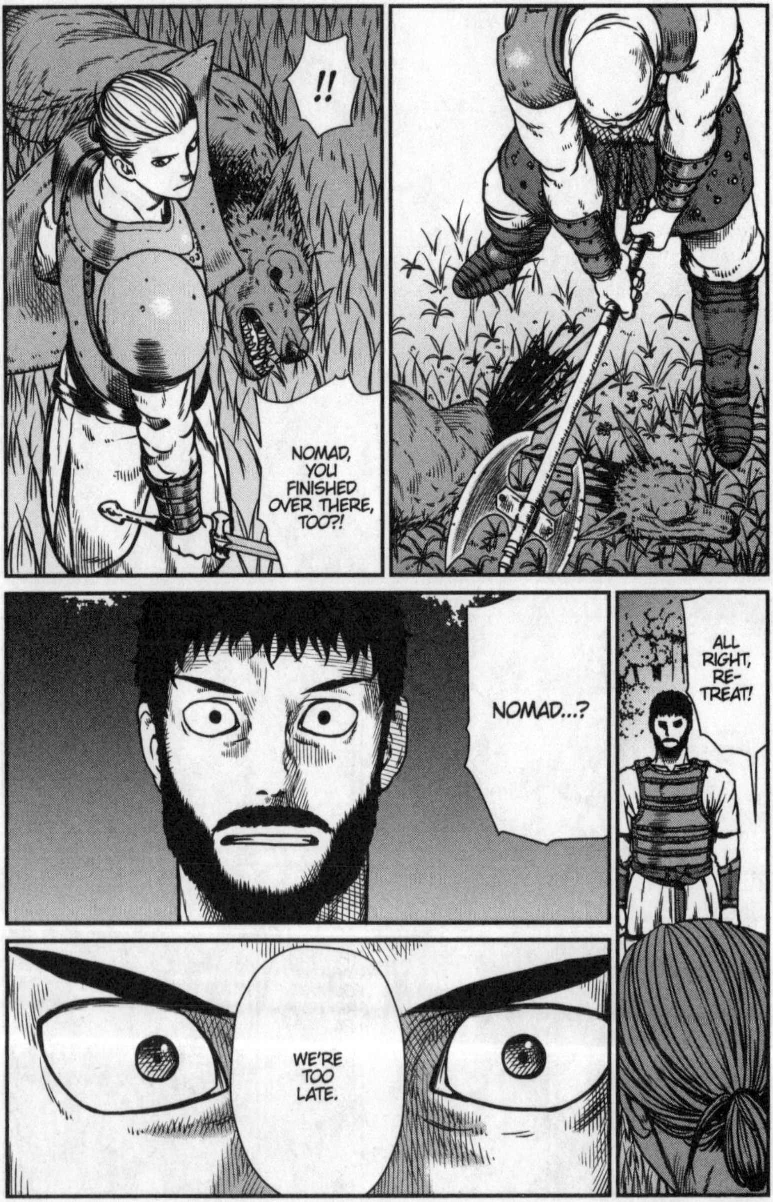
!!
NOMAD, YOU FINISHED OVER THERE, TOO?!
ALL RIGHT, RE-TREAT!
NOMAD...?
WE'RE TOO LATE.

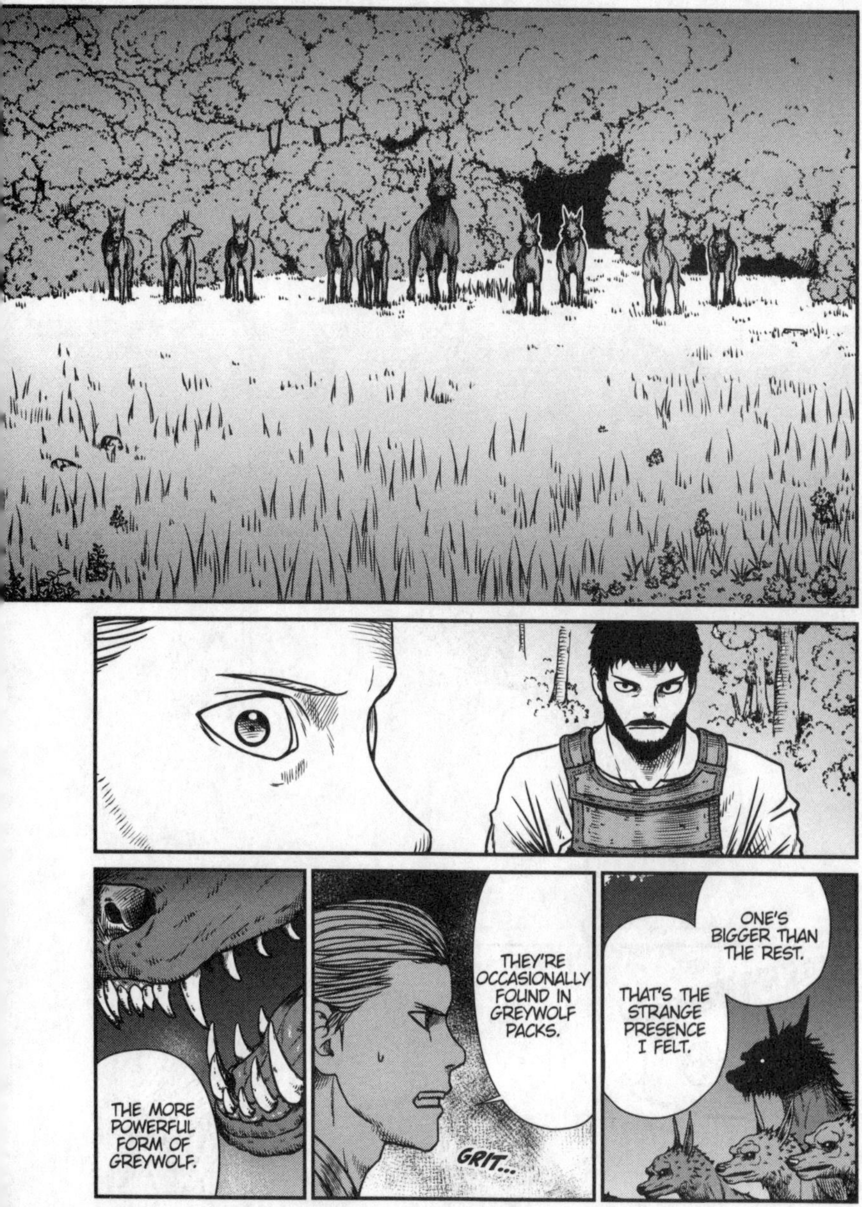
ONE'S BIGGER THAN THE REST.
THAT'S THE STRANGE PRESENCE I FELT.
THEY'RE OCCASIONALLY FOUND IN GREYWOLF PACKS.
GRIT...
THE MORE POWERFUL FORM OF GREYWOLF.

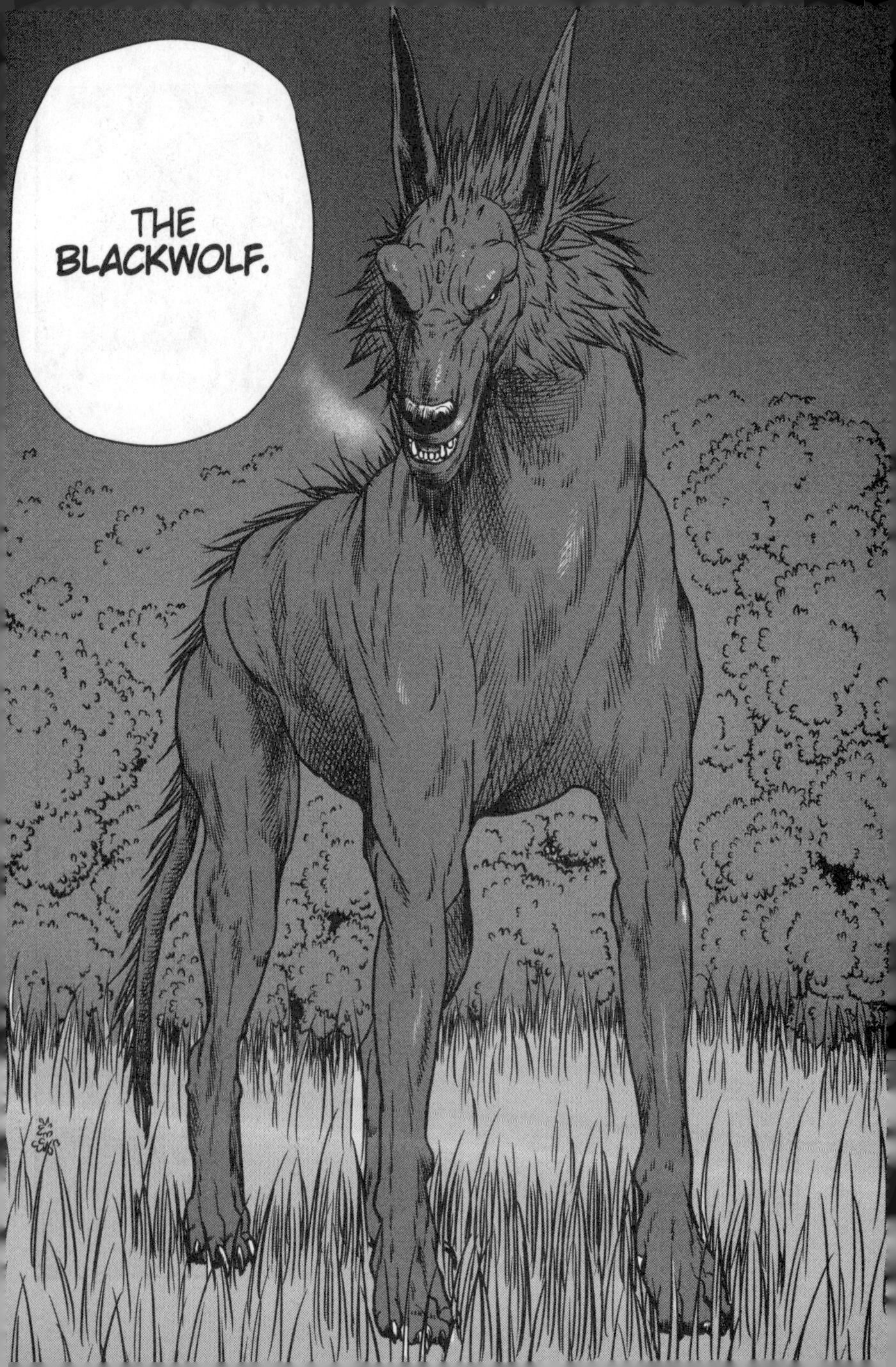
THE BLACKWOLF.

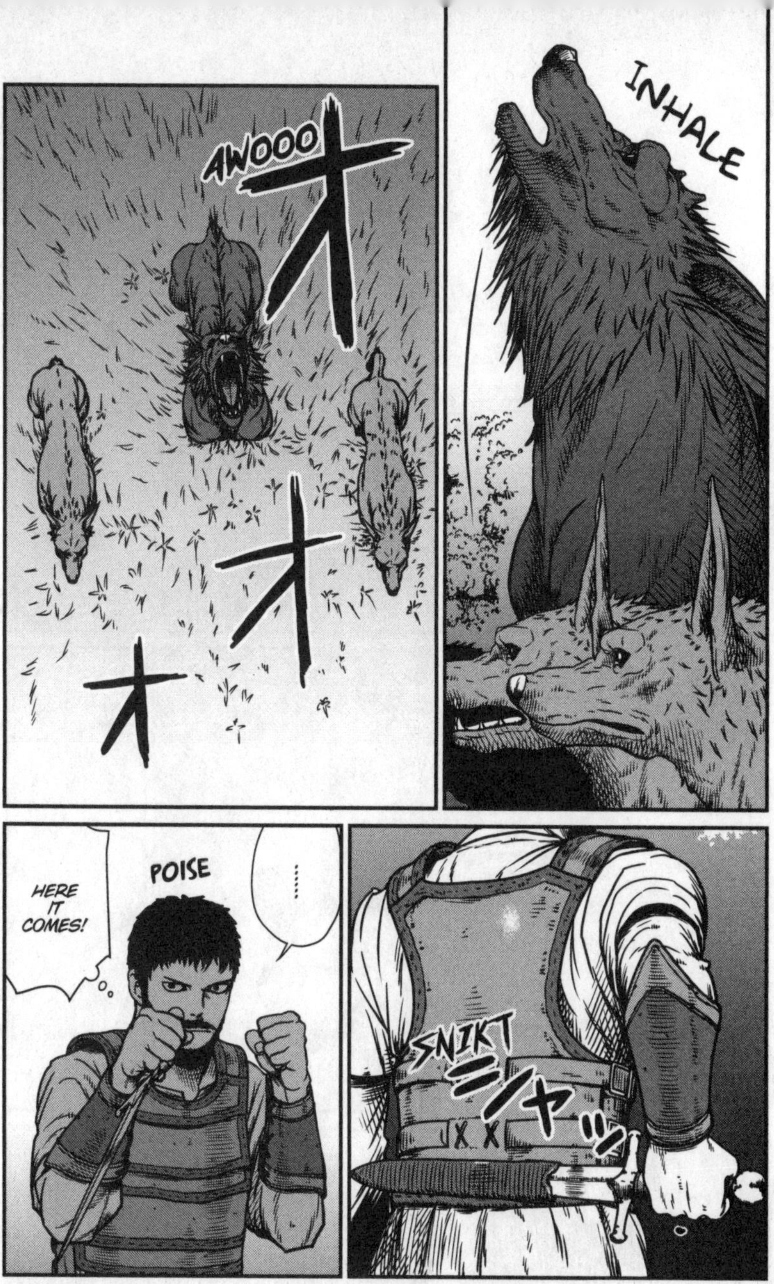
INHALE
AWOOO
オオオオ
SNIKT
シャッ
......
POISE
HERE IT COMES!

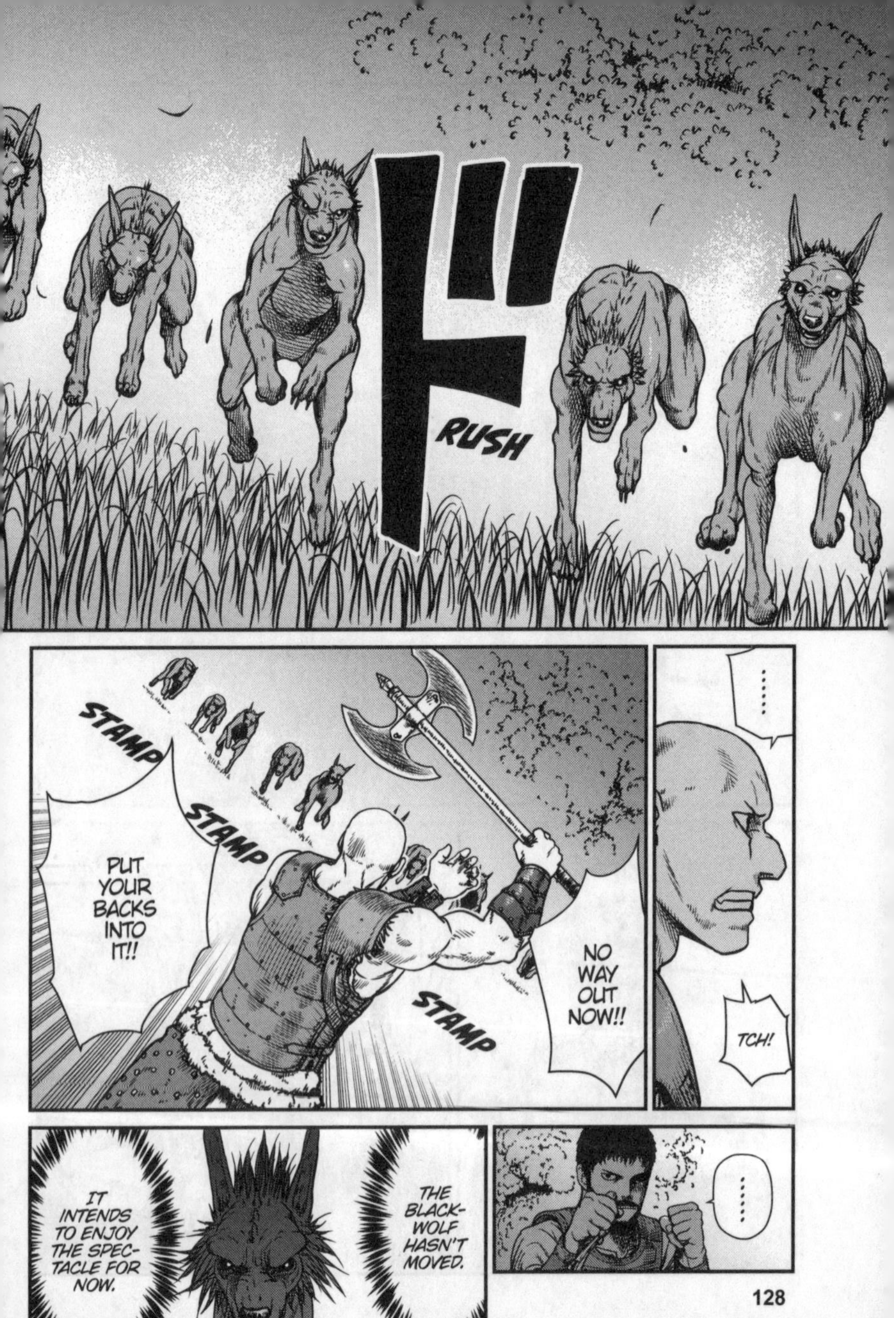
RUSH
......
TCH!
STAMP
STAMP
NO WAY OUT NOW!!
PUT YOUR BACKS INTO IT!!
STAMP
......
THE BLACK-WOLF HASN'T MOVED.
IT INTENDS TO ENJOY THE SPEC-TACLE FOR NOW.

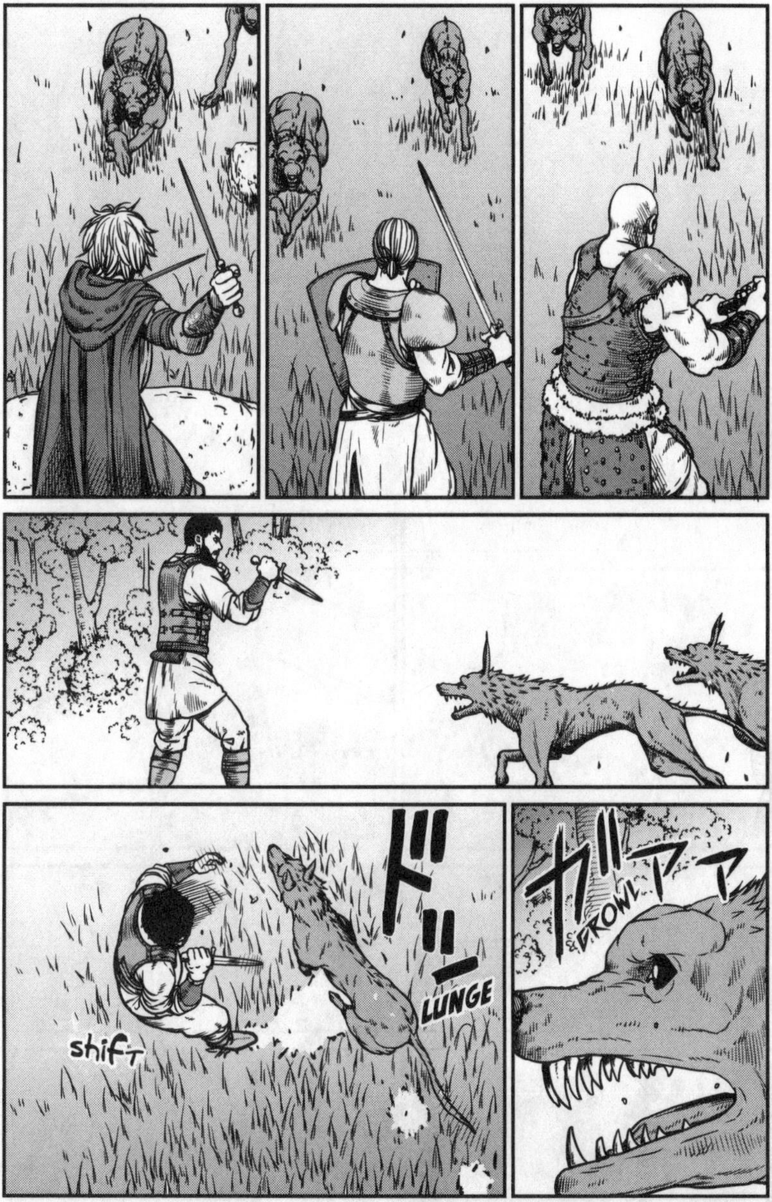
ガアア
GROWL
ドッー
LUNGE
shift

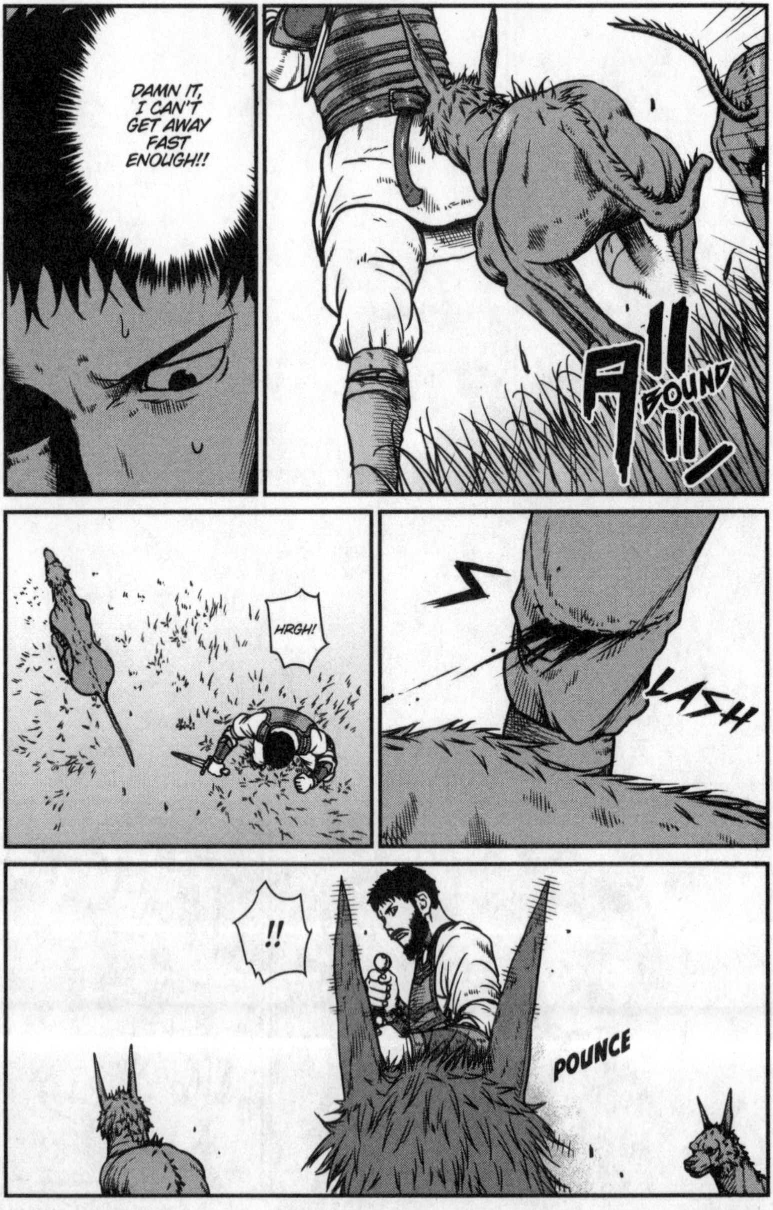
BOUND
DAMN IT, I CAN'T GET AWAY FAST ENOUGH!!
LASH
HRGH!
!!
POUNCE

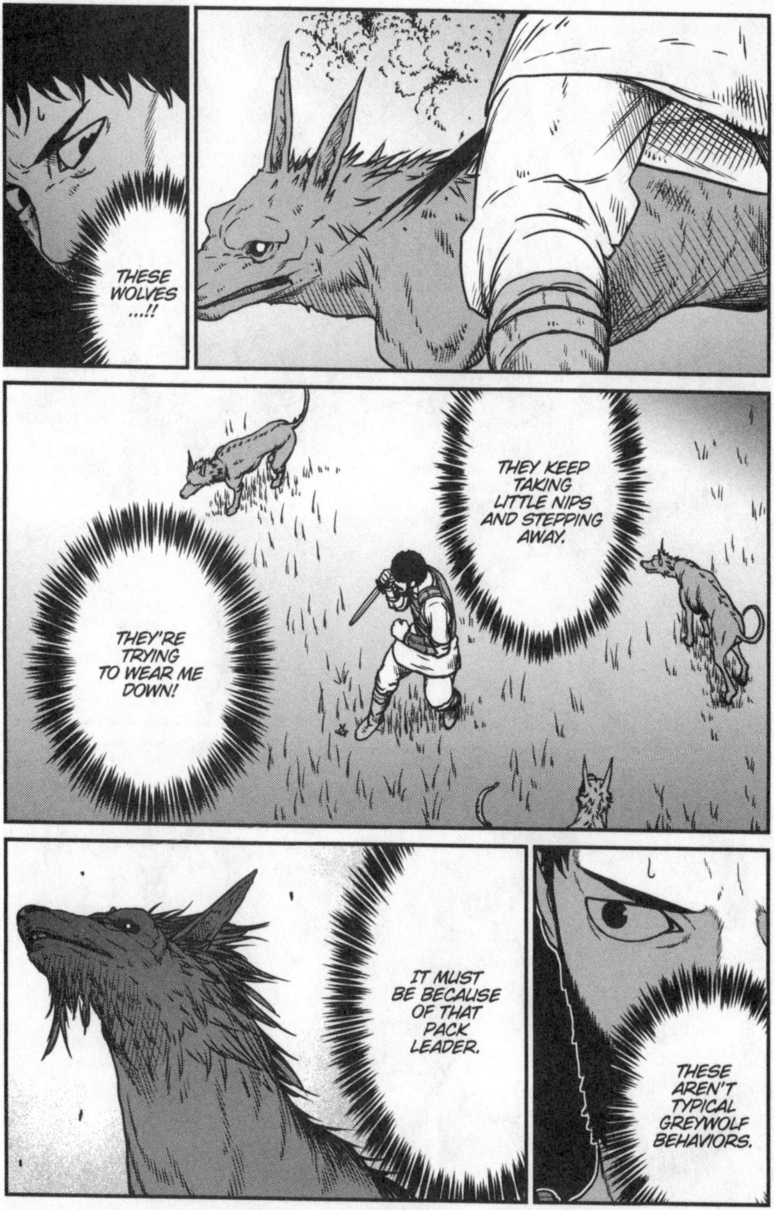
THESE WOLVES ...!!
THEY KEEP TAKING LITTLE NIPS AND STEPPING AWAY.
THEY'RE TRYING TO WEAR ME DOWN!
THESE AREN'T TYPICAL GREYWOLF BEHAVIORS.
IT MUST BE BECAUSE OF THAT PACK LEADER.

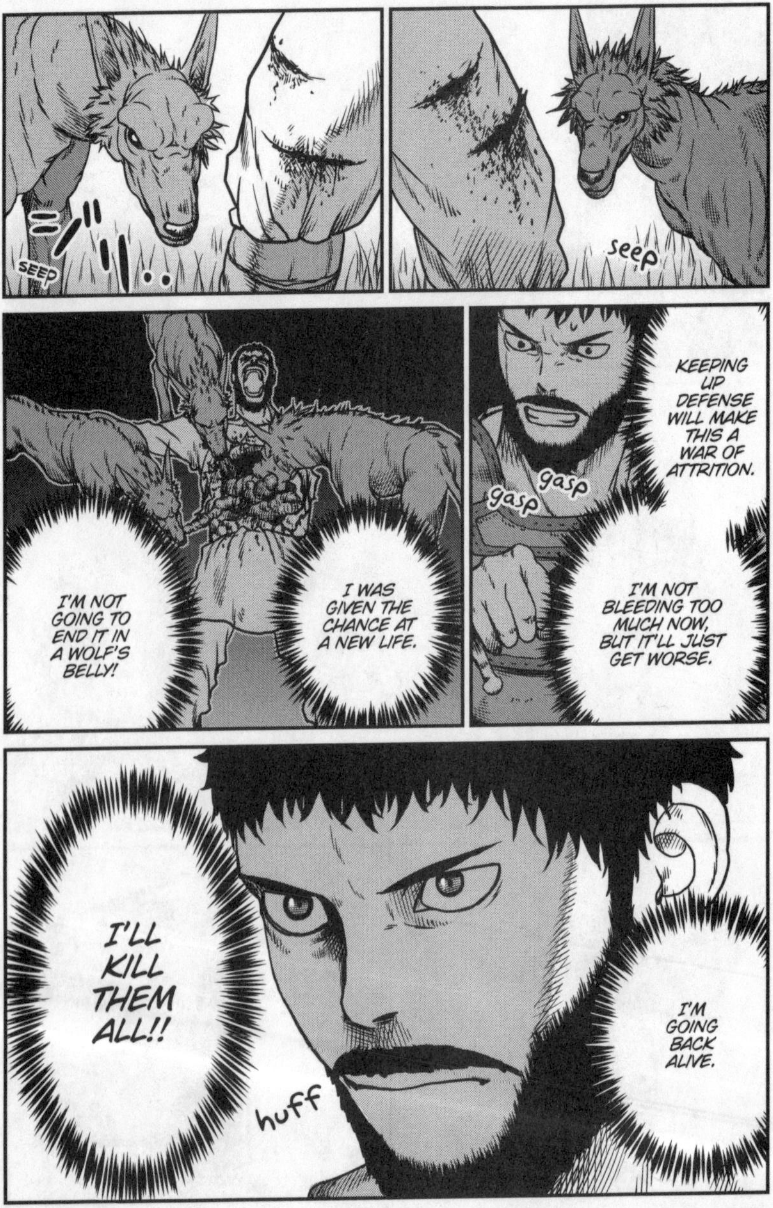
seep
seep
KEEPING UP DEFENSE WILL MAKE THIS A WAR OF ATTRITION.
gasp
gasp
I'M NOT BLEEDING TOO MUCH NOW, BUT IT'LL JUST GET WORSE.
I WAS GIVEN THE CHANCE AT A NEW LIFE.
I'M NOT GOING TO END IT IN A WOLF'S BELLY!
I'M GOING BACK ALIVE.
huff
I'LL KILL THEM ALL!!

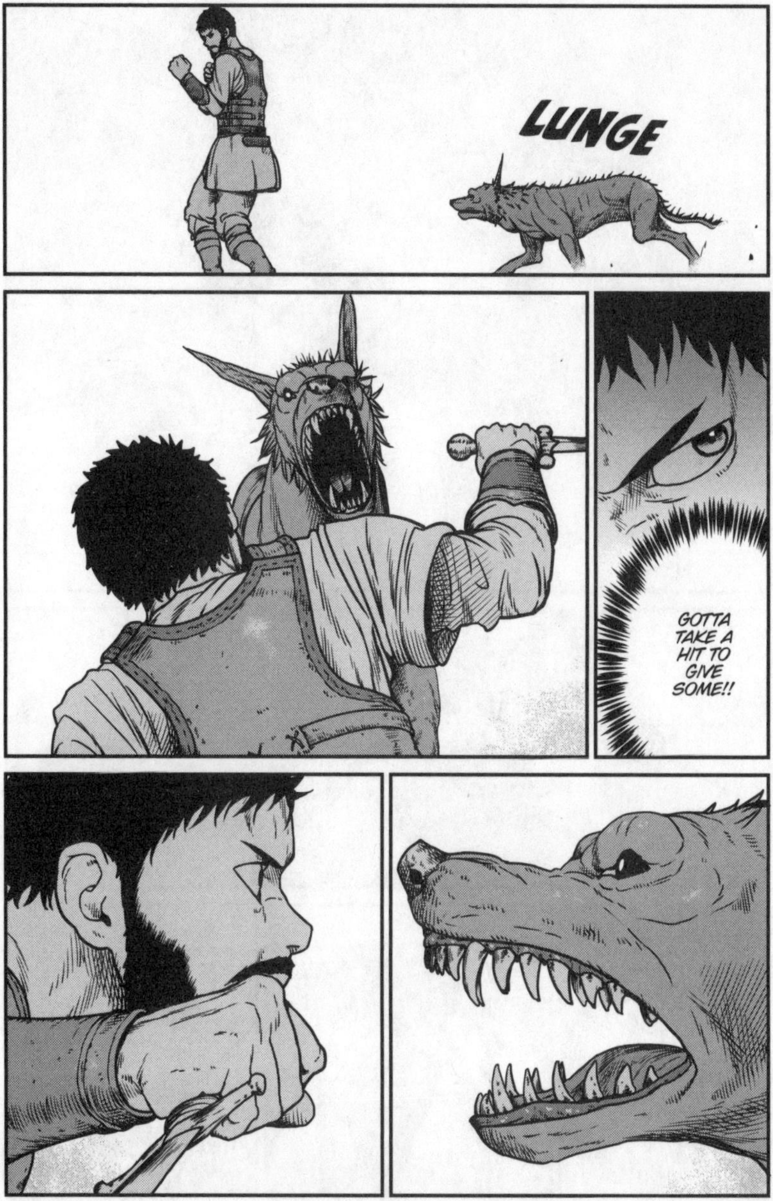
LUNGE
GOTTA TAKE A HIT TO GIVE SOME!!

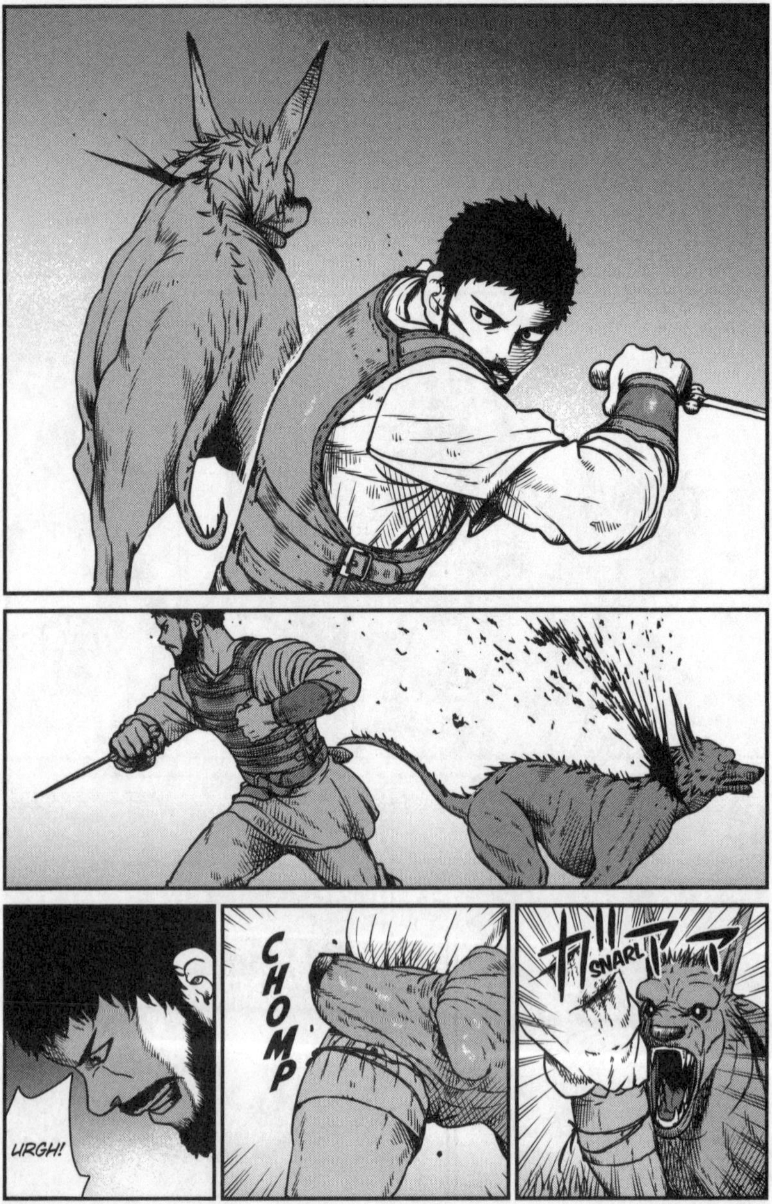
SNARL
CHOMP
URGH!

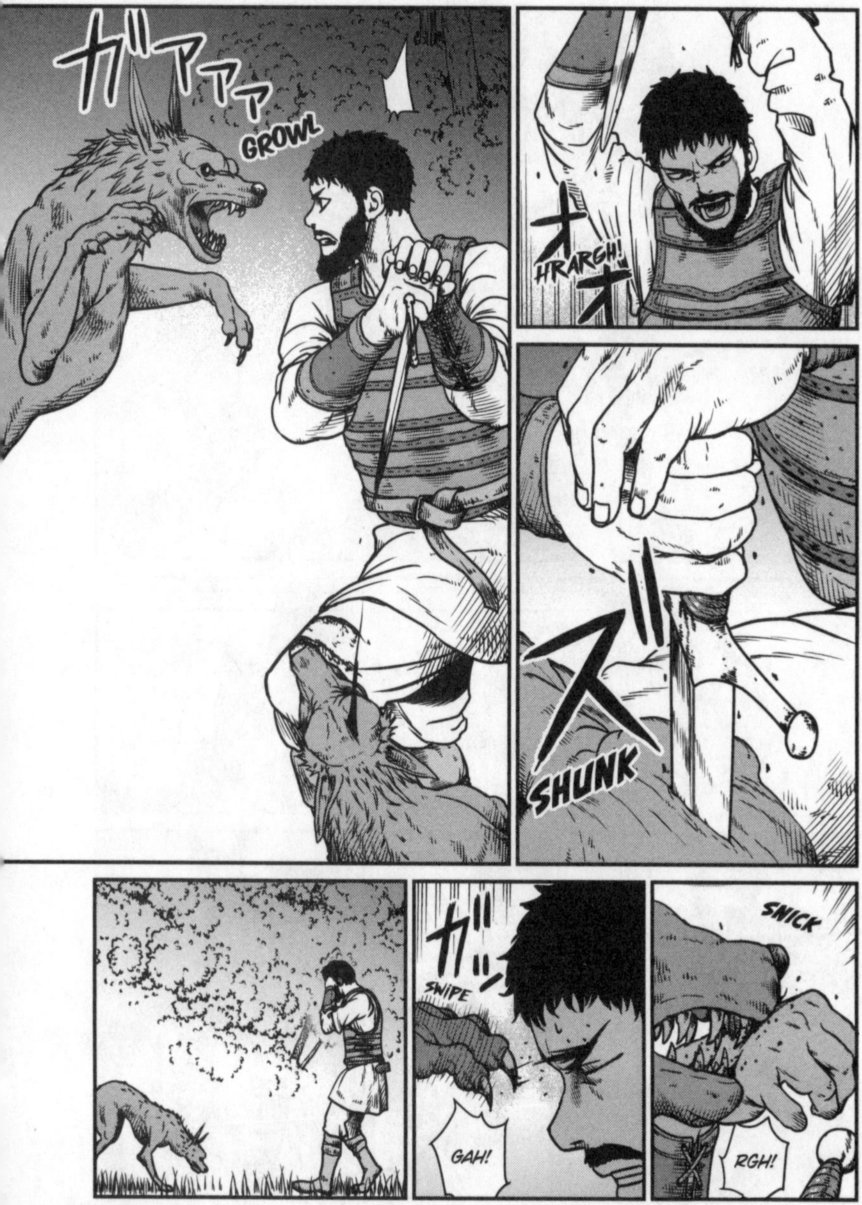
オ
HRARGH!
オ
ズ
SHUNK
ガアァァ
GROWL
SNICK
RGH!
ガッ
SWIPE
GAH!

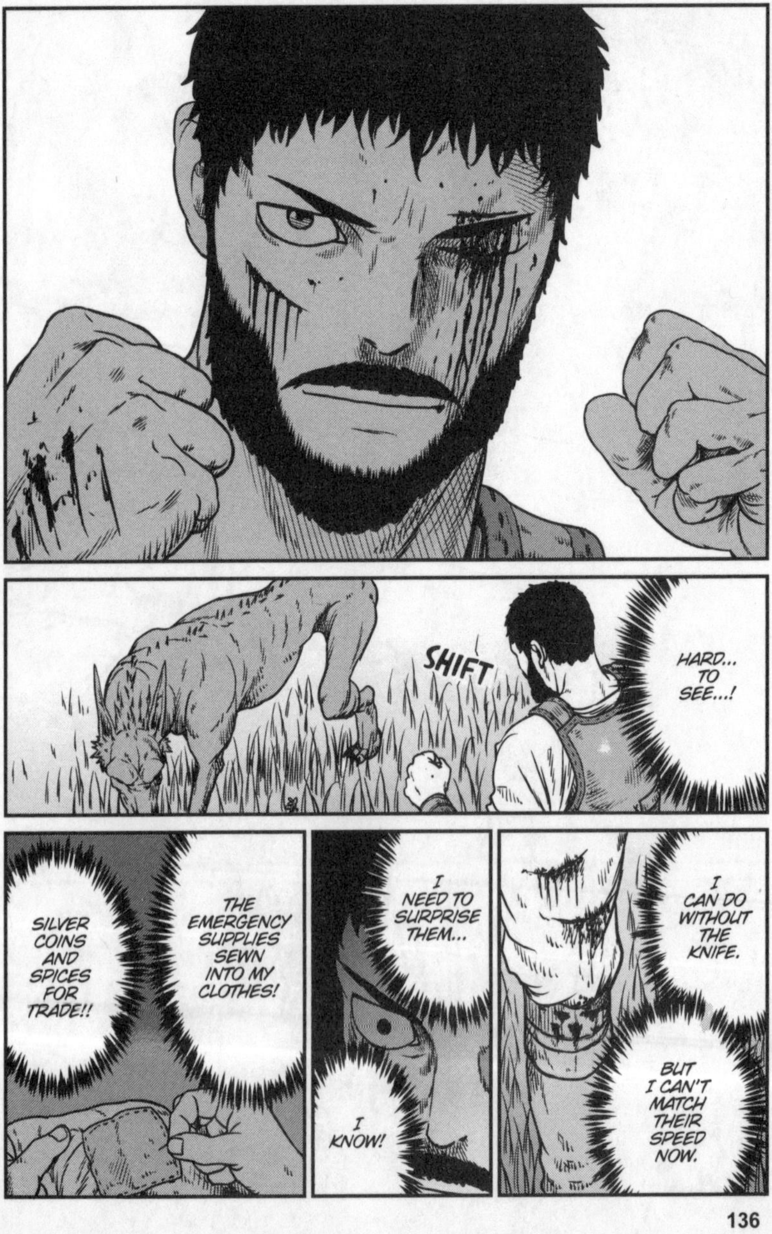
HARD... TO SEE...!
SHIFT
I CAN DO WITHOUT THE KNIFE.
BUT I CAN'T MATCH THEIR SPEED NOW.
I NEED TO SURPRISE THEM...
I KNOW!
THE EMERGENCY SUPPLIES SEWN INTO MY CLOTHES!
SILVER COINS AND SPICES FOR TRADE!!

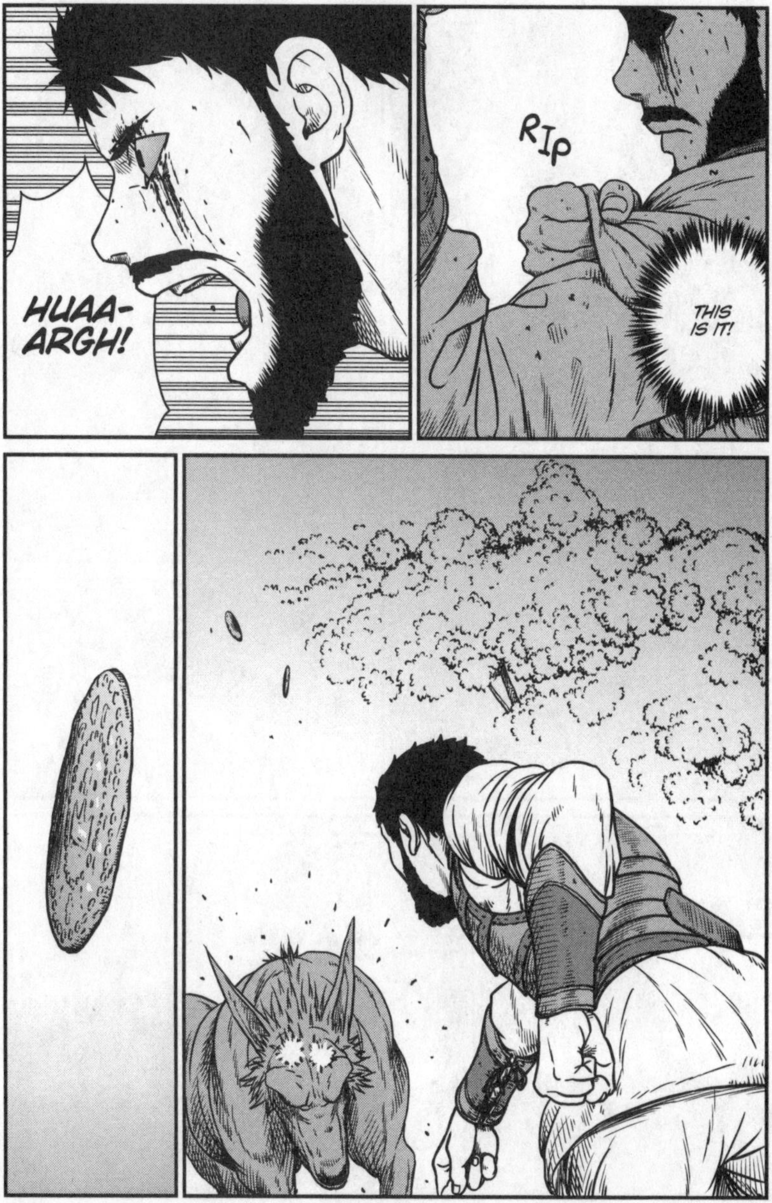
RIP
THIS IS IT!
HUAAA-ARGH!

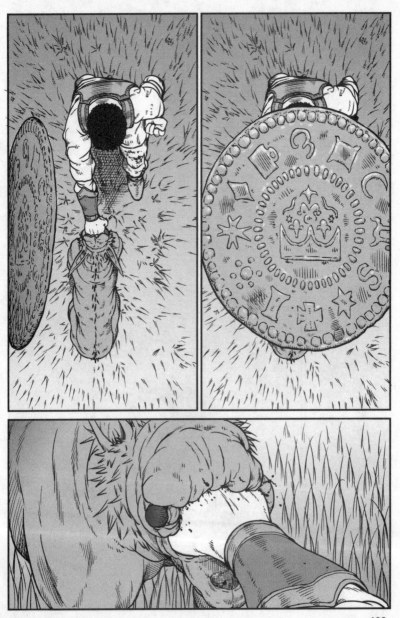

138

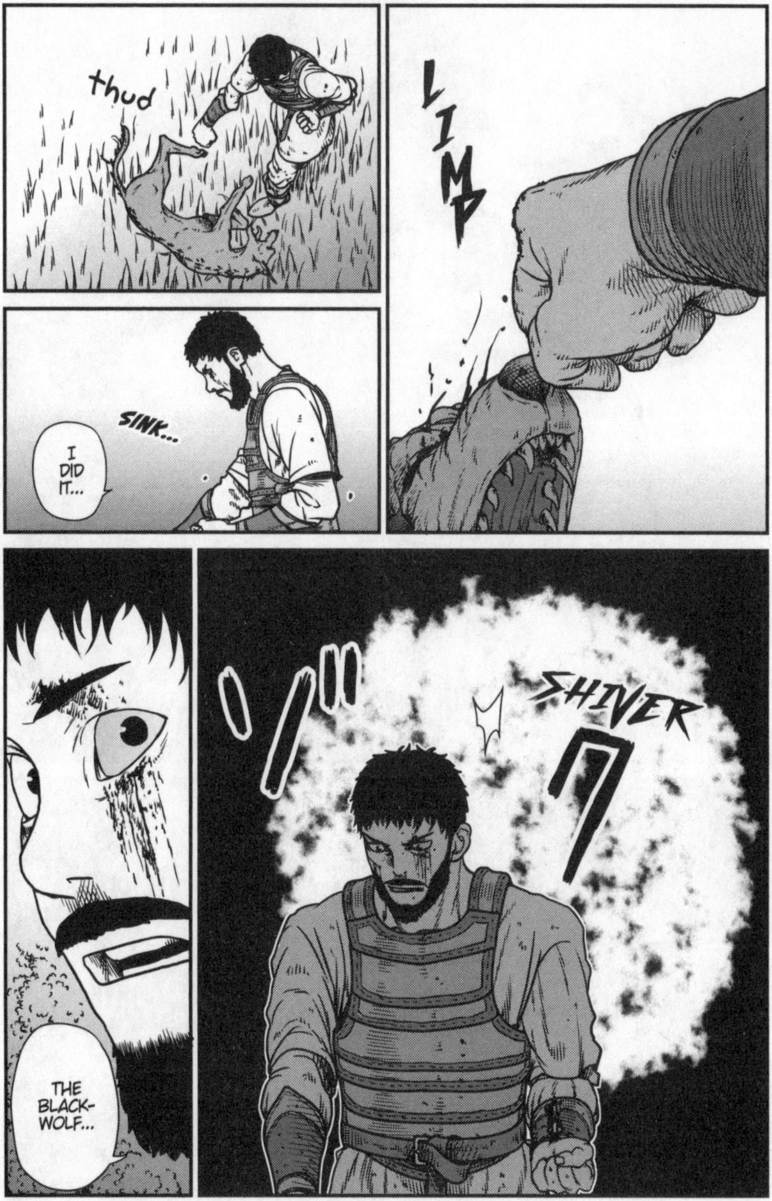
LIMP
thud
SINK...
I DID IT...
SHIVER
THE BLACK-WOLF...

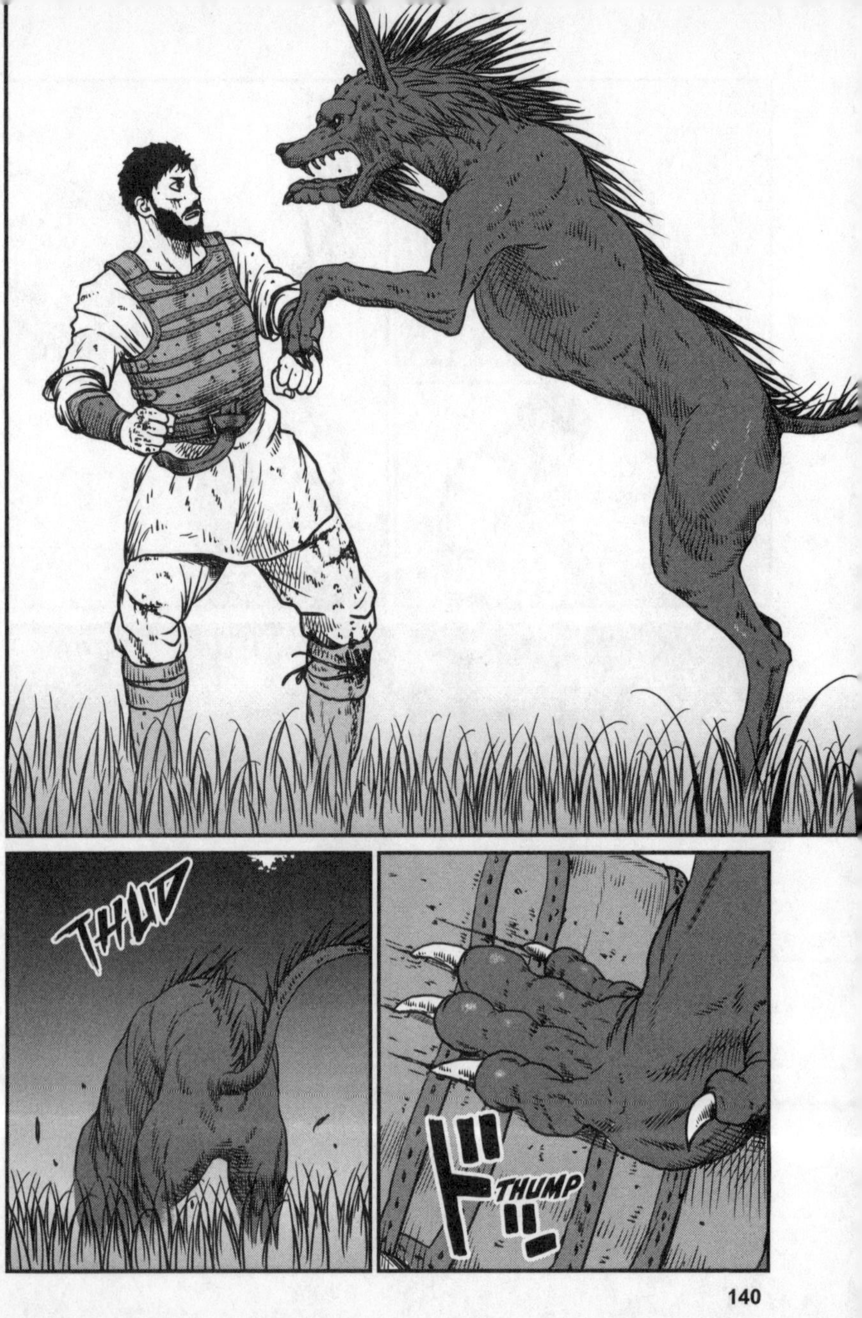
ドッ
THUMP
THUD

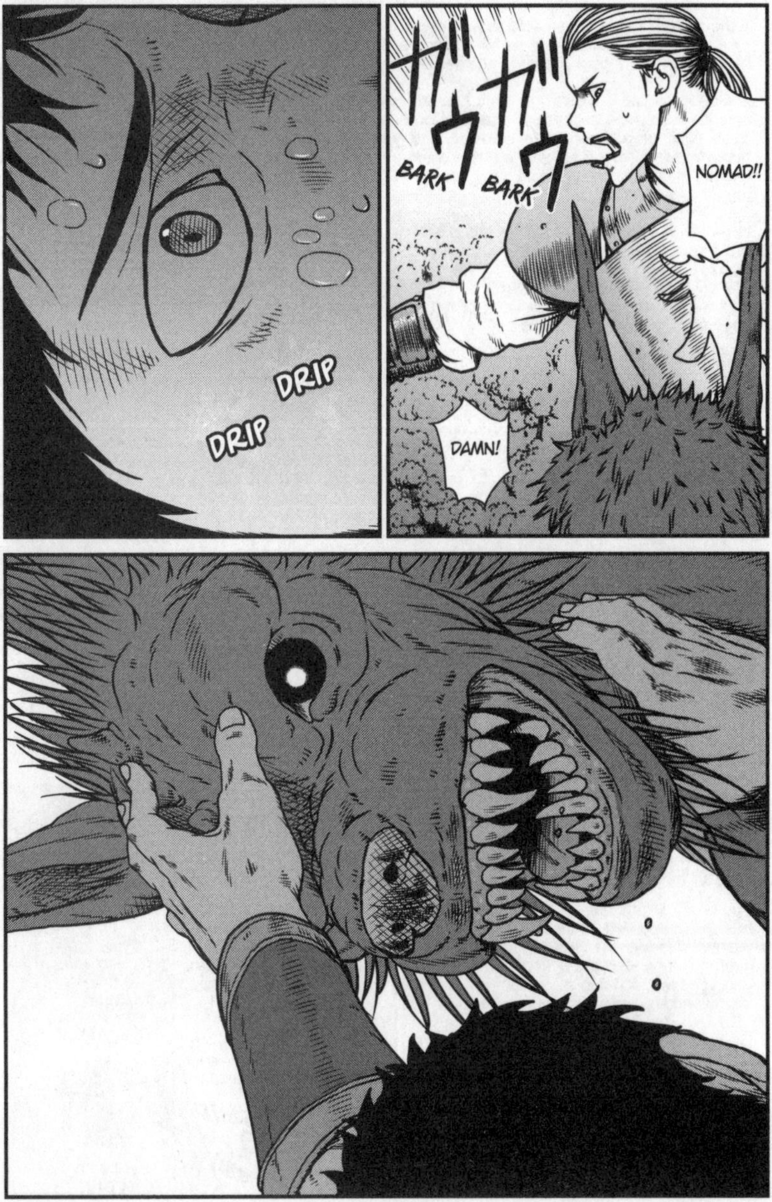
NOMAD!!
ガウ
BARK
ガウ
BARK
DAMN!
DRIP
DRIP

SPECIAL COLUMN BY AUTHOR, YAZIN

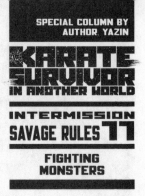

KARATE SURVIVOR IN ANOTHER WORLD

INTERMISSION SAVAGE RULES 11

FIGHTING MONSTERS

Although this might sound arrogant, humans are the supreme rulers of earth. It would not be an exaggeration to state that humans are the most successful species on earth.

But on an individual basis, there are numerous species that we couldn't even hope to compete against. Compare a human to a bear, tiger, or another large predator, and you will find the human completely outmatched in unarmed combat. An inexperienced human would find even a large dog too formidable a foe.

However, humans thrived not thanks to their physical strength, but through their mental abilities. Intelligence combined with acquisitiveness have combined to the point of even affecting the environment around us. As a result, fearsome predators that would have made easy work of individual humans have been brought to near extinction.

Large predators hardly concern us in our daily lives. Our advantage is so great that they have ceased to be a threat at all. But predators were a very real threat to our ancestors before human civilization was well established.

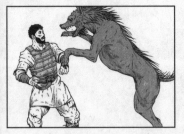

These include the brown bear of Hokkaido, the black bear of Honshu, as well as Japanese wolves and monkeys. Wild animals had to be fought off with primitive weapons, which is an undertaking far more dangerous than we might imagine.

The world that Nomad is sent to runs amok with great predators: the monsters. Their magical powers make them far more powerful than the wild animals of our world. With few exceptions, humans cannot hope to compete against them on base stats alone. Ancient humans had only close-combat weapons such as spears and swords at their disposal. A bout between a human and a monster at the same level would have certainly ended in defeat.

However, humans have a unique weapon at their disposal: intelligence.

Humans can assess the threat level of predators. Humans can specialize and leave combat to the most capable individuals. Crafted weapons increase offensive potential, and protective equipment improves our durability. We can research predator behaviors and use the information to our advantage. Knowledge and cooperation allow humans to defeat foes that no individual would be able to.

The physical capability of humans is not to be scoffed at, either. Although meager compared to bears and tigers, humans are still reasonably weighty. Nomad is 170cm tall and weighs 72kg. He is about as tall as the average Japanese male and a little bit heavier. Even with this rather average build, it would still be possible to crack a concrete block with his elbow and snap a baseball bat with a low kick.

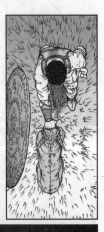

Compare that to the greywolf, which is built similarly to a gray wolf on earth, and weighs between 25-50kg. Despite differences between them and animals of earth, humans still have the advantage in terms of weight, and thus a human could slay a greywolf in close combat.

In addition to this are levels that allow humans to further enhance their physical abilities beyond that on earth. Even with inferior technology, humans of Nomad's world were still able to compete in the race for survival with their strength, culture, and cunning.

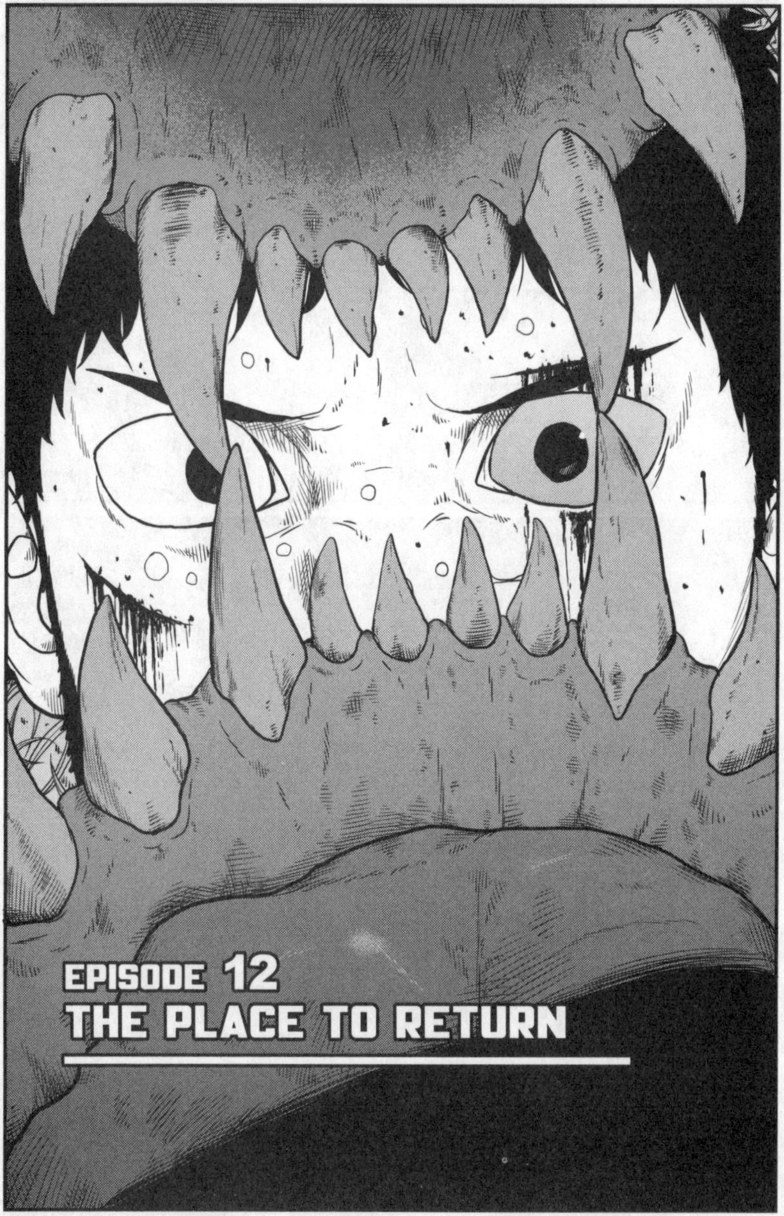
EPISODE 12
THE PLACE TO RETURN

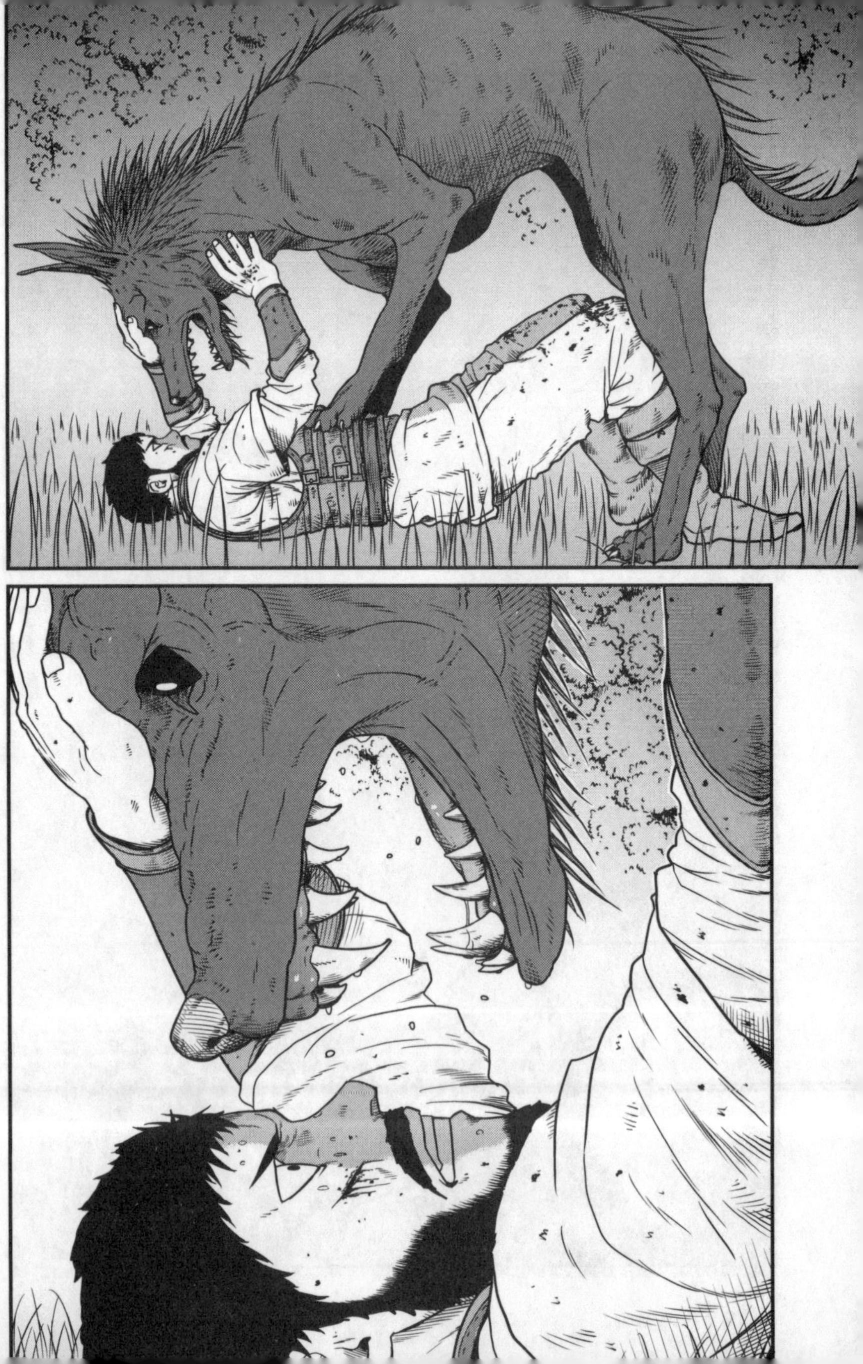

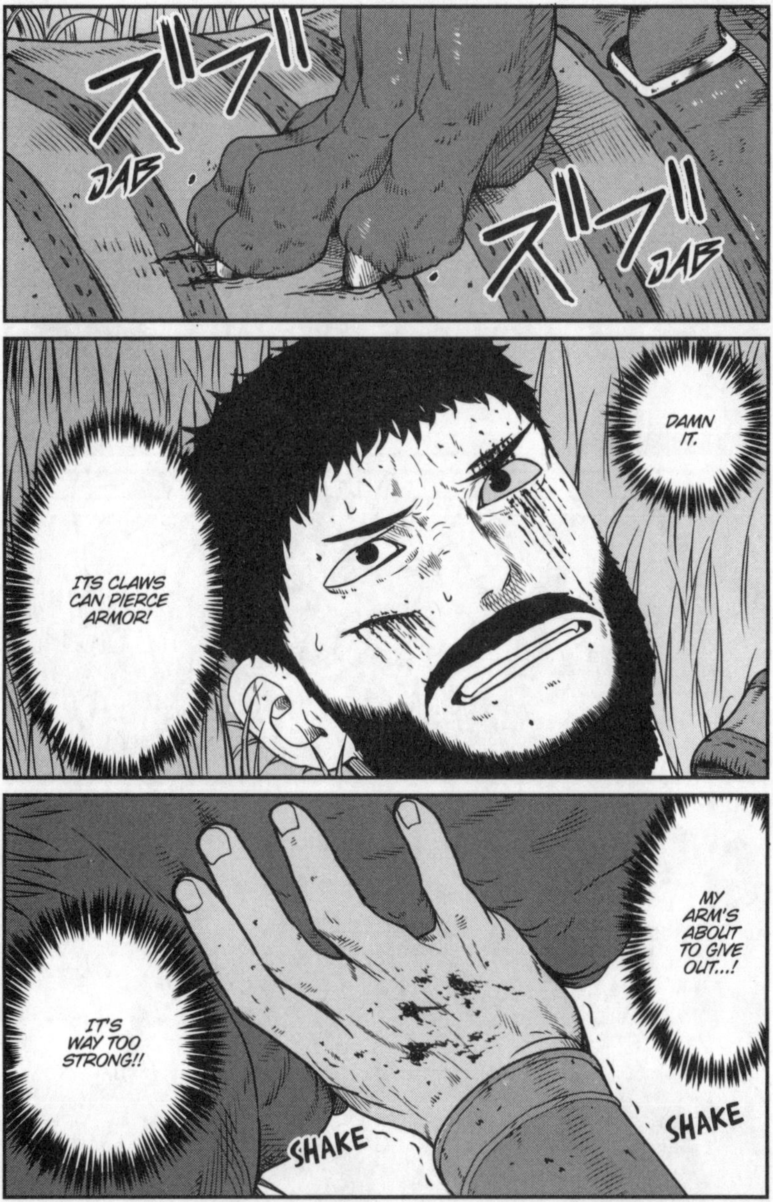
ズブ
JAB
ズブ
JAB
DAMN IT.
ITS CLAWS CAN PIERCE ARMOR!
MY ARM'S ABOUT TO GIVE OUT...!
SHAKE
IT'S WAY TOO STRONG!!
SHAKE

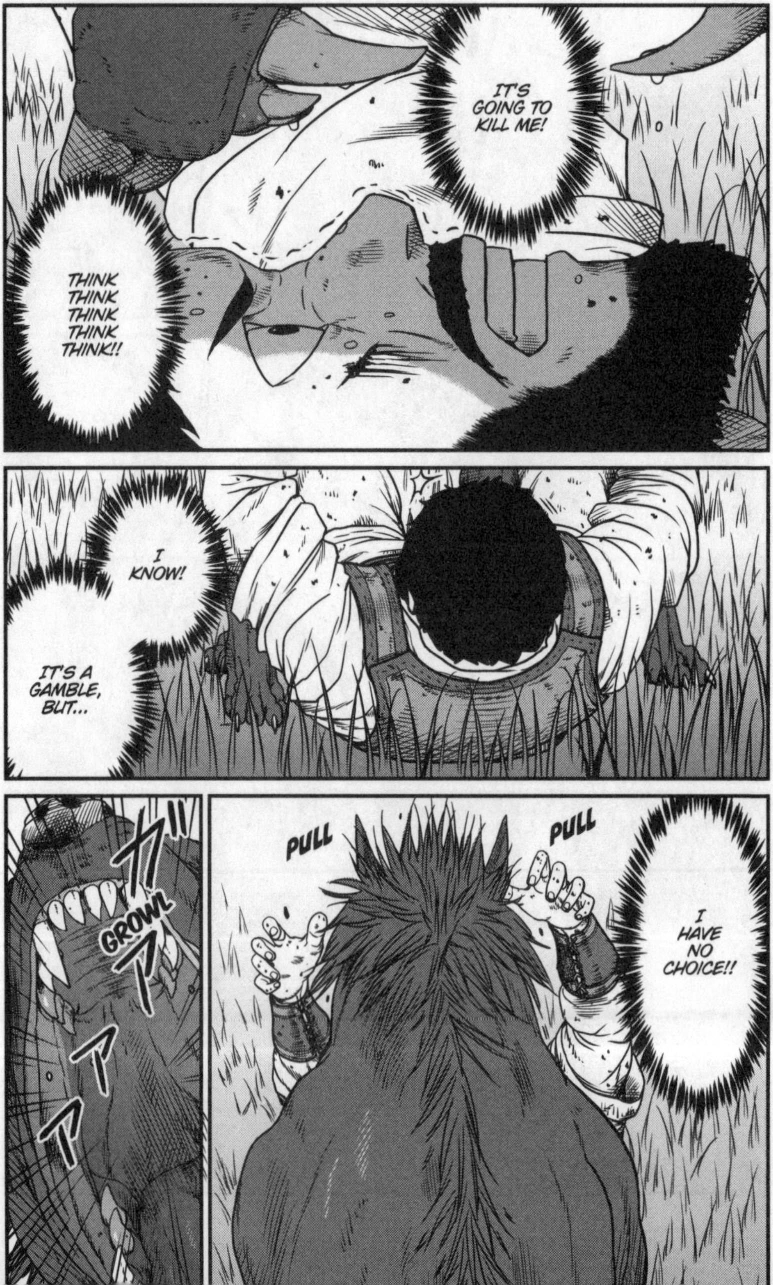
IT'S GOING TO KILL ME!
THINK THINK THINK THINK THINK!!
I KNOW!
IT'S A GAMBLE, BUT...
PULL
PULL
I HAVE NO CHOICE!!
GROWL

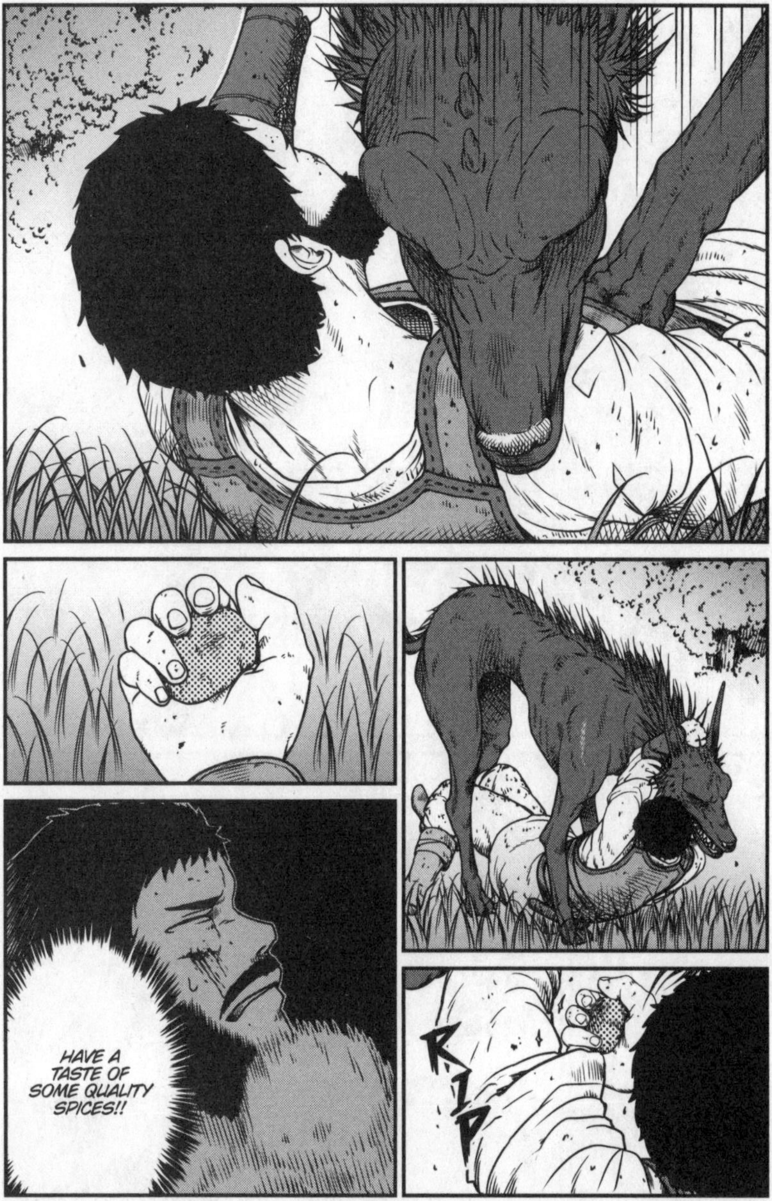
RIP
HAVE A TASTE OF SOME QUALITY SPICES!!

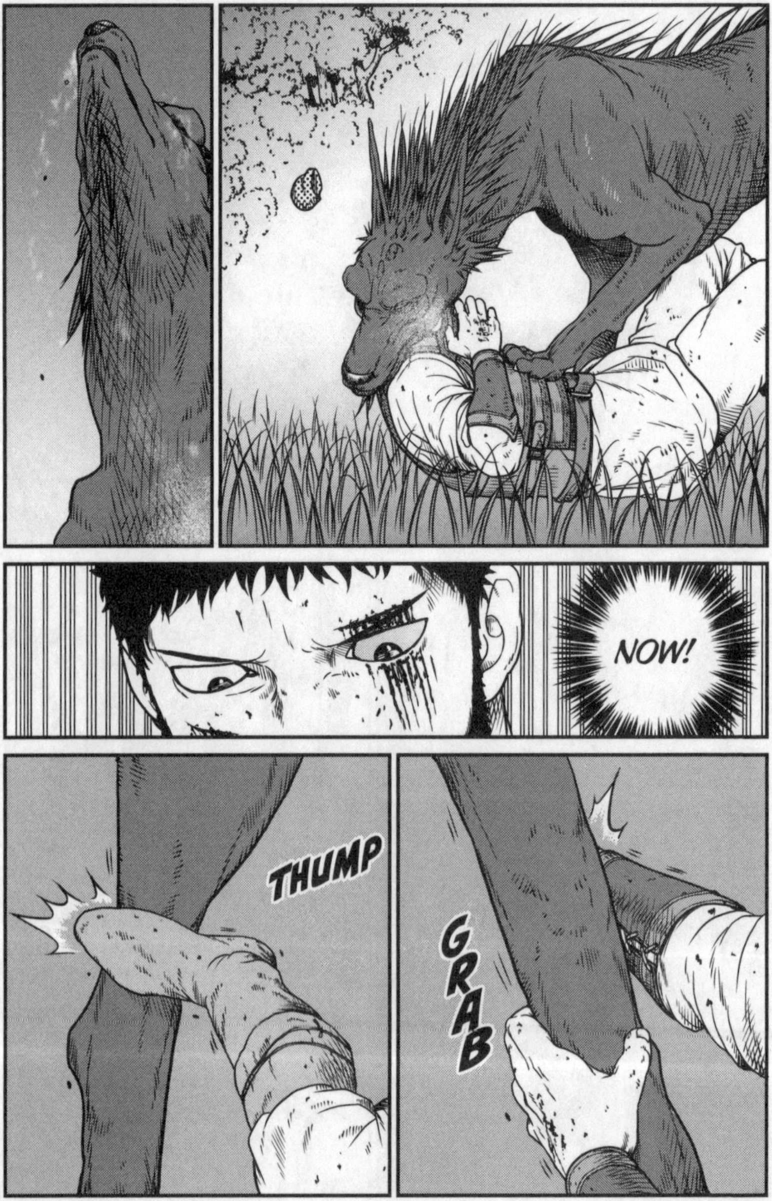
NOW!
GRAB
THUMP

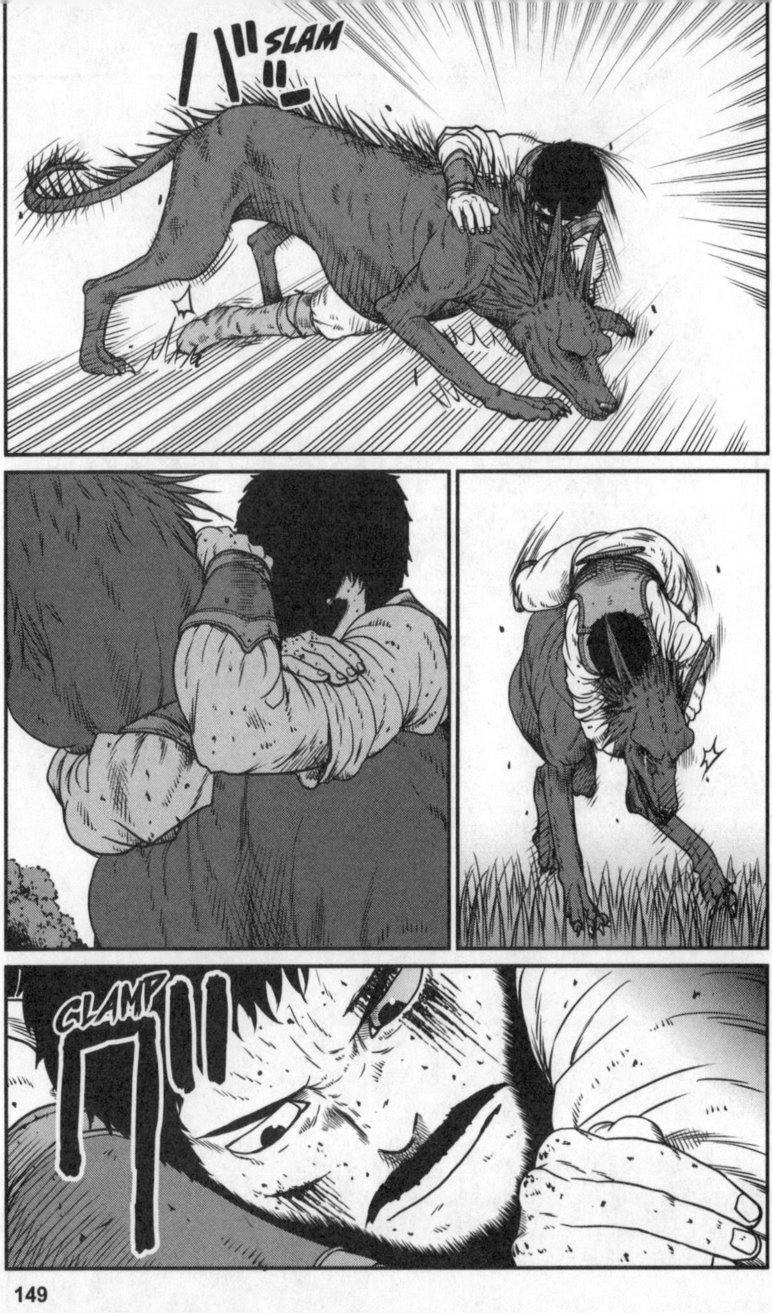
SLAM
CLAMP

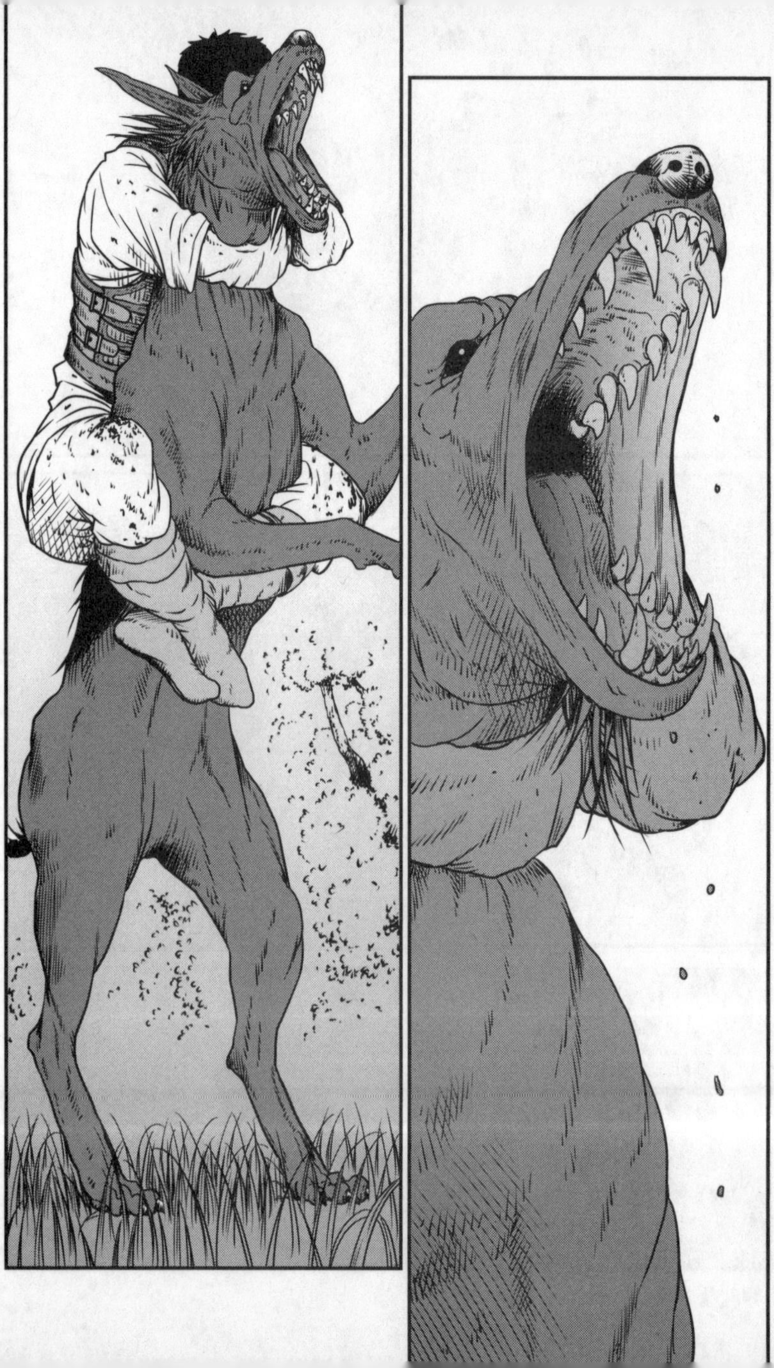

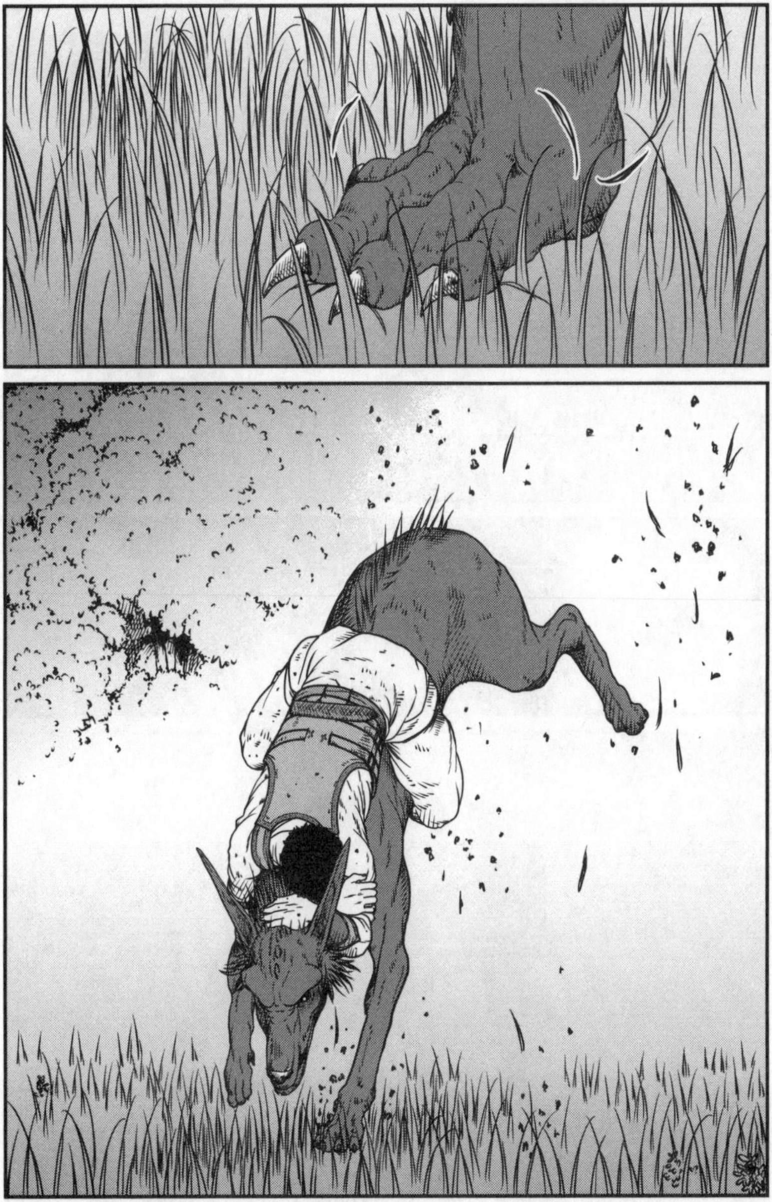

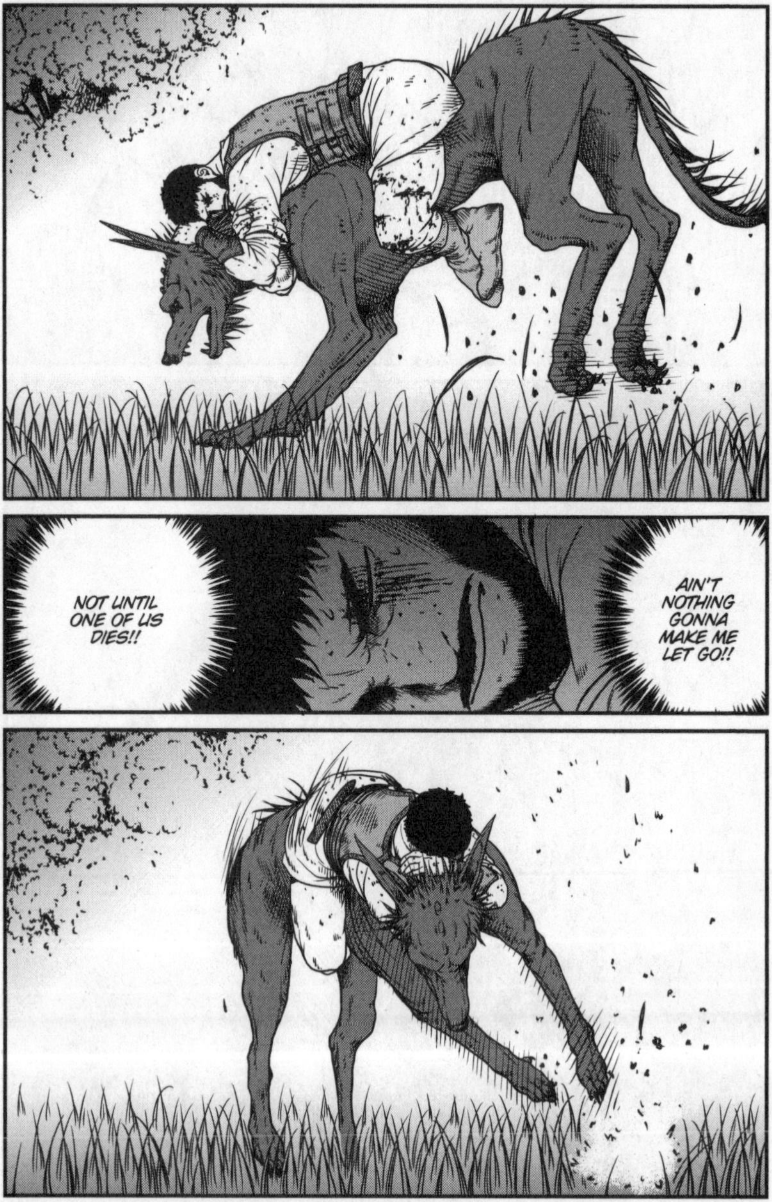
AIN'T NOTHING GONNA MAKE ME LET GO!!
NOT UNTIL ONE OF US DIES!!

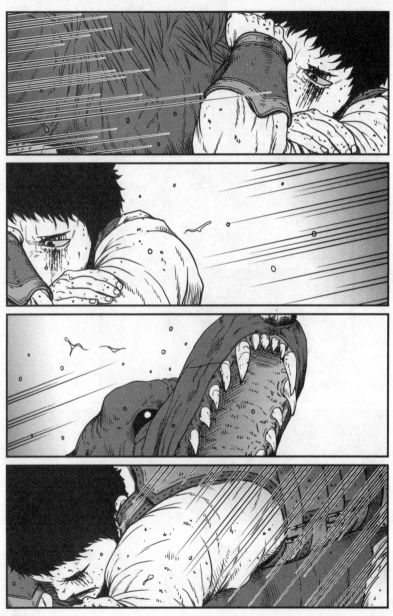

153

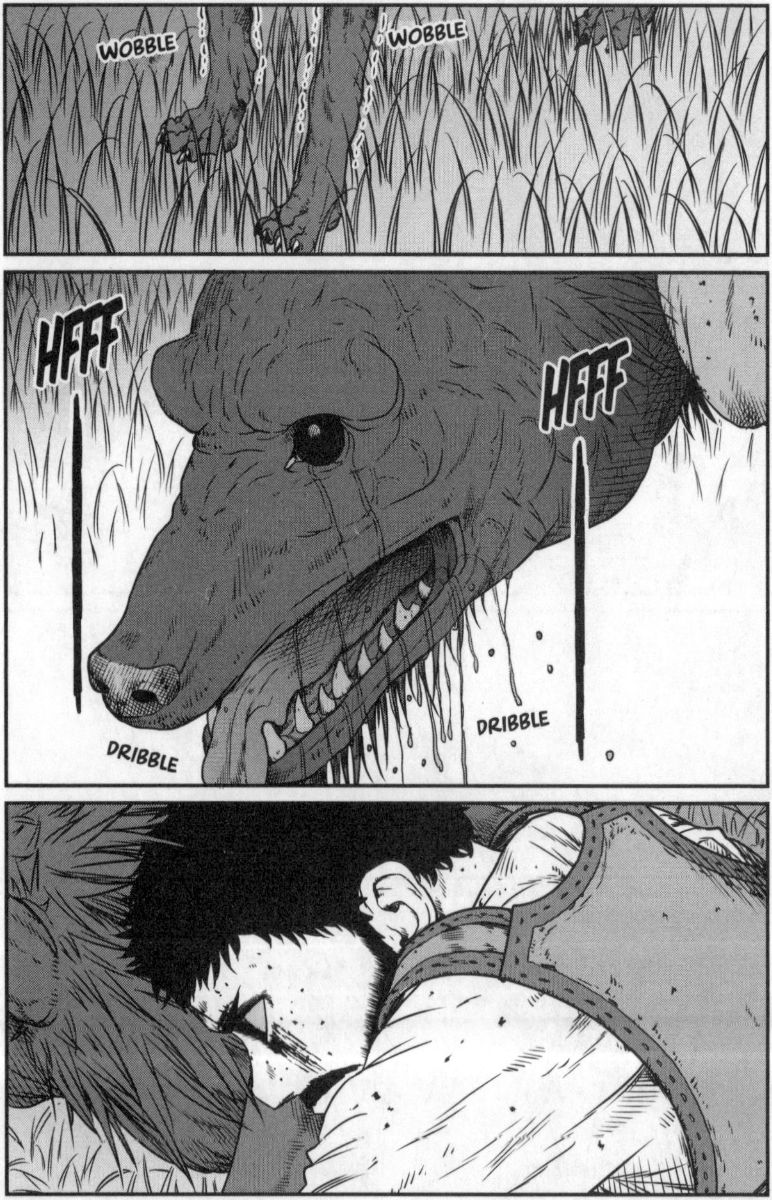
WOBBLE
WOBBLE
HFFF
HFFF
DRIBBLE
DRIBBLE

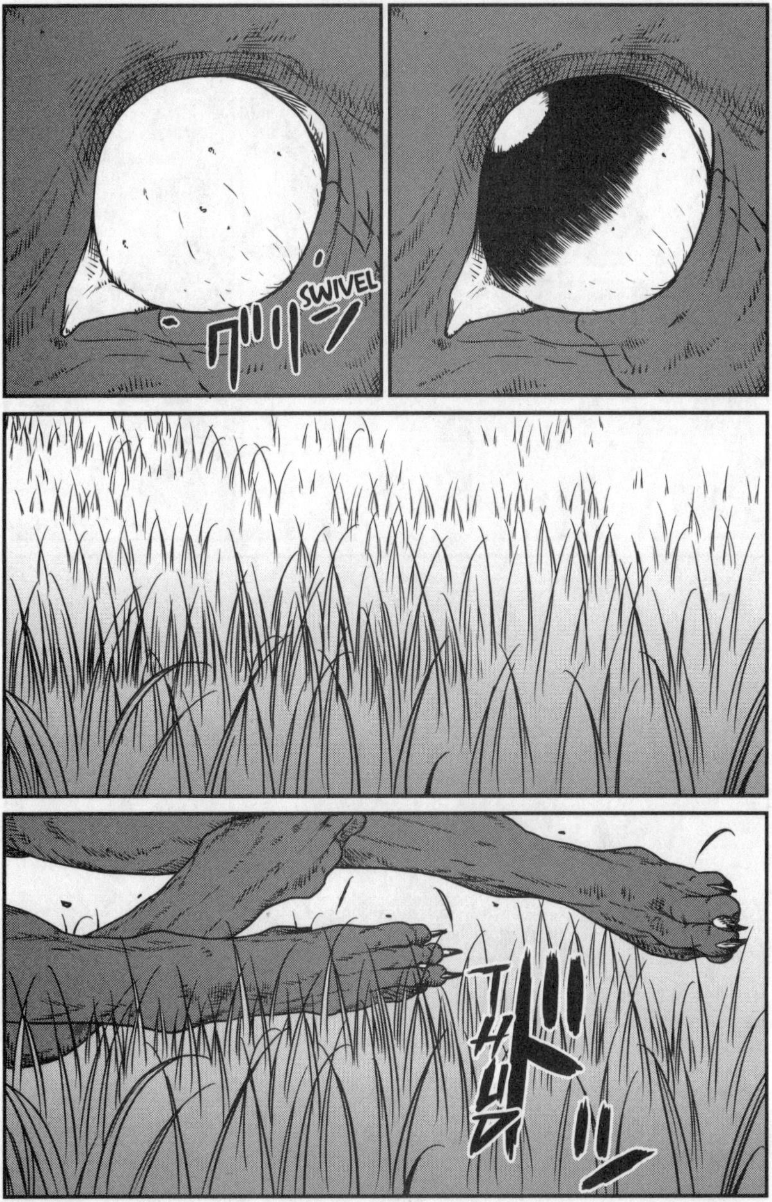
SWIVEL
グリン
THUD
ドッ

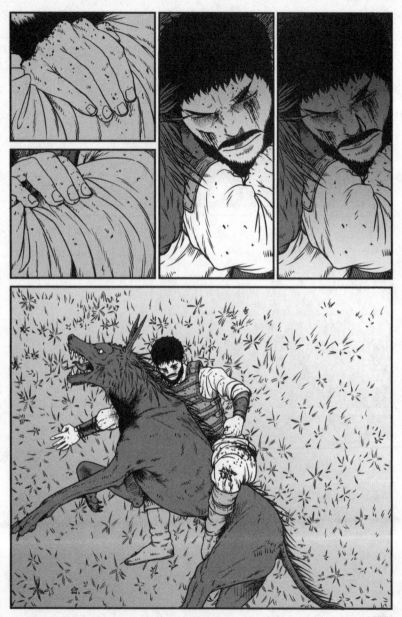

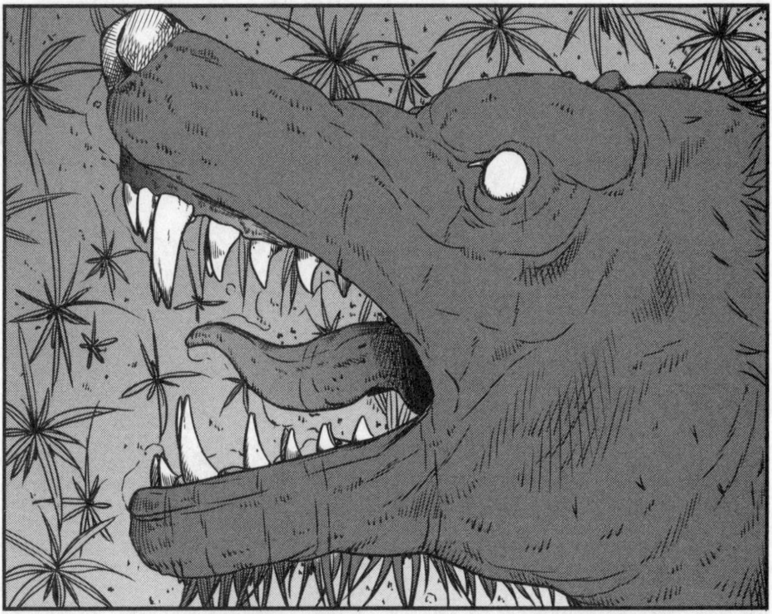

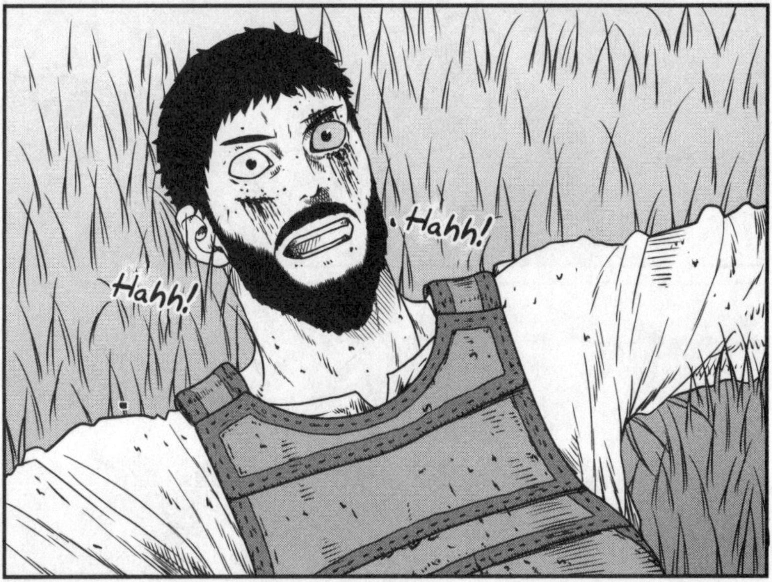
Hahh!
Hahh!

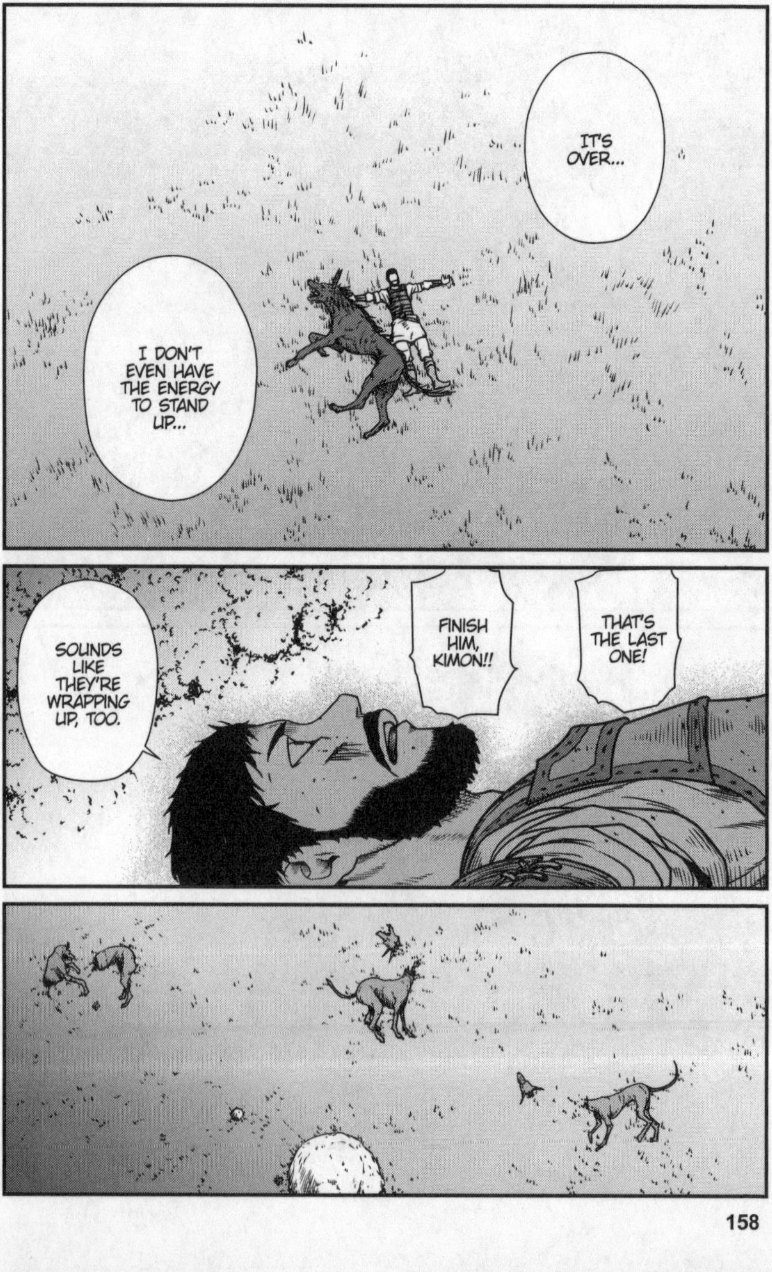
IT'S OVER...
I DON'T EVEN HAVE THE ENERGY TO STAND UP...
THAT'S THE LAST ONE!
FINISH HIM, KIMON!!
SOUNDS LIKE THEY'RE WRAPPING UP, TOO.

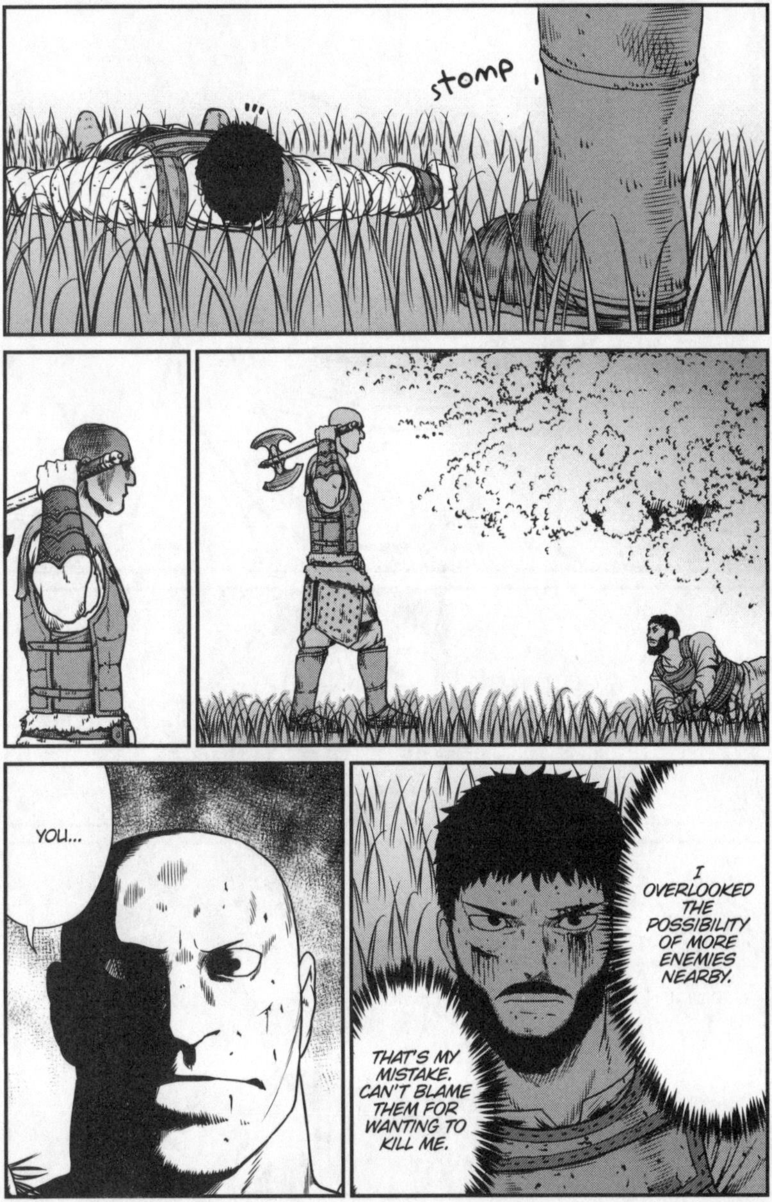
stomp
I OVERLOOKED THE POSSIBILITY OF MORE ENEMIES NEARBY.
THAT'S MY MISTAKE. CAN'T BLAME THEM FOR WANTING TO KILL ME.
YOU...

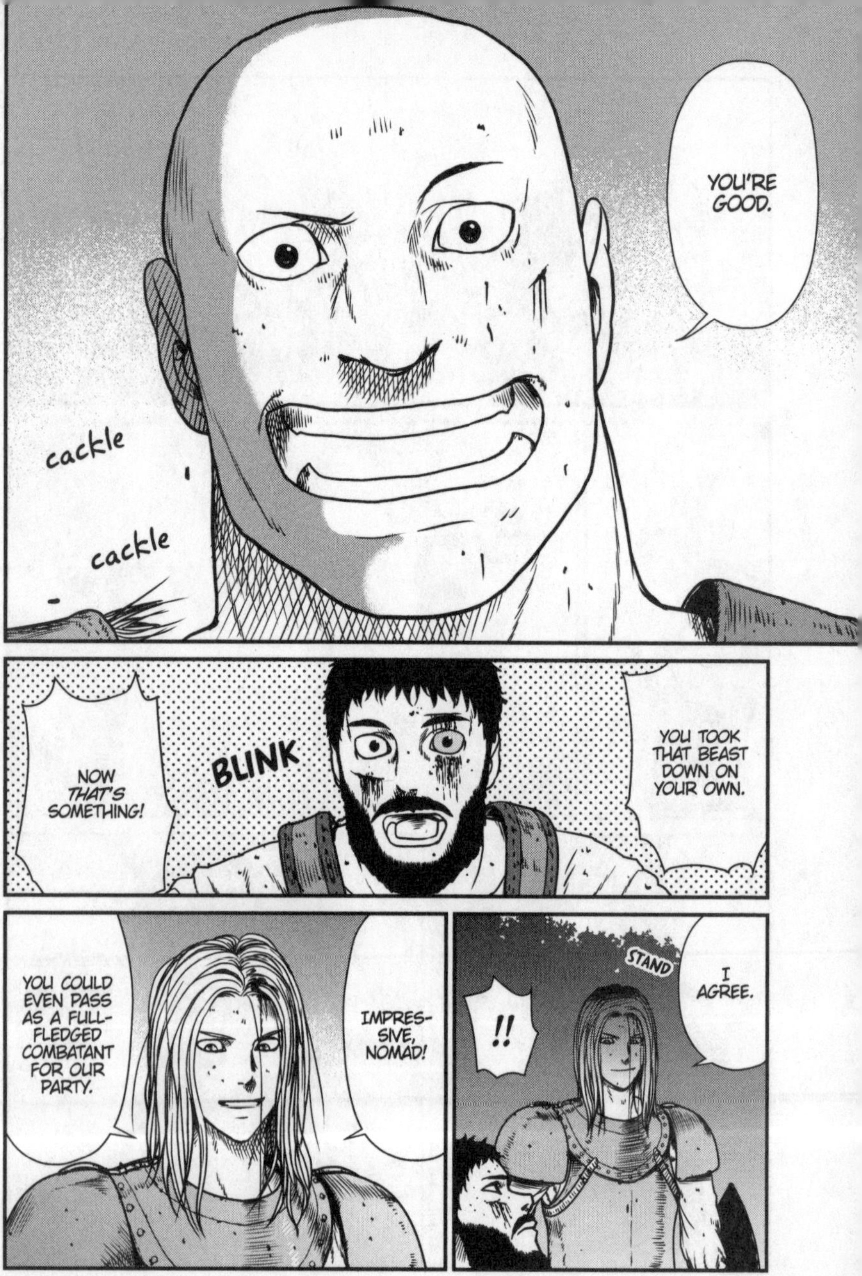
YOU'RE GOOD.
cackle
cackle
YOU TOOK THAT BEAST DOWN ON YOUR OWN.
BLINK
NOW *THAT'S* SOMETHING!
I AGREE.
STAND
!!
IMPRES-SIVE, NOMAD!
YOU COULD EVEN PASS AS A FULL-FLEDGED COMBATANT FOR OUR PARTY.

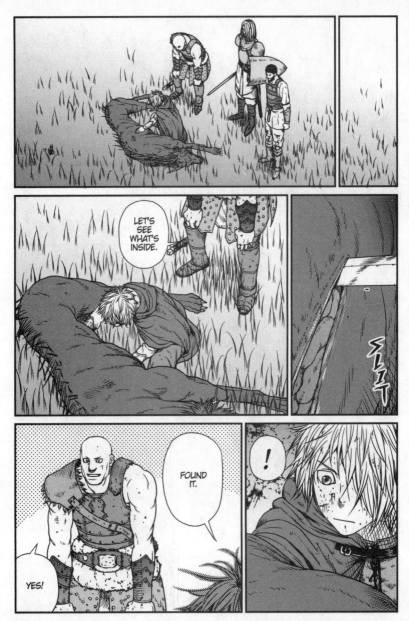

LET'S SEE WHAT'S INSIDE.

SLIT

FOUND IT.

YES!

!

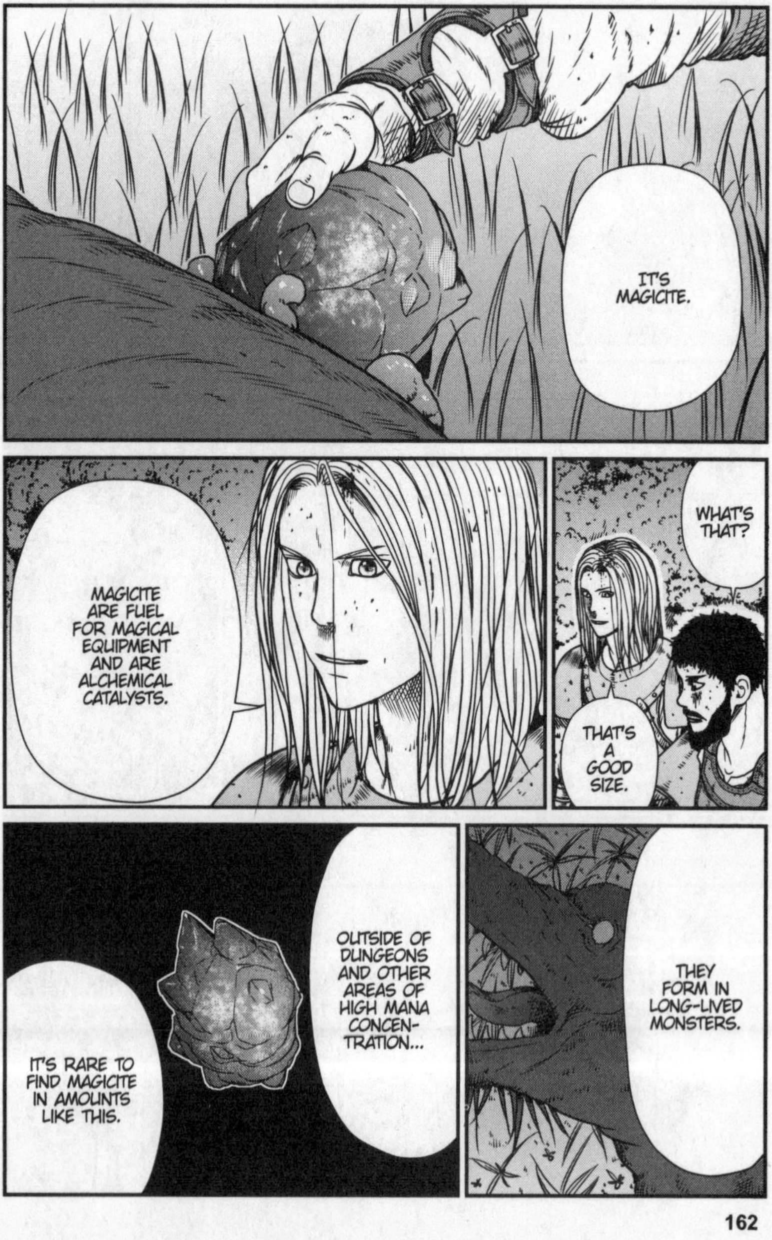
IT'S MAGICITE.
WHAT'S THAT?
THAT'S A GOOD SIZE.
MAGICITE ARE FUEL FOR MAGICAL EQUIPMENT AND ARE ALCHEMICAL CATALYSTS.
THEY FORM IN LONG-LIVED MONSTERS.
OUTSIDE OF DUNGEONS AND OTHER AREAS OF HIGH MANA CONCEN-TRATION...
IT'S RARE TO FIND MAGICITE IN AMOUNTS LIKE THIS.

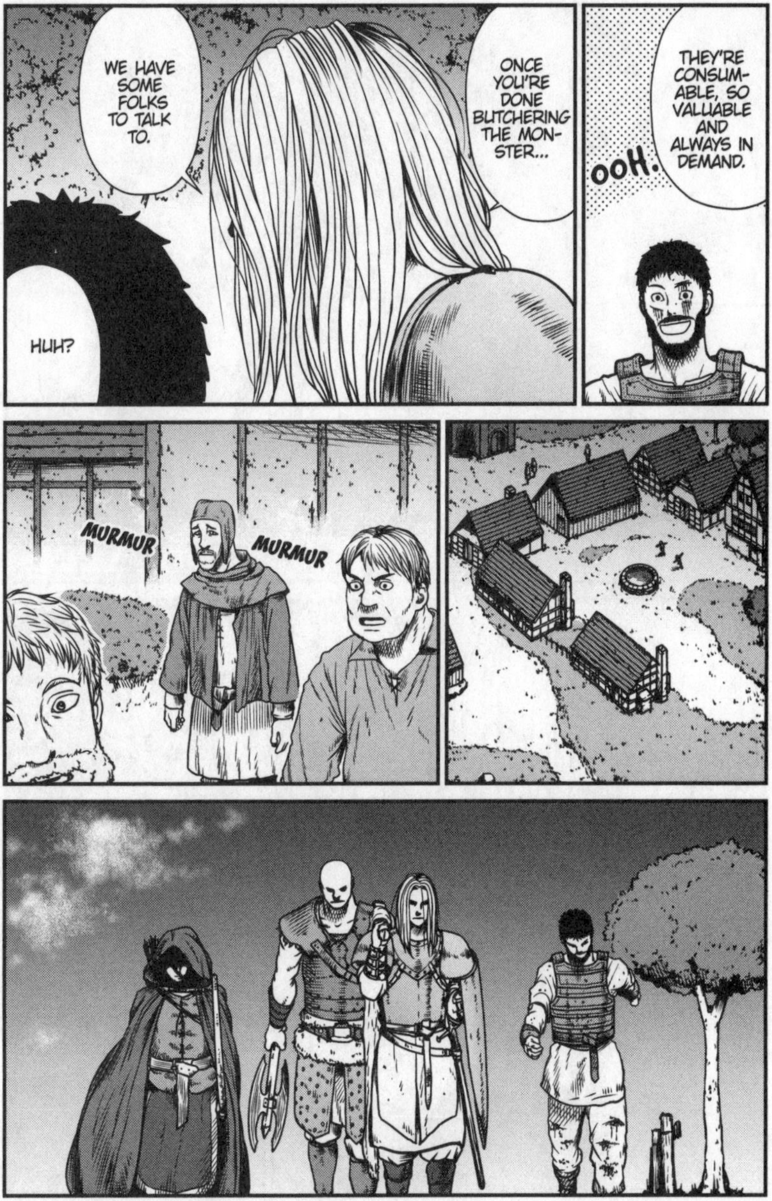
THEY'RE CONSUM-ABLE, SO VALUABLE AND ALWAYS IN DEMAND.
OOH.
ONCE YOU'RE DONE BUTCHERING THE MON-STER...
WE HAVE SOME FOLKS TO TALK TO.
HUH?
MURMUR
MURMUR

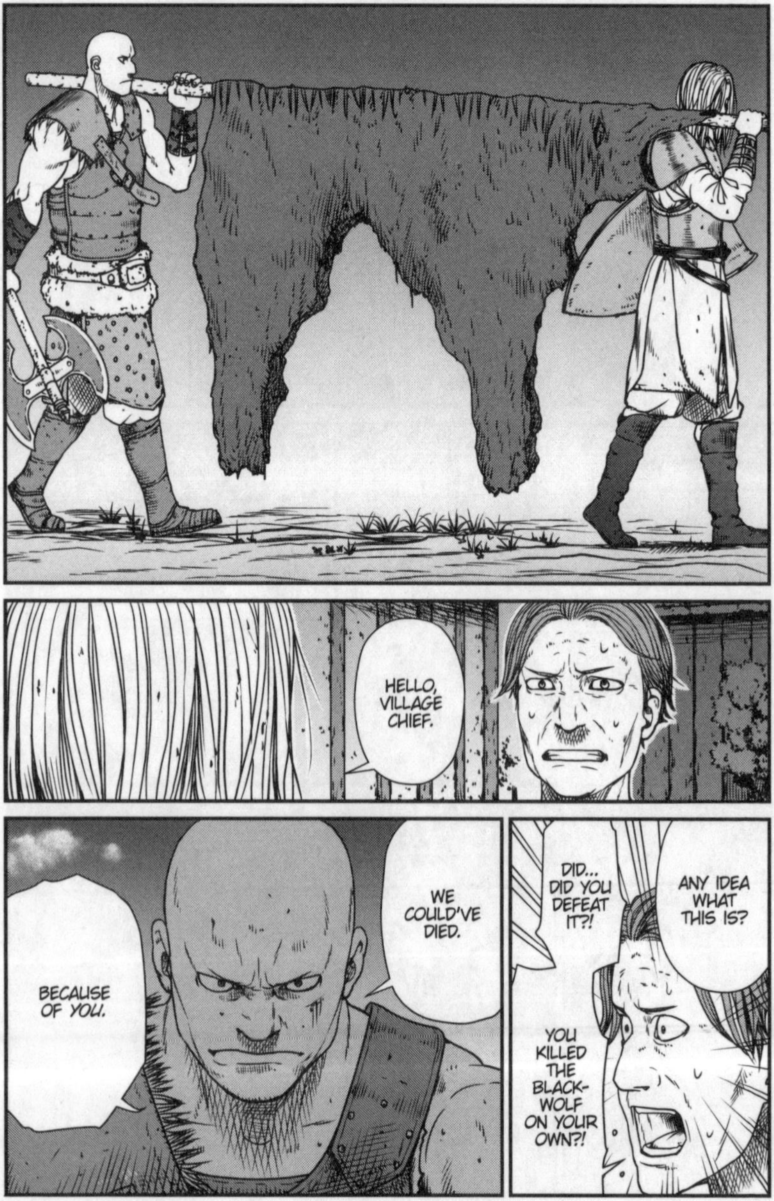
HELLO, VILLAGE CHIEF.
ANY IDEA WHAT THIS IS?
DID... DID YOU DEFEAT IT?!
YOU KILLED THE BLACK-WOLF ON YOUR OWN?!
WE COULD'VE DIED.
BECAUSE OF YOU.

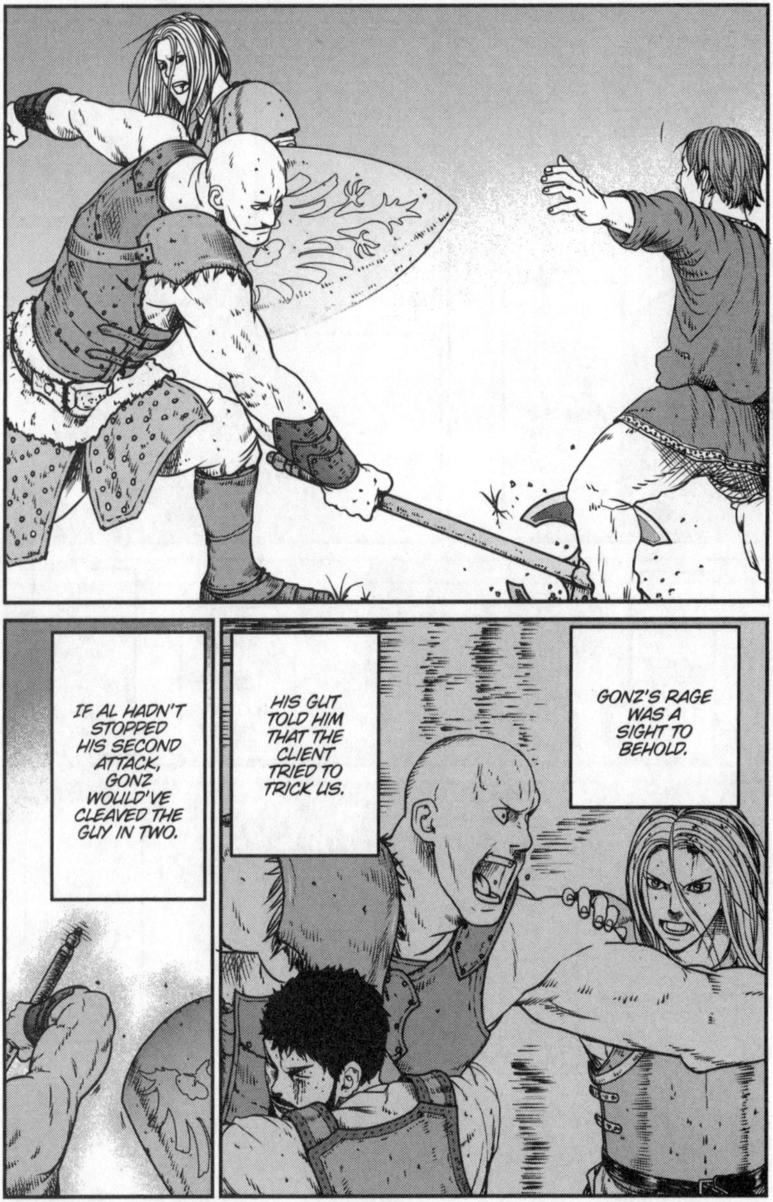
GONZ'S RAGE WAS A SIGHT TO BEHOLD.
HIS GUT TOLD HIM THAT THE CLIENT TRIED TO TRICK US.
IF AL HADN'T STOPPED HIS SECOND ATTACK, GONZ WOULD'VE CLEAVED THE GUY IN TWO.

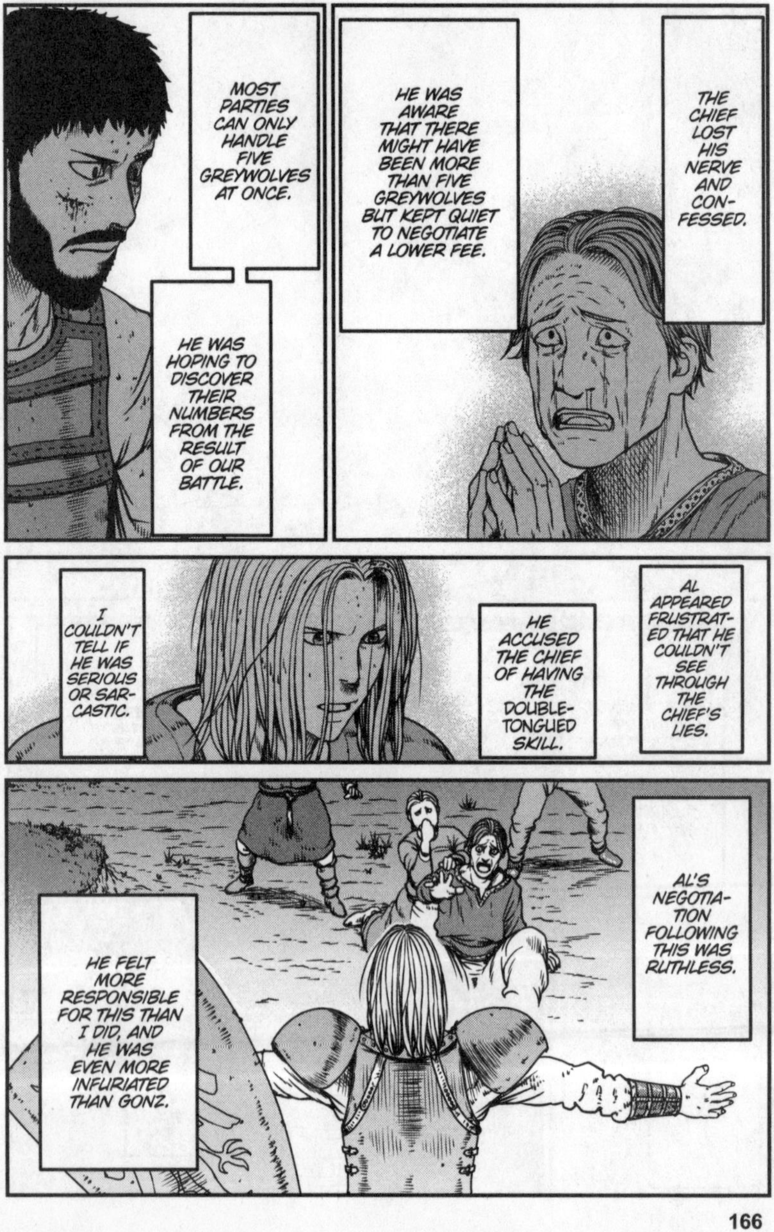
THE CHIEF LOST HIS NERVE AND CONFESSED.
HE WAS AWARE THAT THERE MIGHT HAVE BEEN MORE THAN FIVE GREYWOLVES BUT KEPT QUIET TO NEGOTIATE A LOWER FEE.
MOST PARTIES CAN ONLY HANDLE FIVE GREYWOLVES AT ONCE.
HE WAS HOPING TO DISCOVER THEIR NUMBERS FROM THE RESULT OF OUR BATTLE.
AL APPEARED FRUSTRATED THAT HE COULDN'T SEE THROUGH THE CHIEF'S LIES.
HE ACCUSED THE CHIEF OF HAVING THE DOUBLE-TONGUED SKILL.
I COULDN'T TELL IF HE WAS SERIOUS OR SARCASTIC.
AL'S NEGOTIATION FOLLOWING THIS WAS RUTHLESS.
HE FELT MORE RESPONSIBLE FOR THIS THAN I DID, AND HE WAS EVEN MORE INFURIATED THAN GONZ.

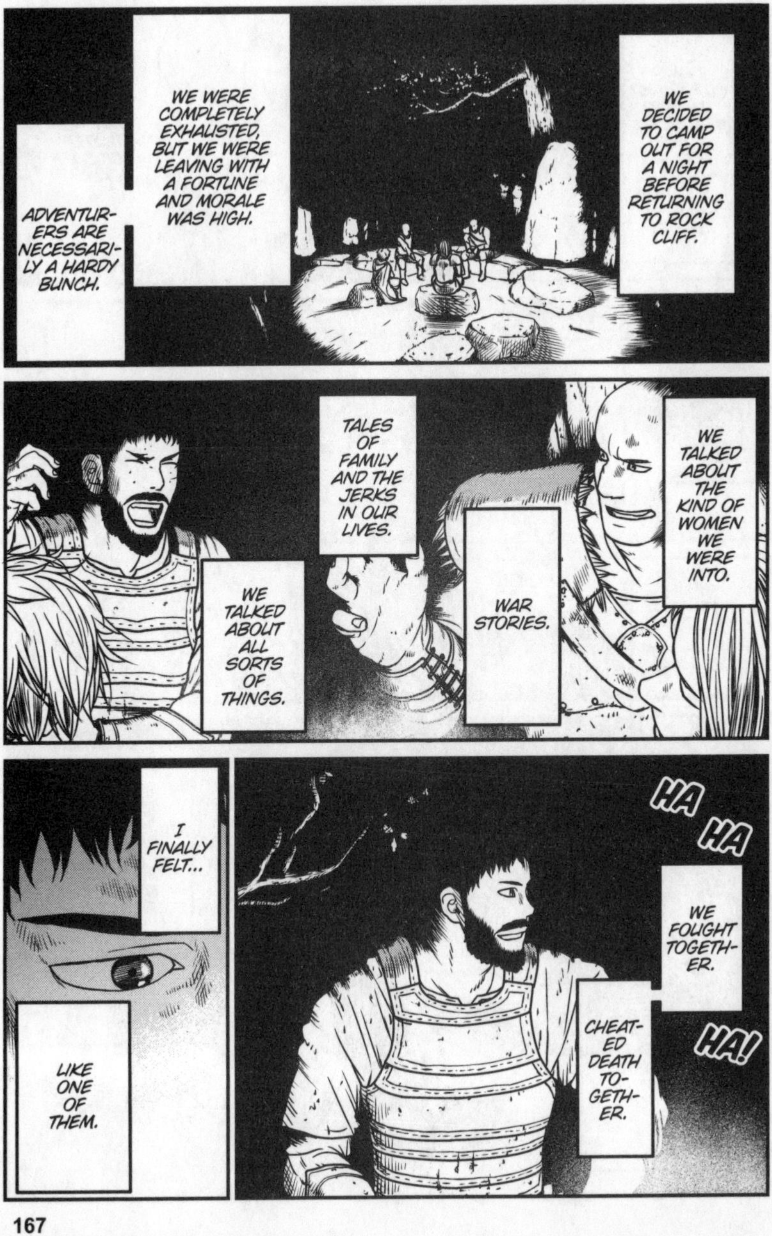
WE DECIDED TO CAMP OUT FOR A NIGHT BEFORE RETURNING TO ROCK CLIFF.
WE WERE COMPLETELY EXHAUSTED, BUT WE WERE LEAVING WITH A FORTUNE AND MORALE WAS HIGH.
ADVENTURERS ARE NECESSARILY A HARDY BUNCH.
WE TALKED ABOUT THE KIND OF WOMEN WE WERE INTO.
WAR STORIES.
TALES OF FAMILY AND THE JERKS IN OUR LIVES.
WE TALKED ABOUT ALL SORTS OF THINGS.
HA HA HA!
WE FOUGHT TOGETHER.
CHEATED DEATH TOGETHER.
I FINALLY FELT...
LIKE ONE OF THEM.

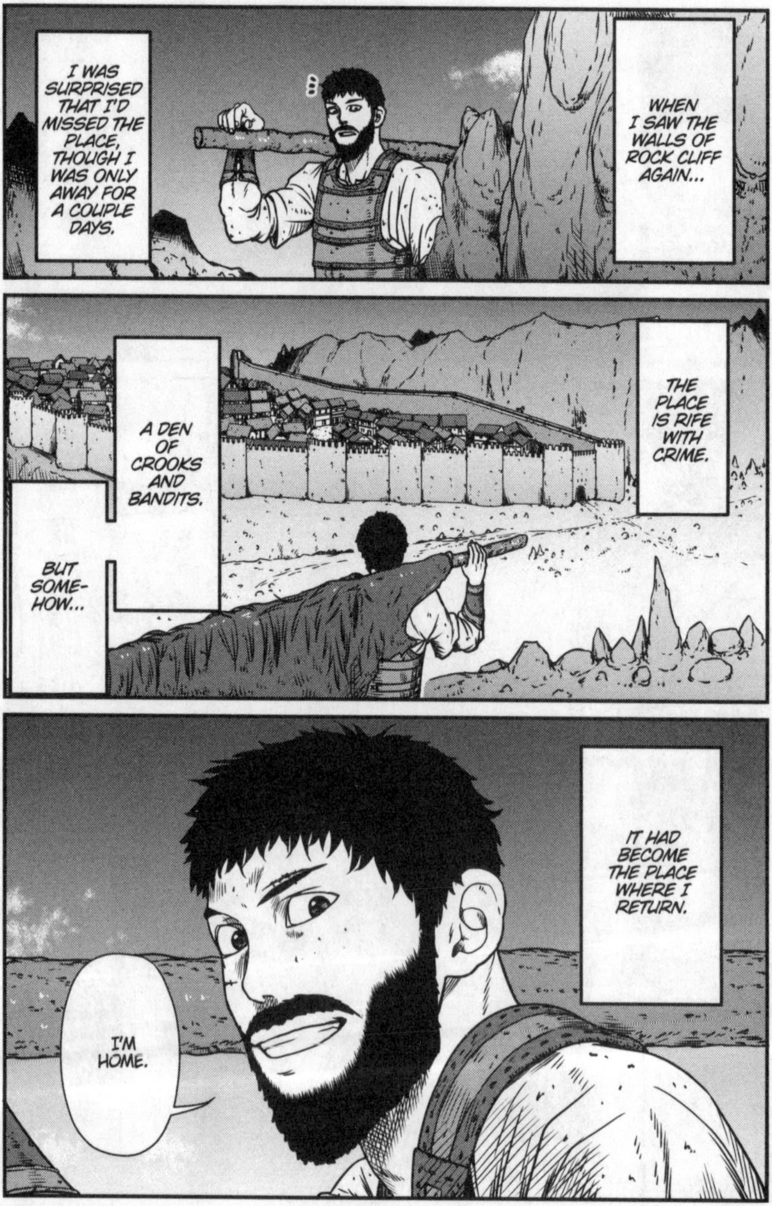
WHEN I SAW THE WALLS OF ROCK CLIFF AGAIN...
I WAS SURPRISED THAT I'D MISSED THE PLACE, THOUGH I WAS ONLY AWAY FOR A COUPLE DAYS.
THE PLACE IS RIFE WITH CRIME.
A DEN OF CROOKS AND BANDITS.
BUT SOME-HOW...
IT HAD BECOME THE PLACE WHERE I RETURN.
I'M HOME.

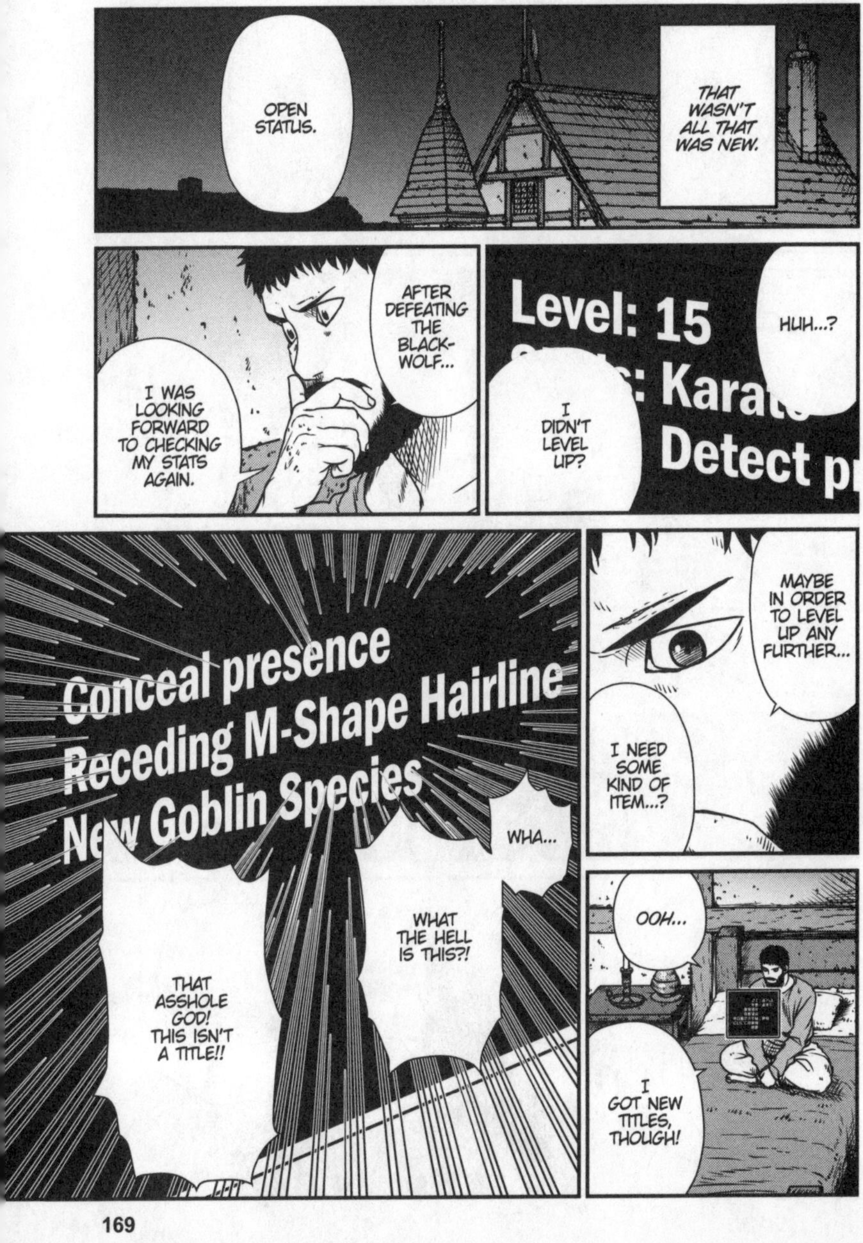
THAT WASN'T ALL THAT WAS NEW.
OPEN STATUS.
HUH...?
Level: 15
: Karat
Detect p
I DIDN'T LEVEL UP?
AFTER DEFEATING THE BLACK-WOLF...
I WAS LOOKING FORWARD TO CHECKING MY STATS AGAIN.
MAYBE IN ORDER TO LEVEL UP ANY FURTHER...
I NEED SOME KIND OF ITEM...?
OOH...
I GOT NEW TITLES, THOUGH!
Conceal presence
Receding M-Shape Hairline
New Goblin Species
WHA...
WHAT THE HELL IS THIS?!
THAT ASSHOLE GOD! THIS ISN'T A TITLE!!

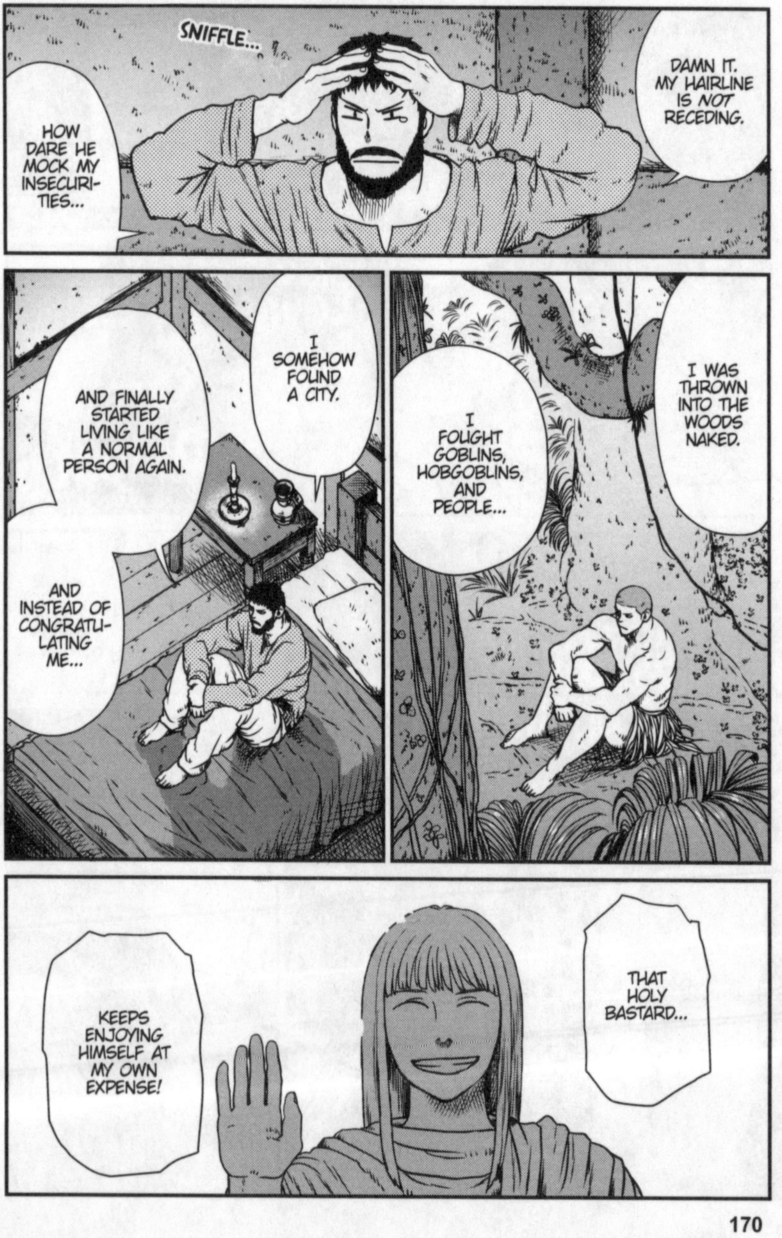
DAMN IT. MY HAIRLINE IS *NOT* RECEDING.
SNIFFLE...
HOW DARE HE MOCK MY INSECURITIES...
I WAS THROWN INTO THE WOODS NAKED.
I FOUGHT GOBLINS, HOBGOBLINS, AND PEOPLE...
I SOMEHOW FOUND A CITY.
AND FINALLY STARTED LIVING LIKE A NORMAL PERSON AGAIN.
AND INSTEAD OF CONGRATULATING ME...
THAT HOLY BASTARD...
KEEPS ENJOYING HIMSELF AT MY OWN EXPENSE!

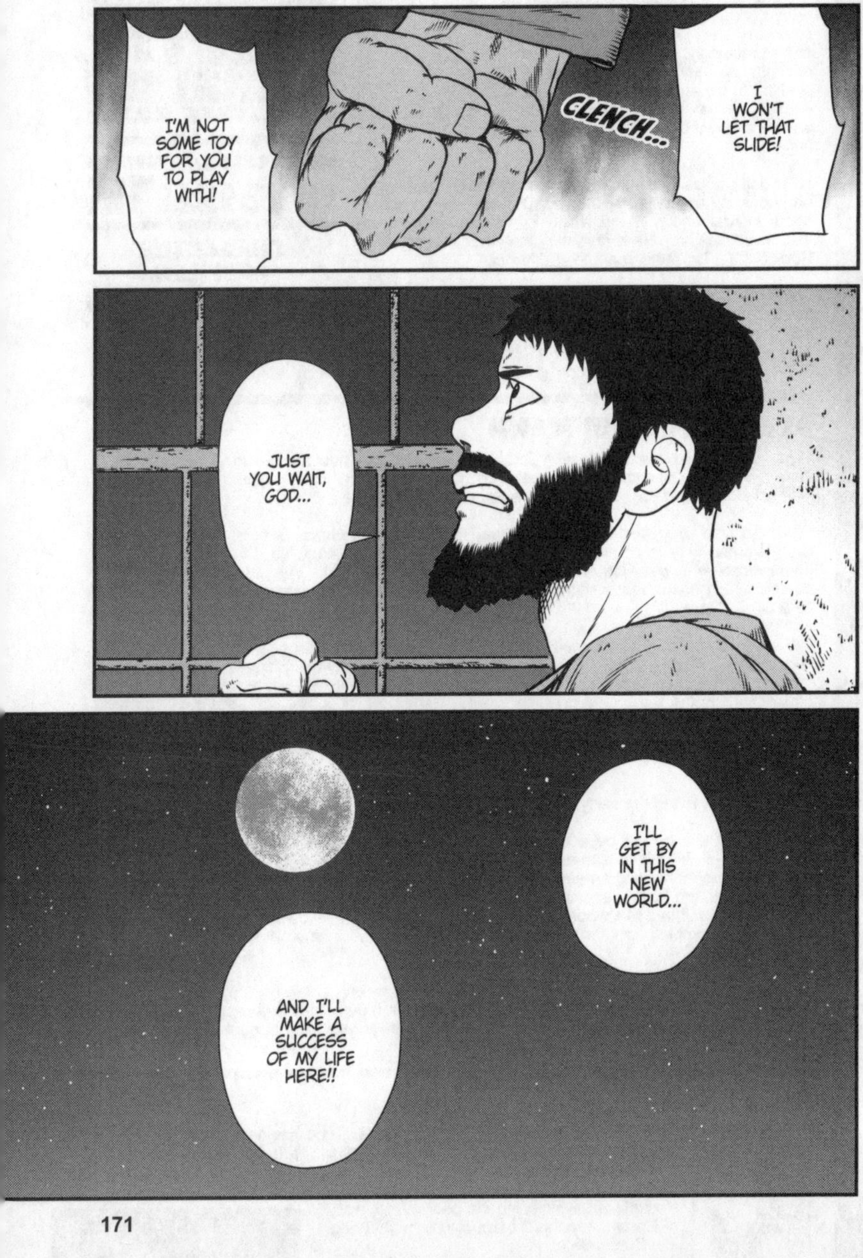
I WON'T LET THAT SLIDE!
CLENCH...
I'M NOT SOME TOY FOR YOU TO PLAY WITH!
JUST YOU WAIT, GOD...
I'LL GET BY IN THIS NEW WORLD...
AND I'LL MAKE A SUCCESS OF MY LIFE HERE!!

SPECIAL COLUMN BY AUTHOR, YAZIN

KARATE SURVIVOR IN ANOTHER WORLD

INTERMISSION

SAVAGE RULES 12

CHARACTER PROFILES

GONZ

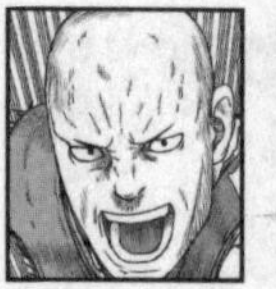

A behemoth with a shaved head. He has great strength befitting his stature, and a surprising level of agility. His base stats are exceedingly high, and his potential strength is near human maximum. In contrast to his amazing physical stats, his intelligence is awfully lacking. He is unable to count beyond the number of his fingers.

He is quick to lose his temper, and the type to let his thoughts be known by action rather than words. He has no qualms about murder and will unleash his trusty axe upon anyone that displeases him. He is feared by the other adventurers of Rock Cliff for his brute strength and ferocity.

As the second son of a village chief, he was raised wanting for nothing. However, he was sidelined in favor of his older and more accomplished brother. One day, Gonz was deceived by a merchant and signed a contract that cost the village heavily. His father lost trust in Gonz and he left the village at the age of twelve. He has been working as an adventurer ever since.

ALBRECHT KAUFMANN

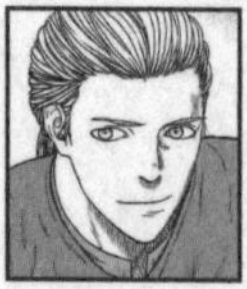

Third son of a baron of the Megado Empire, he excelled in school and would have advanced upon the prestigious path of a bureaucrat. However, an incident led him to fake his death and escape to the city-states.

While he was struggling with his new way of life, he met Gonz. Despite Gonz's proficiency in combat, his intellect was low and he struggled with negotiations. Al was clever but less capable in combat. The two complimented each other's weaknesses, and this two-man party were tied by a bond of trust.

His good looks and elegant mannerisms are in keeping with his noble heritage, though his appearance invited mockery from the other, coarser, adventurers. However, he is known to remove competitors through information he gathers by charming women, and through his connections in the slums and unofficial guilds. Many now recognize him as a more terrifying figure than Gonz.

KIMON

Kimon was invited to the party by Al.

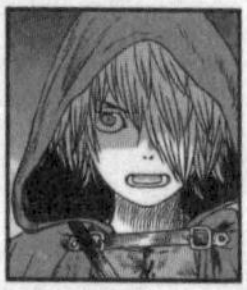

A hunter by trade, he has basic scouting experience, but his real value lies in his archery skills. He is capable of hitting his target through numerous obstacles, even threading an arrow through the trees in a forest. In fact, his scouting skills are basic because of his exceedingly high archery skills. He only had to stroll into the woods and shoot his target from afar before his mission as complete. Kimon never had the opportunity to improve his scouting skills.

Kimon is a boy of few words, although he was a chatterbox in the past. Since his blabbing brought about the death of his master, he has kept his mouth shut, believing his words bring bad luck. His mind is always full of thoughts, but betrays very little through his speech and expressions.

CLEYANNE

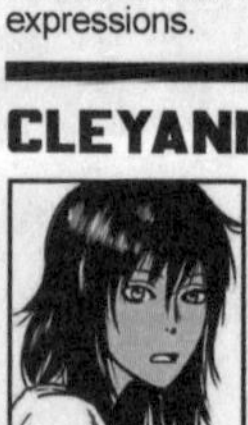

An older and fellow student of Maria-Belle. Since leaving her teacher, she set up an independent practice in Rock Cliff. She is a highly skilled apothecary and was adopted by the regional lord. She has earned the respect of the people of Rock Cliff by treating everyone without discrimination, including the poor. She is wary of Nomad, fearing the trouble he might bring into Belle's life.

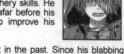

KARATE SURVIVOR IN ANOTHER WORLD

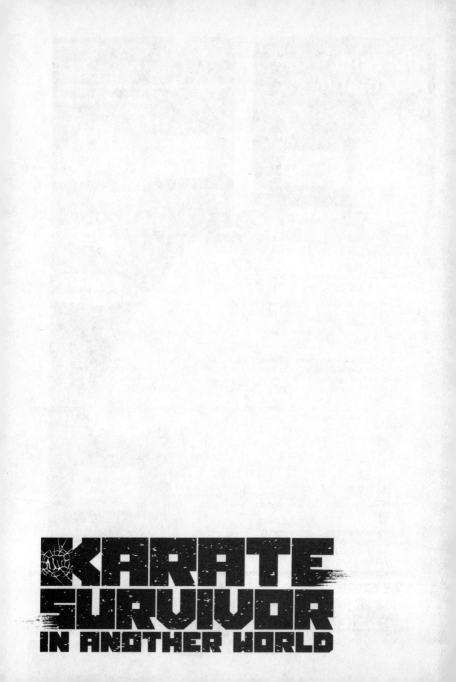

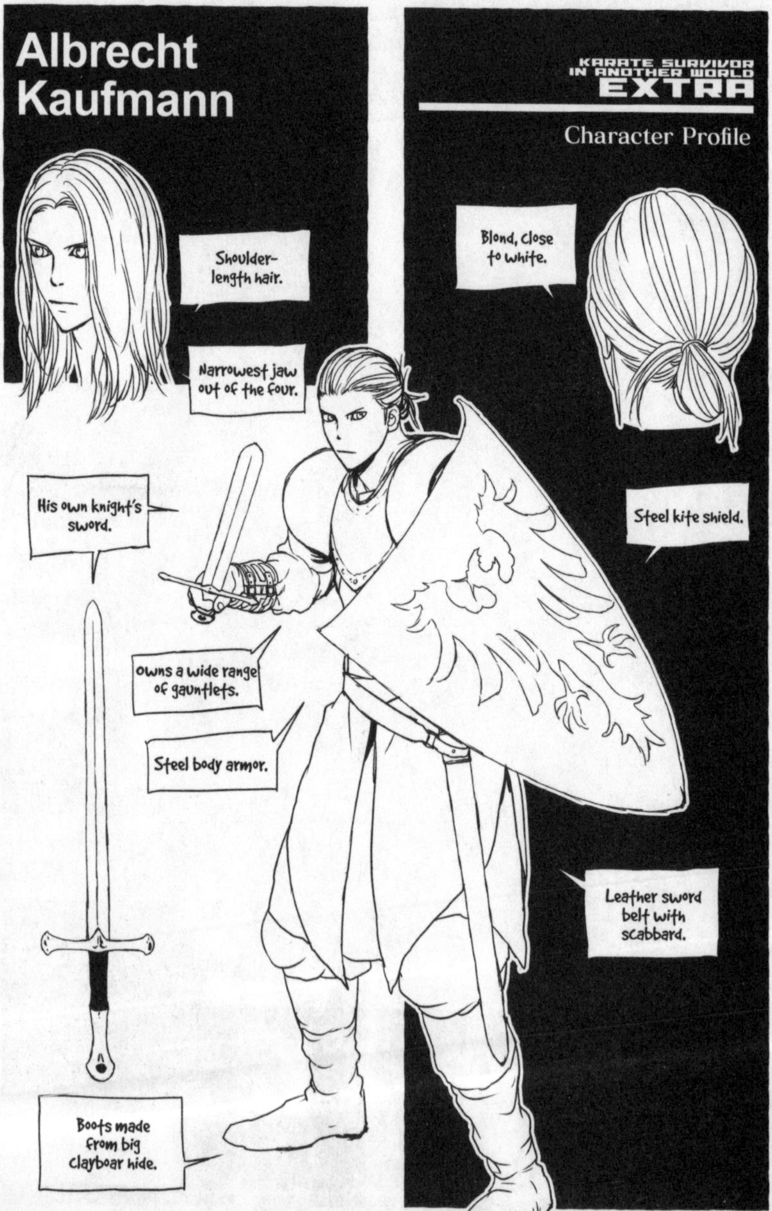
Albrecht Kaufmann
KARATE SURVIVOR IN ANOTHER WORLD
EXTRA
Character Profile
Shoulder-length hair.
Narrowest jaw out of the four.
Blond, close to white.
His own knight's sword.
Steel kite shield.
Owns a wide range of gauntlets.
Steel body armor.
Leather sword belt with scabbard.
Boots made from big clayboar hide.

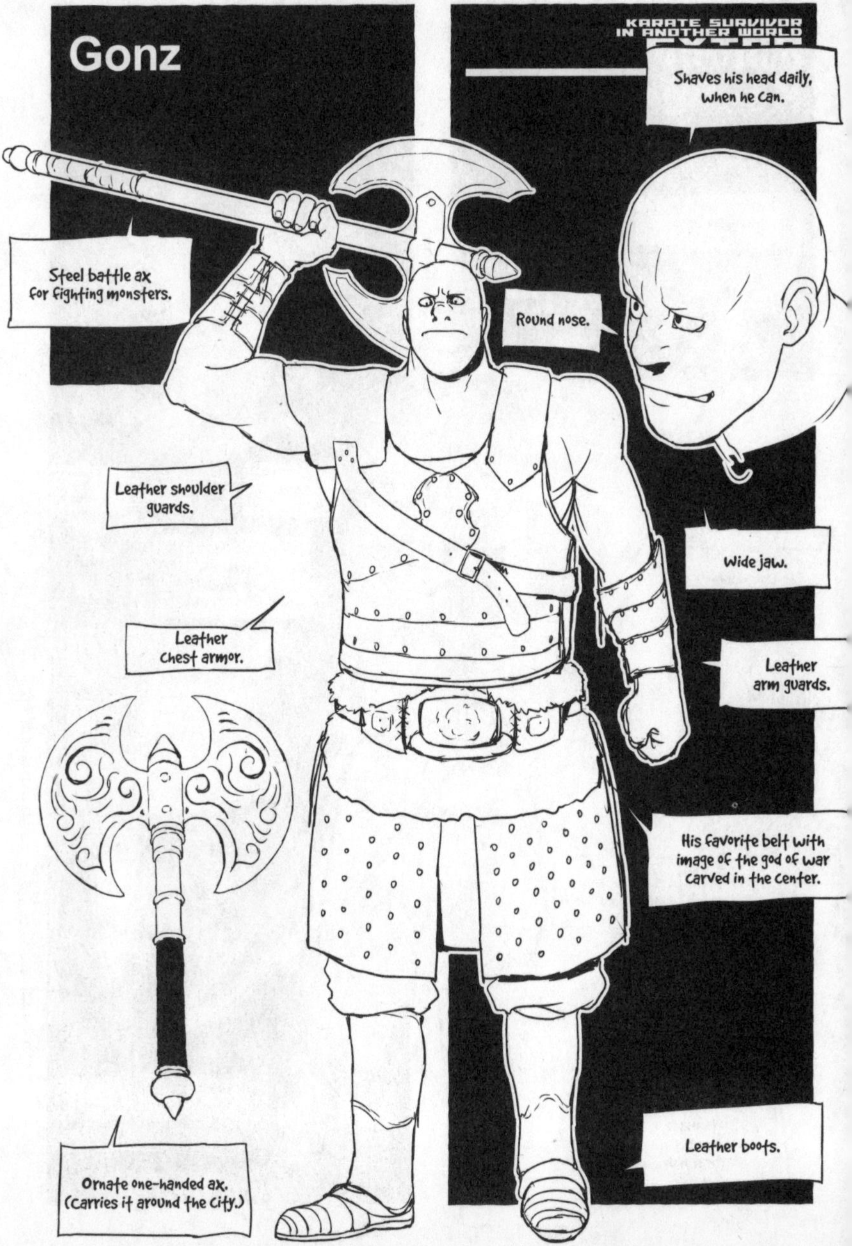
KARATE SURVIVOR IN ANOTHER WORLD
Gonz
Shaves his head daily, when he can.
Steel battle ax for fighting monsters.
Round nose.
Leather shoulder guards.
Wide jaw.
Leather chest armor.
Leather arm guards.
His favorite belt with image of the god of war carved in the center.
Leather boots.
Ornate one-handed ax. (Carries it around the city.)

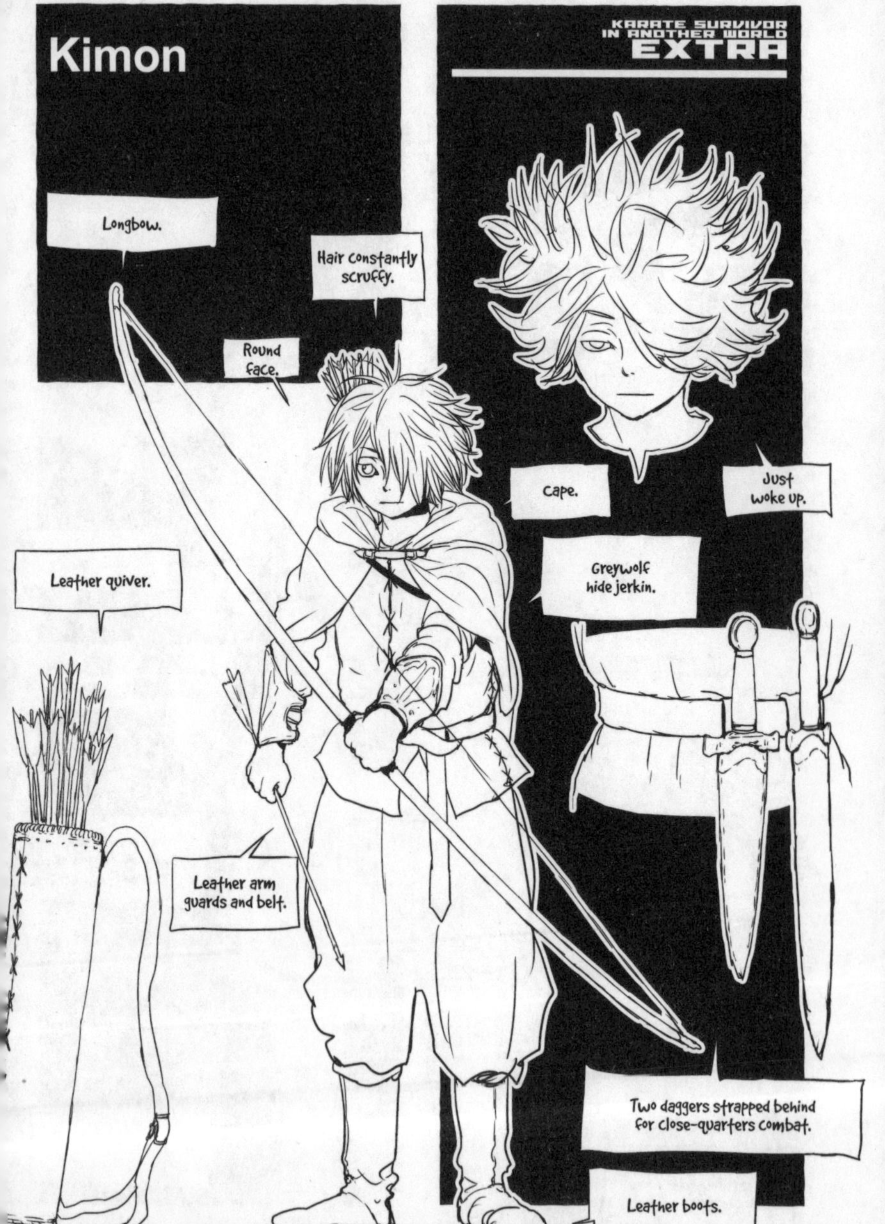
KARATE SURVIVOR IN ANOTHER WORLD
EXTRA
Kimon
Just woke up.
Cape.
Greywolf hide jerkin.
Two daggers strapped behind for close-quarters combat.
Leather boots.
Hair constantly scruffy.
Longbow.
Round face.
Leather quiver.
Leather arm guards and belt.